Laboratory Manual

Prentice Hall

Physical Science

Concepts in Action

With Earth and Space Science

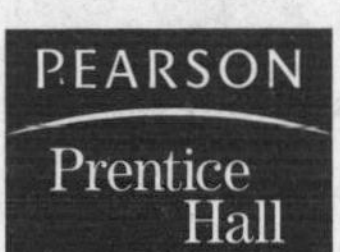

Boston, Massachusetts
Upper Saddle River, New Jersey

Laboratory Manual

Prentice Hall

Physical Science

Concepts in Action

With Earth and Space Science

FIELD TESTERS

Robert W. Arts
Pikeville College
Pikeville, Kentucky

Peggy Lynn Bondurant
Mesquite High School
Gilbert, Arizona

Teresa Casal
Felix Varela Senior High School
Miami, Florida

Richelle Lee Dull
Vance High School
Charlotte, North Carolina

Yvonne Favaro
Englewood Cliffs, New Jersey

Mary Louise Freitas
Peoria High School
Peoria, Arizona

Karen S. Garner
Rutherford County Schools
Murfreesboro, Tennessee

Margaret A. Holzer
Chatham High School
Somerset, New Jersey

Susan McCullen
Big Rapids High School
Big Rapids, Michigan

David Petro
Cardinal Carter Secondary School
Leamington, Ontario, Canada

A. Marie Pool
Clinton High School
Clinton, Oklahoma

Alan Seidman
Margaretville Central School
Margaretville, New York

Evan P. Silberstein
Spring Valley High School
Spring Valley, New York

Lesia Thaisz
Gloversville High School
Gloversville, New York

James R. White
Southside High School
Chocowinity, North Carolina

John P. Wilbur
Caledonia-Mumford Schools
Caledonia, New York

SAFETY REVIEWER

Dr. Kenneth R. Roy
Glastonbury Public Schools
Glastonbury, Connecticut

ISBN 0-13-069975-6

27 20

Contents

Student Safety Manual

The symbol 🔍 denotes Inquiry Lab

The symbol ⚗ denotes Design Your Own Experiment Lab

Laboratory Investigations

Chemistry

Physics

Earth and Space Science

Student Edition Lab Worksheets

(continued)

SI Units and Conversion Table

COMMON SI UNITS

Measurement	Unit	Symbol	Equivalents
Length	1 millimeter	mm	1,000 micrometers (µm)
	1 centimeter	cm	10 millimeters (mm)
	1 meter	m	100 centimeters (cm)
	1 kilometer	km	1,000 meters (m)
Area	1 square meter	m^2	10,000 square centimeters (cm^2)
	1 square kilometer	km^2	1,000,000 square meters (m^2)
Volume	1 milliliter	mL	1 cubic centimeter (cm^3 or cc)
	1 liter	L	1,000 milliliters (mL)
Mass	1 gram	g	1,000 milligrams (mg)
	1 kilogram	kg	1,000 grams (g)
	1 ton	t	1,000 kilograms (kg) = 1 metric ton
Time	1 second	s	
Temperature	1 Kelvin	K	1 degree Celsius (°C)

METRIC CONVERSION TABLES

When You Know	Multiply by	To Find		
		When You Know	Multiply by	To Find
inches	2.54	centimeters	0.394	inches
feet	0.3048	meters	3.281	feet
yards	0.914	meters	1.0936	yards
miles	1.609	kilometers	0.62	miles
square inches	6.45	square centimeters	0.155	square inches
square feet	0.093	square meters	10.76	square feet
square yards	0.836	square meters	1.196	square yards
acres	0.405	hectares	2.471	acres
square miles	2.59	square kilometers	0.386	square miles
cubic inches	16.387	cubic centimeters	0.061	cubic inches
cubic feet	0.028	cubic meters	35.315	cubic feet
cubic yards	0.765	cubic meters	1.31	cubic yards
fluid ounces	29.57	milliliters	0.0338	fluid ounces
quarts	0.946	liters	1.057	quarts
gallons	3.785	liters	0.264	gallons
ounces	28.35	grams	0.0353	ounces
pounds	0.4536	kilograms	2.2046	pounds
tons	0.907	metric tons	1.102	tons

When You Know		
Fahrenheit	subtract 32; then divide by 1.8	to find Celsius
Celsius	multiply by 1.8; then add 32	to find Fahrenheit

Science Safety Rules

To prepare yourself to work safely in the laboratory, read over the following safety rules. Then read them a second time. Make sure you understand and follow each rule. Ask your teacher to explain any rules you do not understand.

Dress Code

1. To protect yourself from injuring your eyes, wear safety goggles whenever you work with chemicals, flames, glassware, or any substance that might get into your eyes. If you wear contact lenses, notify your teacher.
2. Wear an apron or coat whenever you work with corrosive chemicals or substances that can stain.
3. Tie back long hair to keep it away from any chemicals, flames, or equipment.
4. Remove or tie back any article of clothing or jewelry that can hang down and touch chemicals, flames, or equipment. Roll up or secure long sleeves.
5. Never wear open shoes or sandals.

General Precautions

6. Read all directions for an experiment several times before beginning the activity. Carefully follow all written and oral instructions. If you are in doubt about any part of the experiment, ask your teacher for assistance.
7. Never perform activities that are not assigned or authorized by your teacher. Obtain permission before "experimenting" on your own. Never handle any equipment unless you have specific permission.
8. Never perform lab activities without direct supervision.
9. Never eat or drink in the laboratory.
10. Keep work areas clean and tidy at all times. Bring only notebooks and lab manuals or written lab procedures to the work area. All other items, such as purses and backpacks, should be left in a designated area.
11. Do not engage in horseplay.

First Aid

12. Always report all accidents or injuries to your teacher, no matter how minor. Notify your teacher immediately about any fires.
13. Learn what to do in case of specific accidents, such as getting acid in your eyes or on your skin. (Rinse acids from your body with plenty of water.)
14. Be aware of the location of the first-aid kit, but do not use it unless instructed by your teacher. In case of injury, your teacher should administer first aid. Your teacher may also send you to the school nurse or call a physician.
15. Know the location of the emergency equipment such as fire extinguisher and fire blanket.
16. Know the location of the nearest telephone and whom to contact in an emergency.

Heating and Fire Safety

17. Never use a heat source, such as a candle, burner, or hot plate, without wearing safety goggles.
18. Never heat anything unless instructed to do so. A chemical that is harmless when cool may be dangerous when heated.
19. Keep all combustible materials away from flames. Never use a flame or spark near a combustible chemical.
20. Never reach across a flame.
21. Before using a laboratory burner, make sure you know proper procedures for lighting and adjusting the burner, as demonstrated by your teacher. Do not touch the burner. It may be hot. Never

leave a lighted burner unattended. Turn off the burner when not in use.

22. Chemicals can splash or boil out of a heated test tube. When heating a substance in a test tube, make sure that the mouth of the tube is not pointed at you or anyone else.
23. Never heat a liquid in a closed container. The expanding gases produced may shatter the container.
24. Before picking up a container that has been heated, first hold the back of your hand near it. If you can feel heat on the back of your hand, the container is too hot to handle. Use an oven mitt to pick up a container that has been heated.

Using Chemicals Safely

25. Never mix chemicals "for the fun of it." You might produce a dangerous, possibly explosive substance.
26. Never put your face near the mouth of a container that holds chemicals. Many chemicals are poisonous. Never touch, taste, or smell a chemical unless you are instructed by your teacher to do so.
27. Use only those chemicals needed in the activity. Read and double-check labels on supply bottles before removing any chemicals. Take only as much as you need. Keep all containers closed when chemicals are not being used.
28. Dispose of all chemicals as instructed by your teacher. To avoid contamination, never return chemicals to their original containers. Never pour untreated chemicals or other substances into the sink or trash containers.
29. Be extra careful when working with acids or bases. Pour all chemicals over the sink or a container, not over your work surface.
30. If you are instructed to test for odors, use a wafting motion to direct the odors to your nose. Do not inhale the fumes directly from the container.
31. When mixing an acid and water, always pour the water into the container first then add the acid to the water. Never pour water into an acid.
32. Take extreme care not to spill any material in the laboratory. Wash chemical spills and splashes immediately with plenty of water. Immediately begin rinsing with water any acids that get on your skin or clothing, and notify your teacher of any acid spill at the same time.

Using Glassware Safely

33. Never force glass tubing or a thermometer into a rubber stopper or rubber tubing. Have your teacher insert the glass tubing or thermometer if required for an activity.
34. If you are using a laboratory burner, use a wire screen to protect glassware from any flame. Never heat glassware that is not thoroughly dry on the outside.
35. Keep in mind that hot glassware looks cool. Never pick up glassware without first checking to see if it is hot. Use an oven mitt. See rule 24.
36. Never use broken or chipped glassware. If glassware breaks, notify your teacher and dispose of the glassware in the proper broken-glassware container.
37. Never eat or drink from glassware.
38. Thoroughly clean glassware before putting it away.

Using Sharp Instruments

39. Handle scalpels or other sharp instruments with extreme care. Never cut material toward you; cut away from you.
40. Immediately notify your teacher if you cut your skil while working in the laboratory.

Field Safety

41. When leaving the classroom or in the field, do not disrupt the activities of others. Do not leave your group unless you notify a teacher first.

42. Your teacher will instruct you as to how to conduct your research or experiment outside the classroom.

43. Never touch any animals or plants that you encounter in the field unless your teacher instructs you in the proper handling of that species.

44. Clean your hands thoroughly after handling anything in the field.

End-of-Experiment Rules

45. After an experiment has been completed, turn off all burners or hot plates. If you used a gas burner, check that the gas-line valve to the burner is off. Unplug hot plates.

46. Turn off and unplug any other electrical equipment that you used.

47 Clean up your work area and return all equipment to its proper place.

48. Dispose of waste materials as instructed by your teacher.

49. Wash your hands after every experiment.

Safety Symbols

These symbols alert you to possible dangers in the laboratory and remind you to work carefully.

General Safety Awareness You may see this symbol when none of the symbols described below appears. In this case, follow the specific instructions provided. You may also see this symbol when you are asked to develop your own procedure in a lab. Have the teacher approve your plan before you go further.

Physical Safety When an experiment involves physical activity, take precautions to avoid injuring yourself or others. Follow instructions from the teacher. Alert the teacher if there is any reason you should not participate in the activity.

Safety Goggles Always wear safety goggles to protect your eyes in any activity involving chemicals, flames or heating, or the possibility of broken glassware.

Lab Apron Wear a laboratory apron to protect your skin and clothing from damage.

Plastic Gloves Wear disposable plastic gloves to protect yourself from chemicals or organisms that could be harmful. Keep your hands away from your face. Dispose of the gloves according to your teacher's instructions at the end of the activity.

Heating Use a clamp or tongs to pick up hot glassware. Do not touch hot objects with your bare hands.

Heat-Resistant Gloves Use an oven mitt or other hand protection when handling hot materials. Hot plates, hot glassware, or hot water can cause burns. Do not touch hot objects with your bare hands.

Flames You may be working with flames from a lab burner, candle, or matches. Tie back loose hair and clothing. Follow instructions from the teacher about lighting and extinguishing flames.

No Flames Flammable materials may be present. Make sure there are no flames, sparks, or other exposed heat sources present.

Electric Shock Avoid the possibility of electric shock. Never use electrical equipment around water, or when the equipment is wet or your hands are wet. Be sure cords are untangled and cannot trip anyone. Disconnect the equipment when it is not in use.

Breakage You are working with materials that may be breakable, such as glass containers, glass tubing, thermometers, or funnels. Handle breakable materials with care. Do not touch broken glassware.

Corrosive Chemical You are working with an acid or another corrosive chemical. Avoid getting it on your skin or clothing, or in your eyes. Do not inhale the vapors. Wash your hands when you are finished with the activity.

Poison Do not let any poisonous chemical come in contact with your skin, and do not inhale its vapors. Wash your hands when you are finished with the activity.

Fumes When poisonous or unpleasant vapors may be involved, work in a ventilated area. Avoid inhaling vapors directly. Only test an odor when directed to do so by the teacher, and use a wafting motion to direct the vapor toward your nose.

Sharp Object Pointed-tip scissors, scalpels, knives, needles, pins, or tacks are sharp. They can cut or puncture your skin. Always direct a sharp edge or point away from yourself and others. Use sharp instruments only as instructed.

Disposal **Chemicals** and other laboratory materials used in the activity must be disposed of safely. Follow the instructions from the teacher.

Hand Washing Wash your hands thoroughly when finished with the activity. Use antibacterial soap and warm water. Lather both sides of your hands and between your fingers. Rinse well.

LABORATORY SAFETY CONTRACT

I, ______________________________, have read the Science Safety Rules and Safety Symbols sections on pages x–xiii of this manual, understand their contents completely, and agree to demonstrate compliance with all safety rules and guidelines that have been established in each of the following categories:

(please check)

- ☐ Dress Code
- ☐ General Precautions
- ☐ First Aid
- ☐ Heating and Fire Safety
- ☐ Using Chemicals Safely
- ☐ Using Glassware Safely
- ☐ Using Sharp Instruments
- ☐ Field Safety
- ☐ End-of-Experiment Rules

Signature ____

Date ____

Name ______________________ Class ________________ Date ____________

Recognizing Laboratory Safety

Pre-Lab Discussion

An important part of your study of science will be working in a laboratory. In the laboratory, you and your classmates will learn about the natural world by conducting experiments. Working directly with household objects, laboratory equipment, and even living things will help you to better understand the concepts you read about in your textbook or in class.

Most of the laboratory work you will do is quite safe. However, some laboratory equipment, chemicals, and specimens can be dangerous if handled improperly. Laboratory accidents do not just happen. They are caused by carelessness, improper handling of equipment, or inappropriate behavior.

In this investigation, you will learn how to prevent accidents and thus work safely in a laboratory. You will review some safety guidelines and become acquainted with the location and proper use of safety equipment in your classroom laboratory.

Problem

What are the proper practices for working safely in a science laboratory?

Materials *(per group)*

Science textbook

Laboratory safety equipment (for demonstration)

Procedure

Part A: Reviewing Laboratory Safety Rules and Symbols

1. Carefully read the list of laboratory safety rules listed on pages x – xii of this lab manual.
2. Special symbols are used throughout this lab book to call attention to investigations that require extra caution. Use pages xii and xiii as a reference to describe what each symbol means in numbers 1 through 7 of Observations.

Part B: Location of Safety Equipment in Your Science Laboratory

1. The teacher will point out the location of the safety equipment in your classroom laboratory. Pay special attention to instructions for using such equipment as fire extinguishers, eyewash fountains, fire blankets, safety showers, and items in first-aid kits. Use the space provided in Part B under Observations to list the location of all safety equipment in your laboratory.

Name ______________________ Class ________________ Date ____________

RECOGNIZING LABORATORY SAFETY (continued)

Observations

Part A

1. ____

2. ____

3. ____

4. ____

5. ____

6. ____

7. ____

Part B

Analyze and Conclude

Look at each of the following drawings and explain why the laboratory activities pictured are unsafe.

1.

2.

3.

Critical Thinking and Applications

In each of the following situations, write yes if the proper safety procedures are being followed and no if they are not. Then give a reason for your answer.

1. Gina is thirsty. She rinses a beaker with water, refills it with water, and takes a drink.

____

____

2. Bram notices that the electrical cord on his microscope is frayed near the plug. He takes the microscope to his teacher and asks for permission to use another one.

____

____

3. The printed directions in the lab book tell a student to pour a small amount of hydrochloric acid into a beaker. Jamal puts on safety goggles before pouring the acid into the beaker.

____

____

4. It is rather warm in the laboratory during a late spring day. Anna slips off her shoes and walks barefoot to the sink to clean her glassware.

____

____

5. While washing glassware, Mike splashes some water on Evon. To get even, Evon splashes him back.

____

____

6. During an experiment, Lindsey decides to mix two chemicals that the lab procedure does not say to mix, because she is curious about what will happen.

____

____

Name ______________________ Class ______________ Date ____________

Laboratory Skills Checkup 1

Defining Elements of a Scientific Method

Laboratory activities and experiments involve the use of the scientific method. Listed in the left column are the names of parts of this method. The right column contains definitions. Next to each word in the left column, write the letter of the definition that best matches that word.

_____ **1.** Hypothesis	**A.** Prediction about the outcome of an experiment
_____ **2.** Manipulated Variable	**B.** What you measure or observe to obtain your results
_____ **3.** Responding Variable	**C.** Measurements and other observations
_____ **4.** Controlling Variables	**D.** Statement that sums up what you learn from an experiment
_____ **5.** Observation	**E.** Factor that is changed in an experiment
_____ **6.** Data	**F.** What the person performing the activity sees, hears, feels, smells, or tastes
_____ **7.** Conclusion	**G.** Keeping all variables the same except the manipulated variable

Name ______________________ Class ______________ Date ____________

Laboratory Skills Checkup 2

Analyzing Elements of a Scientific Method

Read the following statements and then answer the questions.

1. You and your friend are walking along a beach in Maine on January 15, at 8:00 am.
2. You notice a thermometer on a nearby building that reads −1°C.
3. You also notice that there is snow on the roof of the building and icicles hanging from the roof.
4. You further notice a pool of sea water in the sand near the ocean.
5. Your friend looks at the icicles and the pool and says, "How come the water on the roof is frozen and the sea water is not?"
6. You answer, "I think that the salt in the sea water keeps it from freezing at −1°C."
7. You go on to say, "And I think under the same conditions, the same thing will happen tomorrow."
8. Your friend asks, "How can you be sure?" You answer, "I'm going to get some fresh water and some salt water and expose them to a temperature of −1°C and see what happens."

Questions

A. In which statement is a prediction made?

____

B. Which statement states a problem?

____

C. In which statement is an experiment described?

____

D. Which statement contains a hypothesis?

____

E. Which statements contain data?

____

F. Which statements describe observations?

____

Name ______________________ Class ______________________ Date ______________

Laboratory Skills Checkup 3

Performing an Experiment

Read the following statements and then answer the questions.

1. A scientist wants to find out why sea water freezes at a lower temperature than fresh water.
2. The scientist goes to the library and reads a number of articles about the physical properties of solutions.
3. The scientist also reads about the composition of sea water.
4. The scientist travels to a nearby beach and observes the conditions there. The scientist notes the taste of the sea water and other factors such as waves, wind, air pressure, temperature, and humidity.
5. After considering all this information, the scientist sits at a desk and writes, "If sea water has salt in it, it will freeze at a lower temperature than fresh water."
6. The scientist goes back to the laboratory and does the following:
   - **a.** Fills each of two beakers with 1 liter of fresh water.
   - **b.** Dissolves 35 grams of table salt in one of the beakers.
   - **c.** Places both beakers in a freezer at a temperature of −1°C.
   - **d.** Leaves the beakers in the freezer for 24 hours.
7. After 24 hours, the scientist examines both beakers and finds the fresh water to be frozen. The salt water is still liquid.
8. The scientist writes in a notebook, "It appears that salt water freezes at a lower temperature than fresh water does."
9. The scientist continues, "I suggest that the reason sea water freezes at a lower temperature is that sea water contains dissolved salts, while fresh water does not."

Questions

A. Which statement(s) contain conclusions? ______________________

B. Which statement(s) contains a hypothesis? ______________________

C. Which statement(s) contain observations? ______________________

D. Which statement(s) describe an experiment? ______________________

E. In which statement is the problem described? ______________________

F. Which statement(s) contain data? ______________________

G. Which is the manipulated variable in the experiment? ______________________

H. What is the responding variable in the experiment? ______________________

Name ______________________ Class ______________ Date __________

Laboratory Skills Checkup 4

Identifying Errors

Read the following paragraph and then answer the questions.

Andrew arrived at school and went directly to his earth science class. He took off his cap and coat and sat down at his desk. His teacher gave him a large rock and asked him to find its density. Realizing that the rock was too large to work with, Andrew got a hammer from the supply cabinet and hit the rock several times until he broke off a chip small enough to work with. He partly filled a graduated cylinder with water and suspended the rock in the water. The water level rose 2 cm. Andrew committed this measurement to memory. He next weighed the rock on a balance. The rock weighed 4 oz. Andrew then calculated the density of the rock as follows: He divided 2 cm by 4 oz. He then reported to his teacher that the density of the rock was 0.5 cm/oz.

Questions

1. What safety rule(s) did Andrew break?

2. What mistake did Andrew make using measurement units?

3. What should Andrew have done with his data rather than commit them to memory?

4. What is wrong with the statement "He next weighed the rock on a balance"?

5. Why is "4 oz" an inappropriate measurement in a science experiment?

6. What mistake did Andrew make in calculating density?

Some Common Laboratory Equipment

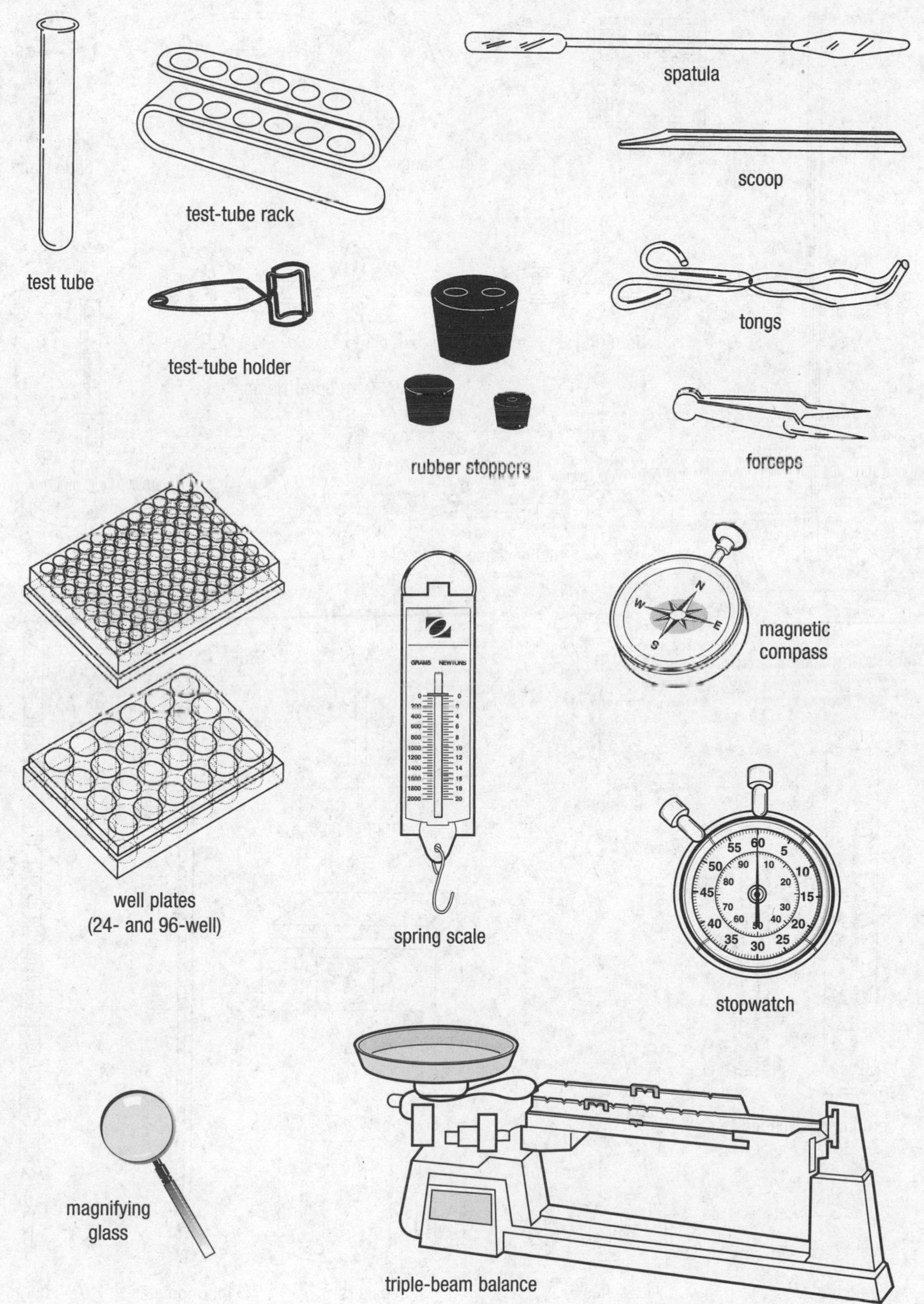

SOME COMMON LABORATORY EQUIPMENT (continued)

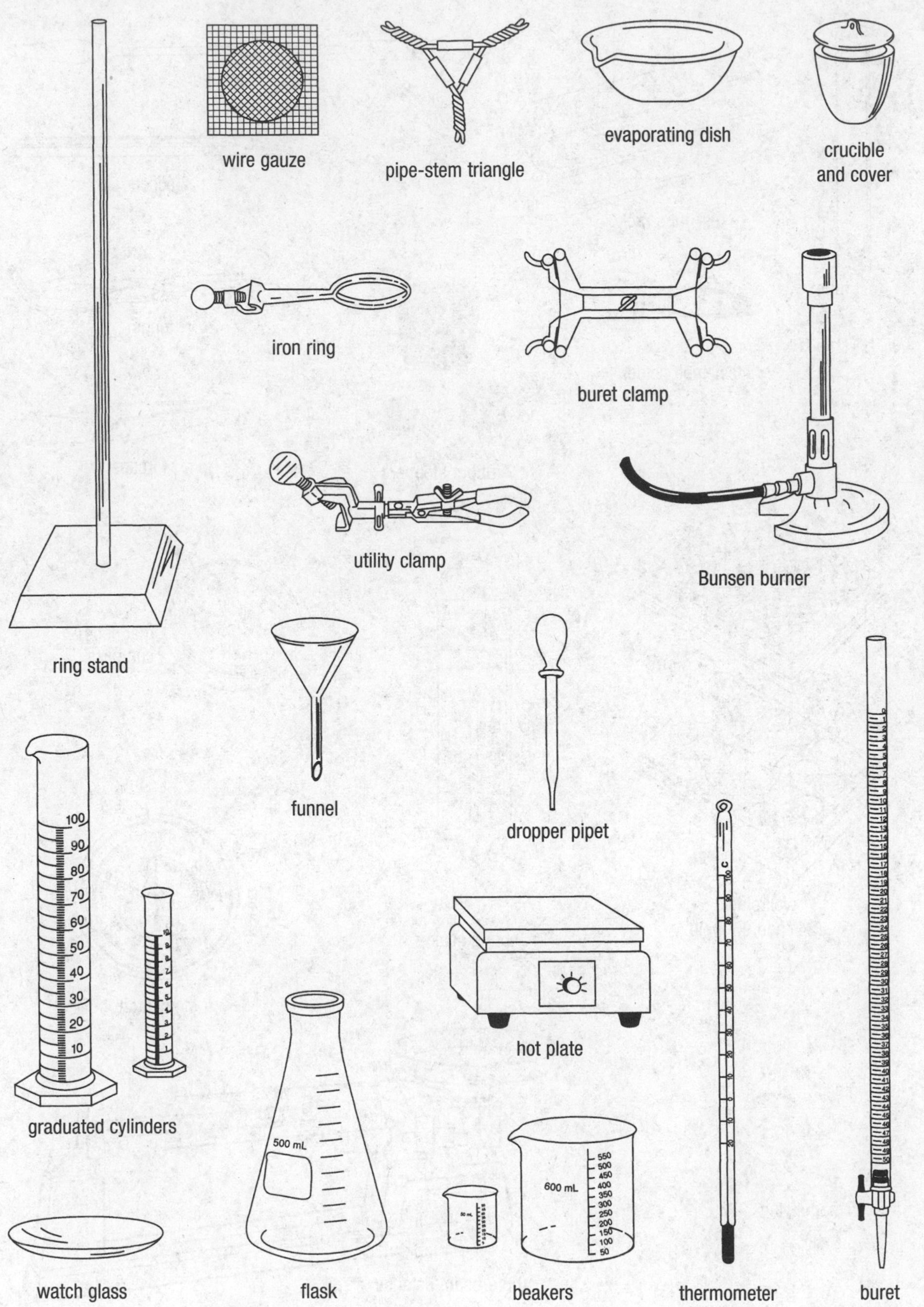

How to Use a Balance

Background Information

The ability to measure accurately the mass of an object is an important skill in the science laboratory. You can use a triple-beam balance to measure mass. As you can see in Figure 1, the balance has several parts. The pan is the flat surface on which you place the object to be measured. The three beams show the mass of the object. Notice that each beam has a different scale. The scale of the middle beam is from 0–500 grams and measures an object to the nearest 100 grams. The scale of the beam in back is from 0–100 grams and measures an object to the nearest 10 grams. The scale of the beam in front is from 0–10 grams and measures an object to the nearest tenth of a gram.

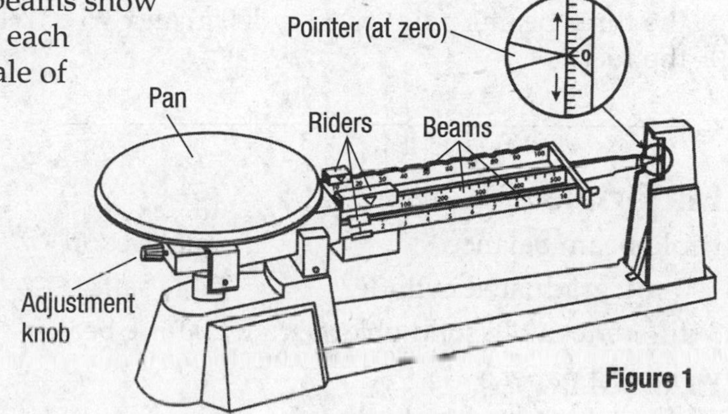

Figure 1

Notice that each beam carries a weight called a rider. You find the mass of an object by placing it on the pan and moving the riders until the pointer on the right of the balance stays pointed to zero.

There are three ways you can use the triple-beam balance to find mass:

Method 1. Measure mass directly. Place the object on the pan and move the riders until the pointer points to zero. Add up the numbers on the beams where the riders are positioned to find mass.

Method 2. Find mass by difference. How could you find the mass of a liquid? First, measure the mass of an empty container that can hold the liquid. Then, measure the combined mass of the container and the liquid. Finally, subtract the mass of the container from the combined mass.

Method 3. Measure out a chemical substance. Suppose you need to obtain 50 g of a powdered chemical. How could you do it? First find the mass of a piece of paper or empty container that will hold the chemical. Then, add this amount to the desired mass of the chemical and preset the riders to this number. Finally, add the chemical to the paper a little at a time until the pointer points to zero.

In this investigation, you will learn how to measure accurately the mass of various objects by using the three methods described above.

Problem

What is the proper way to use the triple-beam balance to measure the mass of different objects?

Name ______________________ Class ________________ Date __________

Pre-Lab Discussion

Read the entire investigation. Then, work with a partner to answer the following questions.

1. What does it mean when the pointer of the balance reads "zero"?

____

____

2. Suppose a rock is balanced on a triple-beam balance. The riders on the three beams point to 60 g, 300 g, and 3.5 g. What is the mass of the rock?

____

Materials *(per group)*

triple-beam balance
100-mL graduated cylinder
3 different small, solid objects
weighing paper
small scoop
table salt
200-mL beaker

Safety ⚠

Review the safety guidelines in the front of your lab book. Note all safety alert symbols next to the steps in the Procedure and review the meaning of each symbol by referring to the Safety Symbols on page xiii.

Procedure

Before you measure the mass of any object, be sure that the riders are moved all the way to the left and that the pointer rests on zero. If necessary, slowly turn the adjustment knob until the pointer rests on zero. This is called zeroing the balance.

Part A: Measuring Mass Directly

1. Place a small, solid object on the balance pan. The beams will rise and the pointer will point above zero.
2. Move the rider on the middle beam on notch at a time until the pointer drops and stays below zero. Move the rider back one notch.
3. Move the rider on the back beam one notch at a time until the pointer again drops and stays below zero. Move the rider back one notch.
4. Slide the rider along the front beam until the pointer stops at zero. The mass of the object is equal to the sum of the readings on the three beams.
5. Record the mass to the nearest tenth of a gram in Data Table 1.
6. Remove this object and repeat Steps 1–5 twice, using two other solid objects.

Name ______________________ Class ________________ Date ____________

Part B: Finding Mass by Difference

7. Find the mass of an empty 250-mL beaker. Record the mass in Data Table 2.
8. Using the graduated cylinder, obtain 50 mL of water.
9. Pour the water into the beaker and find the mass of the beaker and water. Record the mass in Data Table 2.

Part C: Measuring Out a Chemical Substance

10. Place a piece of weighing paper on the balance pan and find its mass. Record the mass in Data Table 3.
11. Add 5 g to the mass of the weighing paper and move the riders to this number.
12. Obtain a sample of table salt from the teacher. Using the scoop, add a small amount of salt at a time to the paper on the balance until the pointer rests on zero. Record the total mass of the weighing paper and salt in Data Table 3.
13. Dispose of the table salt in the container provided by the teacher.

Observations

DATA TABLE 1

Object	Mass (g)

DATA TABLE 2

Mass of Empty Beaker (g)	Mass of Beaker with 50 mL of Water (g)

DATA TABLE 3

Mass of Weighing Paper (g)	Mass of Weighing Paper and Table Salt (g)

Analyze and Conclude

1. What is the mass of 50 mL of water? How did you find this mass?

____

____

____

2. Which rider on the balance should always be moved first when finding the mass of an object? Why?

____

____

____

3. What is the mass of the largest object your balance is able to measure?

____

____

4. What is the mass of the smallest object your balance is able to measure accurately?

5. After using your balance, how should it always be left?

6. Suppose you did not zero the balance before finding the mass of an object. How might that affect your measurement?

7. In this lab, you found the mass of 50 mL of water. Calculate the mass of 1 mL of water. (Do not use the balance.)

8. Describe how you could find the mass of a certain quantity of milk that you poured into a drinking glass.

9. If you were baking a dessert and the recipe called for 250 g of sugar, how could you use the triple-beam balance to obtain this amount?

Go Further

Design a balance that finds mass by comparing the mass of a known object to the mass of an unknown object. Study the triple-beam balance used in this activity and think about how you could balance two or more objects. Construct your balance and use it to find the mass of an object. How could you improve your balance?

Evaluating Precision

Background Information

When an object is measured more than once, the measurements may vary. The closeness of a set of measured values to each other is called **precision.** Many people confuse precision with accuracy. **Accuracy** is a measure of how close the values are to the actual value. A set of values can be in close agreement, or precise, without being accurate.

For example, suppose you repeatedly measure the mass of a 4.00-g object by using a balance that reads too low by 3.00 g every time. You might get nearly identical readings—for example, 1.00 g, 1.01 g, and 0.99 g. These readings are quite precise because they are close together. However, they differ from the actual value by a large amount. Therefore, the measurements are very inaccurate.

In this investigation, you will make several measurements of length, temperature, and volume. Then, you will evaluate the precision of your measurements by comparing them to measurements made by your classmates.

Problem

How can you determine the precision and accuracy of measurements?

Pre-Lab Discussion

Read the entire investigation. Then, work with a partner to answer the following questions.

1. **Applying Concepts** Use the example of a series of repeated length measurements to explain the meaning of precision.

____

____

____

____

____

____

2. **Inferring** What information would you need to determine the accuracy of a measurement?

____

____

____

____

____

Name ______________________ Class ________________ Date ____________

3. **Drawing Conclusions** In this investigation, you will compare measurements that you make to measurements that your classmates make. Will you do this to determine the accuracy or the precision of your measurements?

4. **Designing Experiments** Identify the manipulated, responding, and controlled variables in this investigation.

   a. Manipulated variable

   b. Responding variable

   c. Controlled variables

5. **Analyzing Data** Two students measure the mass of a wooden disk, using the same balance. The first student repeats the weighing three times and obtains mass readings of 47 g, 52 g, and 51 g. The second student obtains mass readings of 45 g, 55 g, and 50 g. Explain which set of measurements is more precise. Can you tell if the measurements are accurate? Why or why not?

Name ______________________ Class ________________ Date ____________

Materials *(per group)*

meter stick

Celsius thermometer

500-mL beaker filled with room-temperature water

10 pennies

50-mL graduated cylinder

Safety

Put on safety goggles and a lab apron. Be careful to avoid breakage when working with glassware. Note all safety alert symbols next to the steps in the Procedure and review the meaning of each symbol by referring to the Safety Symbols on page xiii.

Procedure

1. You and your partner make up a team. Your team and two other teams will make up a group of six. Your teacher will tell you and your partner whether you are Team A, B, or C of your group. The three teams in your group will measure the same objects separately. You will not share your measurements with the other teams in your group until you complete the procedure.
2. Working with your partner, use the meter stick to measure the length of a desk indicated by your teacher. Measure as carefully as possible, to the nearest millimeter. Record the length of the desk in the data table. (*Hint:* Do not reveal the measurements you make to the other teams in your group. They must make the same measurements and must not be influenced by your results.)
3. Use the thermometer to measure the temperature of the beaker of room-temperature water. **CAUTION:** *Do not let the thermometer hit the beaker.* Record this measurement in the data table.
4. Place 25 mL of tap water in the graduated cylinder. Measure the volume of the water. Record this volume in the data table to the nearest 0.1 mL. (*Hint:* Remember to read the volume at the bottom of the meniscus.)
5. Add the 10 pennies to the graduated cylinder. Read the volume of the water and pennies. Record this volume in the data table to the nearest 0.1 mL.
6. Subtract the volume of the water from the volume of the water and pennies. The result is a measurement of the volume of the pennies. Record this value in the data table.
7. After all three teams in your group have finished measuring the same objects for length, temperature, and volume, share your results with the other two teams. Record their measurements in the data table.

Name ______________________ Class ______________ Date ____________

Observations

DATA TABLE

Measurement	Team A	Team B	Team C
Length of desk (mm)			
Temperature of water (°C)			
Volume of water (mL)			
Volume of water and pennies (mL)			
Volume of pennies (mL)			

Analysis and Conclusions

1. Calculating Average the three length measurements you compared by adding them together and dividing the result by 3. Find the range of values by calculating the difference between the largest and smallest values. Record the results of your calculations in the space below.

a. Average of length measurements (mm)

____

b. Range of length measurements (mm)

____

2. **Making Generalizations** Would it be correct to use the range of values you calculated in Question 1 to describe the precision of the measurements? The accuracy of the measurements? Explain your answer.

3. **Analyzing Data** Which of the three sets of measurements had the least spread among the measurements? Suggest reasons for the precision of these measurements.

4. **Applying Concepts** Figure 1 shows the results of three people's attempts to shoot as many bull's-eyes as possible. Below Figure 1, label each of the results as *accurate* or *not accurate,* and as *precise* or *not precise.*

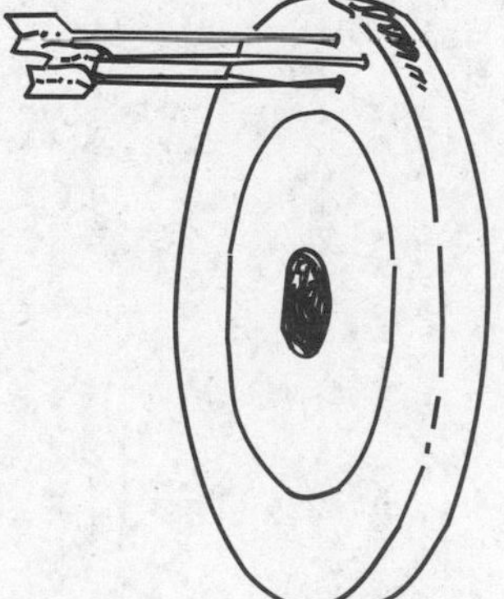

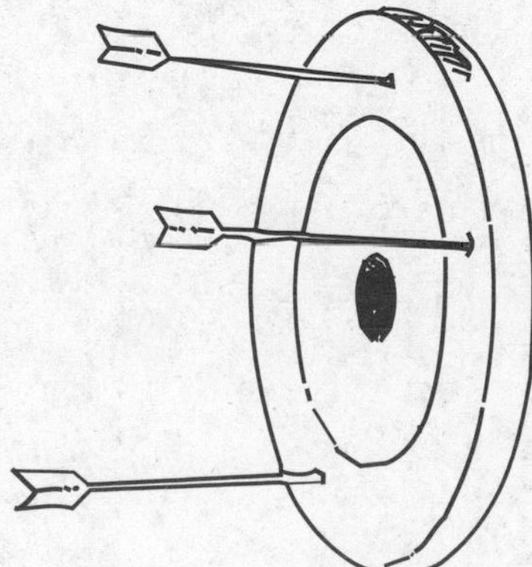

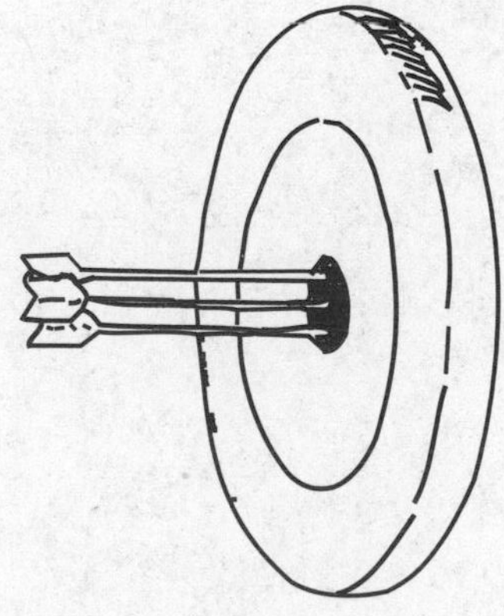

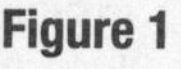

Figure 1

Name ______________________ Class __________________ Date ______________

5. **Evaluating and Revising** Discuss the reasons for the differences among the teams' measurements with the members of your group. Describe these reasons and explain how the measurements could be made more precise.

Go Further

Design an experiment to compare the precision of two or more measuring instruments. Is the precision of each instrument the same throughout its range of measurements? Write a procedure you would follow to answer these questions. After your teacher approves your procedure, carry out the experiment and report your results.

Measuring Volume and Temperature

Background Information

The amount of space an object takes up is called its volume. A commonly used unit of volume is the liter (L). Smaller volumes can be measured in milliliters (mL). One milliliter is equal to 1/1000 of a liter. In the laboratory, the graduated cylinder is often used to measure the volume of liquids.

Temperature is measured with a thermometer. The unit of measurement for temperature is the degree Celsius (°C).

In this investigation, you will practice making measurements of the volume and temperature of a liquid.

Problem

How can you accurately measure the volume and temperature of a liquid?

Pre-Lab Discussion

Read the entire investigation. Then, work with a partner to answer the following questions.

1. **Measuring** How many significant figures are there in the measurement shown in Figure 1?

____

2. **Inferring** Why is it important to read the volume of water in a graduated cylinder by using the bottom of the meniscus?

____

____

____

____

3. **Designing Experiments** Why should you leave the thermometer in beaker B when you add ice?

____

____

____

____

4. **Measuring** If each mark on a thermometer represents 1°C, which part of a temperature measurement will be the estimated digit?

____

____

Name ______________________ Class ________________ Date ____________

Materials *(per group)*

2 150-mL beakers
100-mL graduated cylinder
glass-marking pencil
2 Celsius thermometers
watch or clock
ice cube

Safety

Put on safety goggles and a lab apron. Be careful to avoid breakage when working with glassware. Note all safety alert symbols next to the steps in the Procedure and review the meaning of each symbol by referring to the Safety Symbols on page xiii.

Procedure

Part A: Measuring the Volume of a Liquid

1. Fill a beaker halfway with water.
2. Pour the water in the beaker into the graduated cylinder.
3. Measure the amount of water in the graduated cylinder. To accurately measure the volume, your eye must be at the same level as the bottom of the meniscus, as shown in Figure 1. The meniscus is the curved surface of the water.

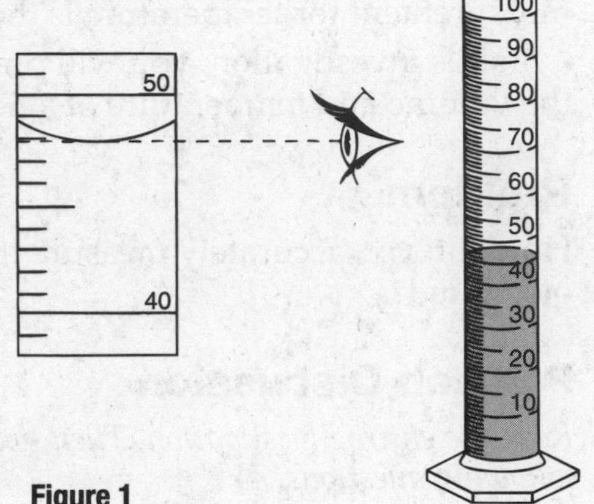

Figure 1

4. Estimate the volume of water to the nearest 0.1 mL. Record this volume in Data Table 1.
5. Repeat Steps 1 through 4, but this time fill the beaker only one-fourth full of water.

Part B: Measuring the Temperature of a Liquid

6. Use the glass-marking pencil to label the beakers *A* and *B*.
7. Use the graduated cylinder to put 50 mL of water in each beaker.
8. Place a thermometer in each beaker. In Data Table 2, record the temperature of the water in each beaker.
9. Carefully add one ice cube to the water in beaker B. Note and record the time.
10. After 1 minute, observe the temperature of the water in each beaker. Record these temperatures in Data Table 2.
11. After 5 minutes, observe the temperature of the water in each beaker. Record these temperatures in Data Table 2.
12. After the ice in beaker B has melted, use the graduated cylinder to find the volume of water in each beaker. Record these volumes in Data Table 3.

Name ____________________ Class ______________ Date __________

Observations

DATA TABLE 1

Measurement	Volume of Water (mL)
Half-filled beaker	
One-fourth filled beaker	

DATA TABLE 2

Beaker	Temperature at Beginning	(°C) Temperature After 1 Minute (°C)	Temperature After 5 Minutes (°C)
A			
B			

DATA TABLE 3

Beaker	Volume of Water at Beginning (mL)	Volume of Water at End (mL)
A		
B		

Name ______________________ Class __________________ Date ____________

Analysis and Conclusions

1. **Observing** What is the largest volume of a liquid that the graduated cylinder is able to measure? What is the smallest volume that the graduated cylinder is able to measure?

2. **Analyzing Data** Describe how the temperature of the water in beakers A and B changed during the investigation.

3. **Analyzing Data** How did the volume of water in beakers A and B change during the investigation? What do you think caused this change?

4. **Applying Concepts** Would you use a 100-mL graduated cylinder, a 25-mL graduated cylinder, or 10-mL graduated cylinder to measure 8 mL of a liquid? Explain your answer.

Go Further

Some liquids do not form a meniscus in a graduated cylinder as water does. Use a 10-mL graduated cylinder to measure 8.0 mL each of water, isopropyl (rubbing) alcohol, and vegetable oil. Observe and draw the meniscus of each liquid. Label your drawings to show how you think the volume of each liquid should be measured. Explain why you think that the volumes should be measured in this way.

Recognizing Chemical and Physical Changes

Background Information

Some chemical and physical changes are easy to recognize. Other changes may be easy to observe, but difficult to classify as a chemical or a physical change just by observation. Many events that occur in nature, such as volcanic eruptions, include both chemical and physical changes. When you observe a complicated event, you may need more information before you can identify the chemical and physical changes that have occurred.

In this investigation, you will observe several events and identify the chemical and physical changes involved in each.

Problem

How can you identify chemical and physical changes?

Pre-Lab Discussion

Read the entire investigation. Then, work with a partner to answer the following questions.

1. **Observing** What evidence of chemical changes will you look for in this investigation?

____

____

____

2. **Inferring** What are some examples of physical changes that you might observe in this investigation?

____

____

3. **Predicting** In which step of this investigation is a physical change most likely to occur? Explain your answer.

____

____

4. **Predicting** In which step of this investigation is a chemical change most likely to occur? Explain your answer.

____

____

____

Name ______________________ Class ________________ Date ____________

Materials *(per group)*

4 test tubes
glass-marking pencil
test-tube rack
magnesium chloride solution
sodium carbonate solution
copper sulfate solution
white vinegar (acetic acid solution)
aluminum foil
calcium carbonate chip
paraffin candle
matches
clock or watch

Safety

Put on safety goggles and a lab apron. Be careful to avoid breakage when working with glassware. Always use caution when working with laboratory chemicals, as they may irritate the skin or stain skin or clothing. Never touch or taste any chemical unless instructed to do so. Be careful when using matches. Tie back loose hair and clothing when working with flames. Do not reach over an open flame. Wash your hands thoroughly after carrying out this investigation. Note all safety alert symbols next to the steps in the Procedure and review the meaning of each symbol by referring to the Safety Symbols on page xiii.

Procedure

1. Use the glass-marking pencil to label the test tubes *1* to *4*. Place the test tubes in a test-tube rack.
2. Fill each test tube one-third full with the solution indicated in Data Table 1.
3. Observe each of the solutions and record your observations in Data Table 1.
4. Observe the appearance of the aluminum foil, the calcium carbonate chip, and the paraffin candle. Record your observations in Data Table 1.
5. Pour the sodium carbonate solution from test tube 2 into the magnesium chloride solution in test tube 1. Observe what happens and record your observations in Data Table 2.
6. Crumple up the aluminum foil and drop it into the copper sulfate solution in test tube 3. Observe test tube 3 every 2 minutes for 10 minutes. Record your observations in Data Table 2.
7. Carefully drop the calcium carbonate chip into the vinegar (acetic acid solution) in test tube 4. Record your observations in Data Table 2.

8. Use a match to light the paraffin candle. Observe what happens to the candle for 5 minutes. In Data Table 3, record what happens to the candle. **CAUTION:** *Be careful not to burn yourself or others.*

9. Complete Data Tables 2 and 3, identifying each change you observed as chemical or physical.

10. Follow your teacher's instructions for disposing of the used chemicals. Wash your hands thoroughly with warm water and soap or detergent before leaving the laboratory.

Observations

DATA TABLE 1

Material	Observations
Test tube 1: magnesium chloride solution	
Test tube 2: sodium carbonate solution	
Test tube 3: copper sulfate solution	
Test tube 4: vinegar (acetic acid solution)	
Aluminum foil	
Calcium carbonate	
Paraffin candle	

Name ______________ Class ______________ Date ______________

DATA TABLE 2

Materials	Observations	Type of Change (chemical or physical)
Magnesium chloride and sodium carbonate solutions		
Copper sulfate solution and aluminum foil		
Calcium carbonate and vinegar		

DATA TABLE 3

Observation	Type of Change (chemical or physical)

Name ______________________ Class ______________ Date ____________

Analysis and Conclusions

1. **Inferring** What type of change occurred when you mixed the magnesium chloride solution with the sodium carbonate solution? Explain your answer.

2. **Inferring** What type of change occurred in the copper sulfate solution when you placed the aluminum foil in it? Explain your answer.

3. **Inferring** What type of change occurred in the acetic acid solution when you placed the calcium carbonate chip in it? Explain your answer.

4. **Evaluating** What evidence was there that new substances formed as the candle burned?

5. **Evaluating** What evidence of a physical change did you observe as the candle burned?

6. **Drawing Conclusions** What signs of chemical changes did you observe in this investigation?

7. **Evaluating and Revising** Formation of a solid, formation of a gas, and a color change can also occur during some physical changes. Give examples of physical changes that could produce these clues. What evidence suggests that the changes you observed in test tubes 1–3 were, in fact, chemical changes?

Go Further

Many activities that people do at home on a regular basis can involve both physical and chemical changes. Examples include cooking or gardening. Pick an activity that you participate in at home and make a list of tasks for that activity. Divide the list into tasks during which a physical change occurs and tasks during which a chemical change occurs. Give reasons for your classifications.

Determining the Densities of Liquids

Background Information

Mass and volume are properties of all matter. **Density** is the ratio of an object's mass to its volume. The density of a specific kind of matter helps to identify it and distinguish it from other kinds of matter. It is possible to determine the densities of liquids in grams per milliliter (g/mL).

In this investigation, you will determine the densities of several liquids by measuring their masses and volumes.

Problem

How can you determine the densities of liquids?

Pre-Lab Discussion

Read the entire investigation. Then, work with a partner to answer the following questions.

1. **Formulating Hypotheses** For identical volumes, what will the relationship be between the mass and the density of a sample?

2. **Controlling Variables** What are the manipulated and responding variables in this investigation?

3. **Controlling Variables** What is the controlled variable in this investigation?

4. **Calculating** Why is it necessary to know the mass of the graduated cylinder in order to find the mass of the liquid?

Name ______________________ Class ________________ Date ____________

5. **Predicting** Predict which liquid will be the most dense and which will be the least dense.

____

____

____

Materials *(per group)*

2 100-mL graduated cylinders
triple-beam balance
50 mL denatured ethanol (ethyl alcohol)
50 mL salt water
paper towels

Safety

Put on safety goggles and a lab apron. Be careful to avoid breakage when working with glassware. Always use caution when working with laboratory chemicals, as they may irritate the skin or stain skin or clothing. Never touch or taste any chemical unless instructed to do so. Keep alcohol away from any open flame. Wash your hands thoroughly after carrying out this investigation. Note all safety alert symbols next to the steps in the Procedure and review the meaning of each symbol by referring to the Safety Symbols on page xiii.

Procedure

1. Place a clean graduated cylinder on the laboratory balance. In the data table, record the mass of the graduated cylinder.
2. Place about 50 mL of water in the graduated cylinder. Record the exact volume to the nearest tenth of a milliliter. Use a paper towel to wipe any water from the outside of the cylinder. Find the mass of the graduated cylinder and the water. Record this mass in the data table. **CAUTION:** *Wipe up any spilled liquids immediately to avoid slips and falls.*
3. Calculate the mass of the water by subtracting the mass of the graduated cylinder from the mass of the graduated cylinder and water. Record your answer in the data table.
4. Calculate the density of water, using the following equation. Record the density of water in the data table.

$$\text{Density} = \frac{\text{Mass}}{\text{Volume}}$$

5. Repeat Steps 1 through 4. This time, use a clean graduated cylinder and denatured ethanol instead of water. **CAUTION:** *Denatured ethanol is poisonous and flammable. Do not drink it. Do not use denatured ethanol near an open flame.*
6. Empty the graduated cylinder containing water and dry it thoroughly with a paper towel. Repeat Steps 1 through 4, using this graduated cylinder and the sample of salt water.

Name ____________________ Class ________________ Date ____________

Observations

DATA TABLE

Liquid	Mass of Graduated Cylinder (g)	Mass of Graduated Cylinder and Liquid (g)	Mass of Liquid (g)	Volume of Liquid (mL)	Density of Liquid (g/mL)
Water					
Ethanol					
Salt water					

Analysis and Conclusions

1. **Analyzing Data** List the three liquids you studied in order of increasing density.

____

____

____

2. **Comparing and Contrasting** Which has the greater mass—1 L of water or 1 L of denatured ethanol? Explain your answer.

____

____

____

____

____

3. **Comparing and Contrasting** Which has a greater volume—1000 g of water or 1000 g of denatured ethanol? Explain your answer.

____

____

____

____

____

4. **Inferring** Which is more dense—1 mL of water or 50 L of water? Explain your answer.

5. **Predicting** Predict what would happen to the density of the salt solution if more salt was dissolved in a given volume of solution. Explain your answer.

Go Further

Use your data to predict the position of a small wooden dowel (or small pencil) placed in samples of the liquids used in this investigation. Would more or less of the dowel be visible above the surface of the liquid in each case? Plan a new investigation to test your predictions. Show your plan to your teacher. If your teacher approves your plan, carry out your experiment and report your results.

Desalinization by Distillation

Background Information

"Water, water everywhere, but not a drop to drink." This quotation is from *The Rime of the Ancient Mariner* by Samuel Coleridge, a poem that describes the fate of sailors in a boat that is stranded in the middle of the Pacific Ocean. The sailors are surrounded by water that they cannot drink. Both fresh water and seawater contain dissolved salts. But the amount of dissolved salts in a liter of seawater is much larger. Drinking seawater causes water to flow out of cells in the body, which increases dehydration. This effect is the exact opposite of the desired effect of drinking water.

In regions where the supply of fresh water is limited, seawater can be treated to make it safe to drink. The general name for processes that remove salts from water is desalinization. One method for separating dissolved salts from water is called distillation. During a distillation process, a liquid undergoes phase changes—vaporization followed by condensation.

Temperature and pressure affect the rate of vaporization. At atmospheric pressure, the rate of vaporization will be most rapid when a liquid is at a temperature equal to its boiling point. The container in which the hot vapor is collected must be chilled so that the vapor will rapidly condense. Distilling a liquid at its boiling point requires heat-resistant containers and a source of energy to heat the liquid, such as a gas burner. Sunlight can be used as the source of energy for distillation, but the process will take more time.

In Part A of this investigation, you will distill salt water by heating and boiling the salt water. In Part B of this investigation, you will use sunlight to vaporize the water.

Problem

How is the desalinization of salt water accomplished by distillation?

Pre-Lab Discussion

Read the entire investigation. Then, work with a partner to answer the following questions.

1. **Predicting** In Part A, how will the contents of the cooled flask differ from the contents of the heated flask?

____

____

2. **Measuring** In Part A, are you measuring the temperature of the liquid in the flask or the vapor? Explain your answer.

____

____

____

3. **Designing Experiments** In Part B, why is it important to keep the clear bottle away from direct sunlight?

____

____

____

4. **Formulating Hypotheses** In Part B, why is the bottle containing the salt water placed on a board? (*Hint:* Assume that some water vapor condenses in the plastic tubing.)

____

____

____

5. **Inferring** Differences in what physical property are used to separate the table salt from the water in the salt-water mixture?

____

____

____

Materials *(per group)*

2 250-mL flasks
100-mL graduated cylinder
500-mL beaker
Lab burner
2-hole rubber stopper with glass tubing and non-mercury thermometer inserted
2 40-cm pieces of clear plastic tubing
ring stand and ring
wire gauze
salt water
crushed ice
2 2-L plastic bottles
electrical or masking tape
wooden board, at least 3 cm thick
glass marking pencil
graph paper

Safety

Put on safety goggles and a lab apron. Be careful to avoid breakage when working with glassware. Never touch or taste any chemical unless instructed to do so. Use extreme care when working with heated equipment or materials to avoid burns. Observe proper laboratory procedures when using electrical equipment. Tie back loose hair and clothing when working with flames. Be careful when using matches. Do not reach over an open flame. Note all safety alert symbols next to the steps in the Procedure and review the meaning of each symbol by referring to the Safety Symbols on page xiii.

Procedure

Part A: Distillation of Salt Water By Boiling

1. Set up the apparatus, as shown in Figure 1. **CAUTION:** *Be sure that all glassware used in this investigation is heat-resistant.*
2. Place 100 mL of the salt-water solution in the flask to be heated.
3. Gently push one end of the rubber tubing onto the right-angle glass tubing. Place the stopper containing the right-angle glass tubing and thermometer firmly on the flask of salt water. The bulb of the thermometer should be near the top of the flask and not in the liquid. If necessary, ask your teacher to adjust the position of the thermometer.
4. Fill the beaker with crushed ice and set it away from the burner. Place the second flask in the crushed ice. Insert the open end of the plastic tubing in the middle of the flask, making sure that the tubing does not touch the bottom of the flask.

Figure 1

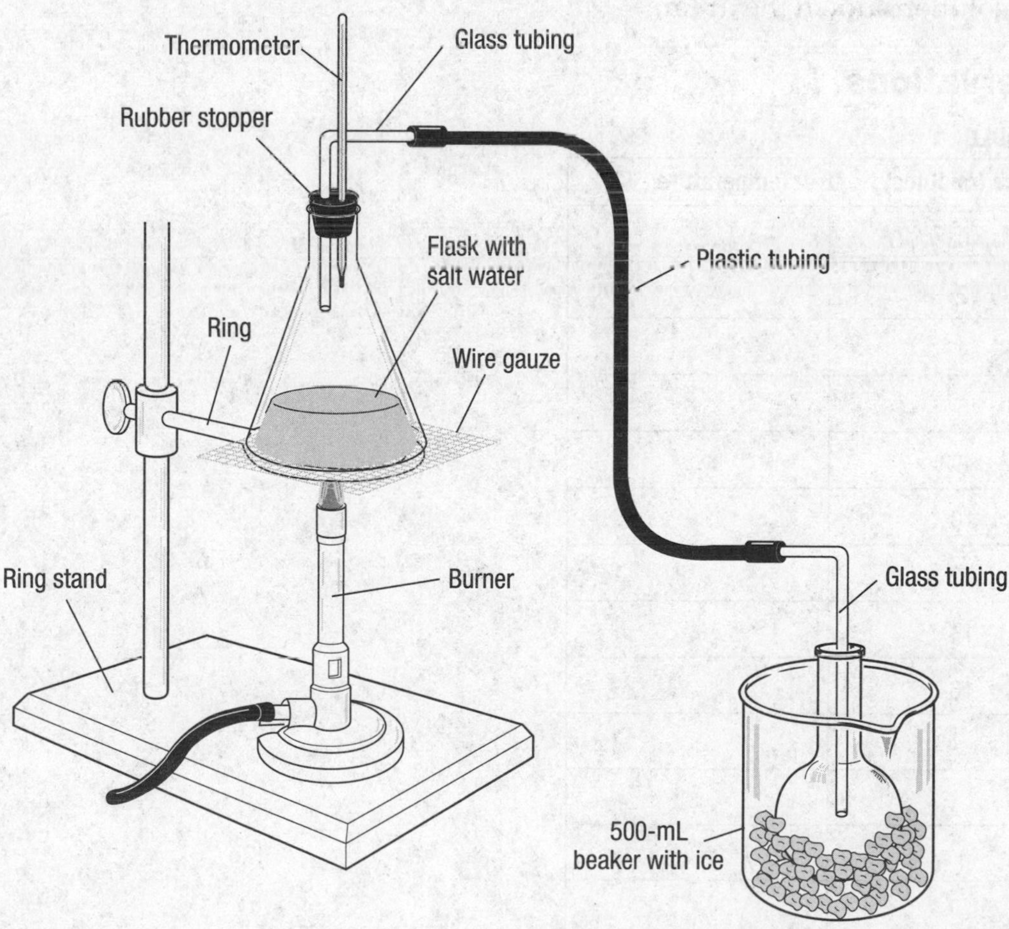

Name ______________________ Class ______________ Date ____________

5. Observe the temperature in the flask containing salt water. Record this temperature in the data table. Turn on the burner. Note and record the temperature at 2-minute intervals as you complete Steps 6 and 7. Attach a separate sheet of paper if you need more space to record the temperature.
6. When the temperature stops rising, you should notice a liquid beginning to collect in the flask in the beaker of crushed ice. Circle the temperature at this time in the data table. **CAUTION:** *Do not allow the plastic tubing to touch the liquid being collected.*
7. Continue collecting liquid in the cooled flask until about three-fourths of the liquid in the heated flask has been vaporized. Turn off the burner.
8. Observe the appearance of the contents of the cooled flask and the heated flask.
9. Allow the heated flask to cool. **CAUTION:** *Be careful in handling equipment that has been heated. Hot glass looks like cold glass. Do not touch the heated flask or burner.*
10. When the flask has cooled enough to handle, pour both of the solutions down the drain.

Observations

DATA TABLE

Time (minutes)	Temperature (°C)
0	
2	
4	
6	
8	
10	
12	
14	
16	

Name ______________________ Class ______________ Date ___________

Part B: Distillation of Salt Water by Evaporation

11. Set up the apparatus, as shown in Figure 2. Wrap the electrical or masking tape around both ends of the plastic tube so that the tube will fit tightly into the necks of the plastic bottles.
12. Place 100 mL of tap water in the clear bottle. Use a glass marking pencil to mark the height of the water. Pour the water down the drain.
13. Place 100 mL of the salt-water solution in the black bottle.
14. Insert one end of the plastic tubing into the neck of the black bottle, and the other end into the neck of the clear bottle.
15. Set both bottles on a window sill that has exposure to sunlight during at least half of the day. Set the black bottle on the wooden board so that it is at a higher position than the clear bottle. Arrange the bottles so that the black bottle receives sunlight as much as possible, while the clear bottle is kept out of the sun as much as possible.
16. Check the bottles daily until at least 75 percent of the liquid has been transferred to the clear bottle.
17. Pour the liquid from the black bottle clear container into a graduated cylinder and record the volume.
18. Observe the appearance of the two liquids. Then pour the liquids down the drain.

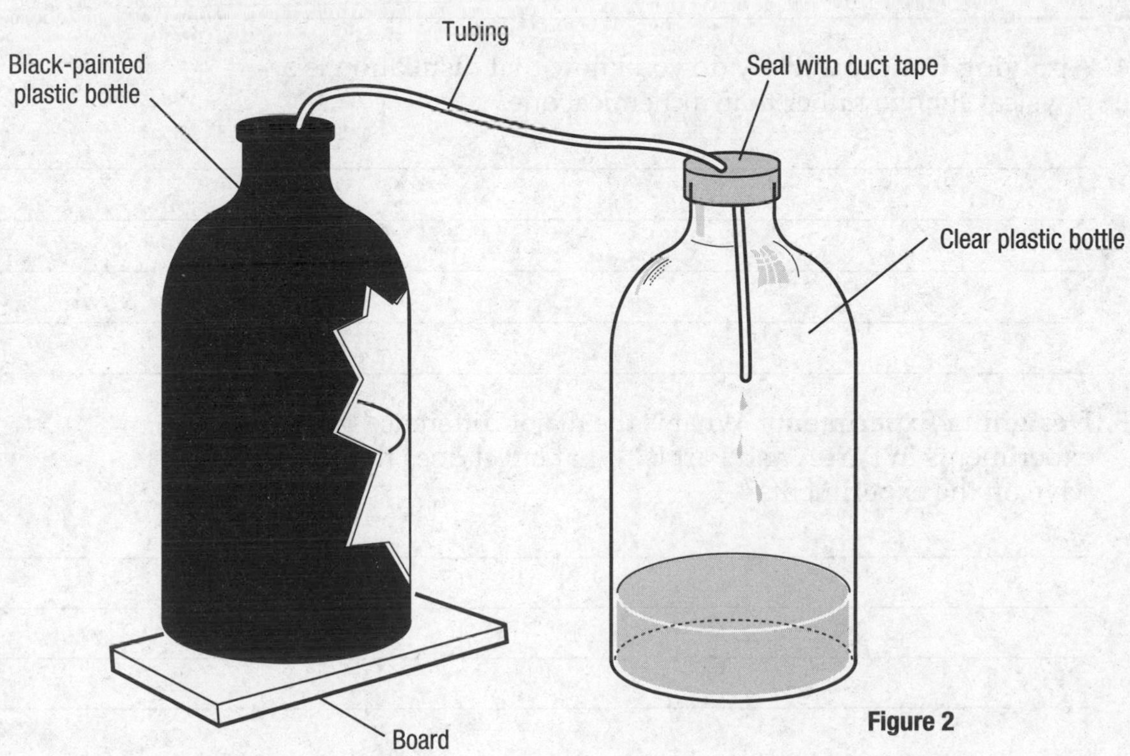

Figure 2

Analysis and Conclusions

1. **Using Tables and Graphs** Draw a graph of your data from Part A. Plot time along the horizontal axis and temperature along the vertical axis. Label the point on your graph that corresponds to the time when you started to collect distilled liquid in the cooled flask.

2. **Observing** Did you observe any evidence that the liquids in the heated and cooled flasks had different compositions?

3. **Designing Experiments** Suggest at least one procedure that you could use to demonstrate that the liquids in the heated and cooled flasks have different compositions.

4. **Applying Concepts** How do you know that distillation is a physical change rather than a chemical one?

5. **Designing Experiments** What is the major difference between the experiments in Part A and Part B? What effect does this difference have on the experiments?

Name ______________________ Class __________________ Date ____________

6. **Comparing and Contrasting** List the advantages of each method used in this investigation for distilling water.

____

____

____

____

____

7. **Classifying** During vaporization, a liquid changes to a gas or a vapor. Explain how the temperature at which vaporization takes place determines whether the process is described as evaporation or boiling. (*Hint:* These terms occur in the titles for Parts A and B of this investigation.)

____

____

____

____

Go Further

Distilled water can be distinguished from salt water based on a difference in density. You can use a fresh, raw egg to demonstrate this difference. Predict what you will observe when you place the egg in the liquids. Have your teacher supervise your experiment. Wash your hands thoroughly with soap or detergent after you complete the experiment.

Investigating Space Between Particles in Matter

Background Information

If you have ever seen water drain through beach sand, you know that there are spaces between the grains of sand. Because the grains of sand are relatively small and separate, you can pour sand almost as if it was a liquid. There are also spaces between the tiny particles that make up all matter.

In this investigation, you will first measure the volume of the space between grains of sand by filling a container with sand and water. Then, you will measure the volume of the space between the particles in a liquid by mixing two liquids together.

Problem

How much space is there between grains of sand or between particles in liquids?

Pre-Lab Discussion

Read the entire investigation. Then, work with a partner to answer the following questions.

1. **Using Analogies** Why is there space between marbles in a bowl? What factors might determine how much space there is between particles in a solid or liquid?

____

____

____

____

____

2. **Predicting** What do you expect to happen to the height of the material in the beaker when you begin to add water to the sand? Explain your answer.

____

____

____

____

____

____

3. **Predicting** In the investigation, you will mix 100 mL of water with 100 mL of isopropyl alcohol. Predict whether the volume of this mixture will be less than, equal to, or more than 200 mL. Explain your answer.

____

____

____

____

____

Materials *(per group)*

2 250-mL graduated cylinders
100-mL graduated cylinder
isopropyl alcohol
sand
glass stirring rod

Safety

Put on safety goggles and a lab apron. Be careful to avoid breakage when working with glassware. Always use caution when working with laboratory chemicals, as they may irritate the skin or stain skin or clothing. Never taste any chemicals unless instructed to do so. Keep alcohol away from any open flame. Wash your hands thoroughly after carrying out this investigation. Note all safety alert symbols next to the steps in the Procedure and review the meaning of each symbol by referring to the Safety Symbols on page xiii.

Procedure

1. Fill a 250-mL graduated cylinder to its 200-mL mark with sand.
2. Fill the 100-mL graduated cylinder to the 100-mL mark with water. Slowly pour a little water into the graduated cylinder containing the sand. Continue pouring until the level of the water in the sand reaches the 200-mL line. Observe the volume of water remaining in the 100-mL graduated cylinder. Record this volume in Data Table 1.
3. Calculate the volume of water added to the sand by subtracting the volume of water remaining in the graduated cylinder from the total volume of water. Record your result in Data Table 1.
4. Pour 100 mL of isopropyl alcohol into the 250-mL graduated cylinder. **CAUTION:** *Isopropyl alcohol is poisonous and flammable.*
5. Fill the 100-mL graduated cylinder to the 100-mL mark with water. Slowly pour the water into the graduated cylinder containing the isopropyl alcohol. Use the glass stirring rod to mix the two liquids. Observe the volume of the mixture. Record this volume in Data Table 2.

Name ______________________ Class ________________ Date __________

6. Subtract the volume of the alcohol-water mixture from the total volume of alcohol and water. Record this difference in Data Table 2. Wash your hands thoroughly after completing the investigation.

Observations

DATA TABLE 1

Material	Volume (mL)
Total water	100
Remaining water	
Water added = total water – remaining water	

DATA TABLE 2

Material	Volume (mL)
Alcohol	100
Water	100
Mixture	
Volume change = mixture – (alcohol + water)	

Analysis and Conclusions

1. **Analyzing Data** What was the total volume of the space between the grains of sand?

2. **Drawing Conclusions** Based on this investigation, how do you know that there is space between the particles in alcohol or water?

3. **Formulating Hypotheses** Why did the total volume of water and alcohol decrease when the liquids were mixed together?

Go Further

If the distances between the particles of a material change, will the volume of the material change? Design an experiment to determine the percentage change in volume that occurs when materials such as water, paraffin, or shortening change from solid to liquid or from liquid to solid. When your teacher has approved your experiment, perform it under your teacher's supervision, using all necessary safety procedures. Report your observations and conclusions.

Name ______________________ Class ________________ Date ____________

Constructing Models of Atoms

Background Information

With an electron microscope, scientists can observe the arrangement of atoms on the surface of a material. But they cannot observe the arrangement of subatomic particles within an atom. Scientists use models to describe the structure of atoms.

Atomic models are revised as scientists learn more about atoms. Thomson revised Dalton's model of atoms as solid spheres when he discovered that atoms contained subatomic particles. To explain why most alpha particles could pass through a thin metal foil without being deflected, Rutherford proposed an atomic model with a dense, positively charged nucleus. The nucleus contains protons and neutrons. In the Bohr model of the atom, electrons move in fixed orbits around the nucleus, like planets around a sun. The currently accepted model of the atom assumes that the movement of electrons is less predictable. In the current model, an electron cloud is used to describe the likely locations for electrons in atoms.

Isotopes are atoms of a given element that contain different numbers of neutrons. Isotopes have the same atomic number, but different mass numbers. In this investigation, you will construct a model of an isotope. Then, you will evaluate your model and identify ways in which it can be improved.

Problem

How might the structure of an atom be modeled?

Pre-Lab Discussion

Read the entire investigation. Then, work with a partner to answer the following questions.

1. **Classifying** How do isotopes of the same element differ?

____

____

2. **Using Tables and Graphs** How can you use the information in Figure 1 to determine the number of protons, neutrons, and electrons in an isotope?

____

____

____

____

3. Using Models What will you use the following items to represent: red pushpins, green pushpins, beads, pipe cleaners?

____

____

____

____

4. Using Models How will you model different isotopes of the same element?

____

____

____

____

5. Drawing Conclusions Which model of the atom does the model you will construct most resemble? Explain your answer.

____

____

____

____

Materials *(per group)*

2 plastic-foam balls
pipe cleaners
red pushpins
green pushpins
beads
2 coat hangers
fishing line
scissors

Safety

Put on safety goggles. Be careful when handling sharp instruments. Note all safety alert symbols next to the steps in the Procedure and review the meaning of each symbol by referring to the Safety Symbols on page xiii.

Name ______________________ Class __________________ Date ____________

Procedure

1. Construct a model of one of the isotopes assigned by your teacher. Use the information in Figure 1 to predict the number of protons, neutrons, and electrons in the isotope. In the data table, record this information and the name of the isotope.

Figure 1

Element	Atomic Number	Stable Isotopes
Hydrogen	1	hydrogen-1, hydrogen 2
Helium	2	helium-3, helium-4
Lithium	3	lithium-6, lithium-7
Boron	5	boron-10, boron-11
Carbon	6	carbon-12, carbon-13
Nitrogen	7	nitrogen-14, nitrogen-15
Oxygen	8	oxygen-16, oxygen-17, oxygen-18
Neon	10	neon-20, neon-21, neon-22
Magnesium	12	magnesium-24, magnesium-25, magnesium-26
Silicon	14	silicon-28, silicon-29, silicon-30
Sulfur	16	sulfur-32, sulfur-33, sulfur-34, sulfur-36
Chlorine	17	chlorine-35, chlorine-37
Argon	18	argon-36, argon-38, argon-40

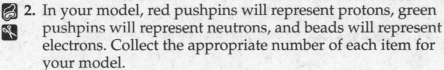

2. In your model, red pushpins will represent protons, green pushpins will represent neutrons, and beads will represent electrons. Collect the appropriate number of each item for your model.
3. The plastic-foam ball will represent the nucleus. Insert the appropriate number of red and green pushpins into the ball to represent the correct number of protons and neutrons.
4. Recall that the first energy level can hold 2 electrons, the second energy level can hold 8 electrons, and the third energy level can hold 18 electrons. Calculate the number of energy levels occupied by electrons when atoms of your isotope are in the ground state. Record this number in the data table.

5. Use pipe cleaners to construct the appropriate number of energy levels for your isotope, as shown in Figure 2. Twist the ends of several pipe cleaners together to make the energy levels long enough to circle the nucleus, but do not close up the pipe-cleaner circles.

Figure 2

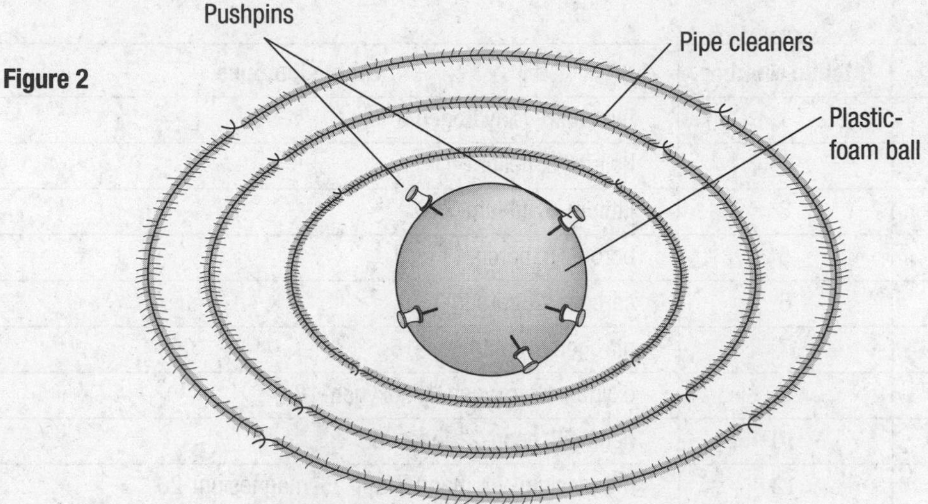

6. Place the appropriate number of beads on each pipe-cleaner circle to represent the electrons in each energy level. In the data table, record the number of electrons in each energy level.
7. Place the energy levels around the nucleus. If there is more than one occupied energy level, place the levels in the correct order.
8. Use fishing line to attach the nucleus and energy levels to a coat hanger, as shown in Figure 3. Your model is now complete.
9. Repeat Steps 1–8 to model the second isotope of your element.

Figure 3

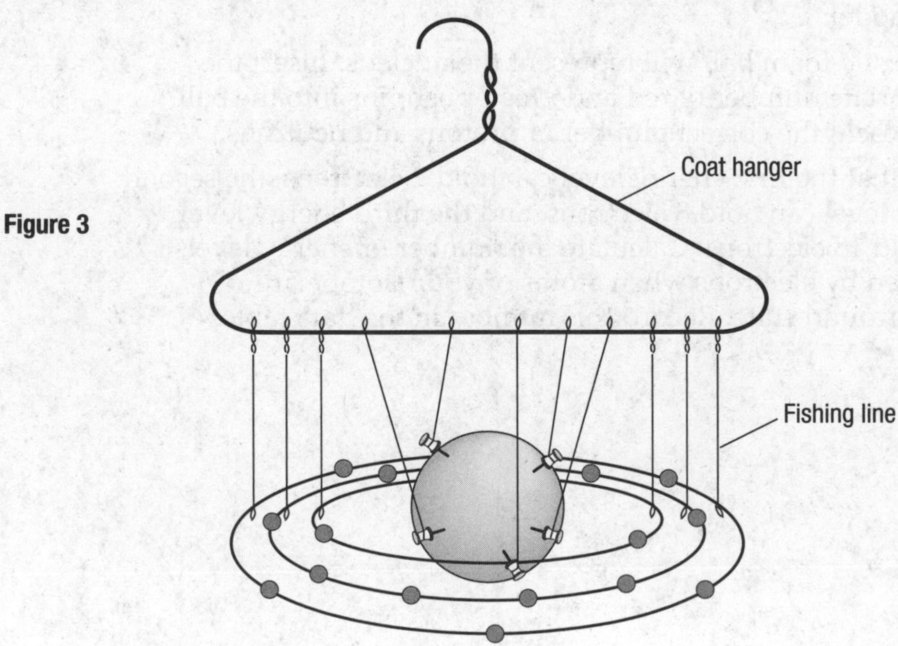

Name ______________________ Class ______________ Date ___________

Observations

DATA TABLE

Isotope		
Atomic number		
Mass number		
Number of protons		
Number of neutrons		
Number of electrons		
Number of energy levels occupied by electrons		
Number of electrons in first energy level		
Number of electrons in second energy level		
Number of electrons in third energy level		

Analysis and Conclusions

1. **Using Models** Why were pushpins with the same mass used to represent protons and neutrons in your model?

____

____

____

____

2. **Using Models** Why were the objects used to represent electrons smaller than the objects used to represent protons and neutrons?

____

____

____

____

3. **Comparing and Contrasting** How were the two models that you constructed similar? How were they different?

____

____

____

____

4. **Applying Concepts** Explain why a model of an atom must always contain the same number of protons and electrons.

5. **Evaluating** What are some inaccuracies in the way your models represent the nucleus?

6. **Evaluating and Revising** In what two ways does your model fail to accurately depict the electrons in an atom?

Go Further

Describe a physical model that could more closely represent the currently accepted model of an atom. Focus on how the model could best represent the behavior of electrons.

Modeling the Location of an Electron in an Atom

Background Information

In the atomic models of the early twentieth century, electrons were said to move around the nucleus along specific paths, much as the planets move around the sun. However, experimental evidence has indicated that the precise position of an electron in an atom cannot be known or predicted. Scientists can speak only of the probability of finding electrons at various locations, not of their exact positions.

Probability is a measure of how often a certain event will occur out of a total number of events. For example, there are two ways a coin can land—with its head facing up or its tail facing up. Each side has a 50 percent (or one out of two) probability of landing face up for any toss.

An **electron cloud** provides a visual model for the probable behavior of an electron in an atom. The electron cloud shows the likelihood that an electron will be found in a given part of the atom around the nucleus. If the electron is not likely to be found at a particular position, the cloud appears less dense. If the electron is more likely to be found at a particular position, the cloud has a denser appearance, as shown in Figure 1.

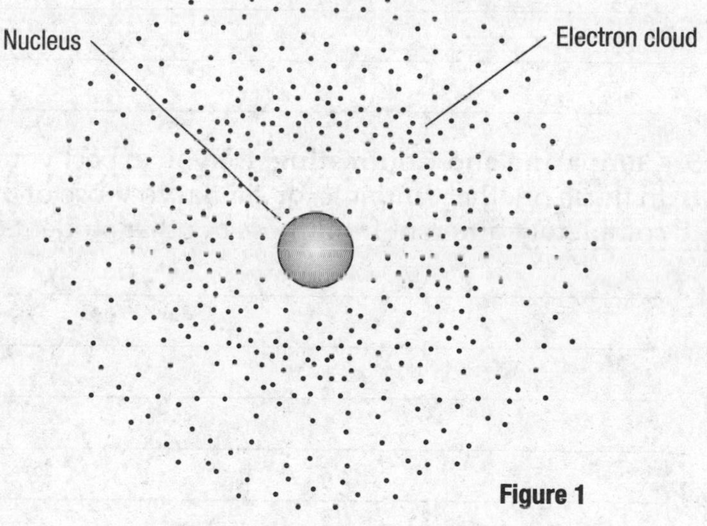

Figure 1

In this investigation, you will use probability to describe the location of an electron in an atom.

Problem

How can the location of an electron in an atom be described?

Pre-Lab Discussion

Read the entire investigation. Then, work with a partner to answer the following questions.

1. **Applying Concepts** Scientists use probability to predict the behavior of electrons in an atom. What is probability?

____

____

____

2. Applying Concepts According to the way you will mark your die at the beginning of this investigation, what is the probability of the electron being found in the zone closest to the "nucleus" (0–4 cm)? In the second closest zone (4–6 cm)? In the third closest zone (6–8 cm)?

____

____

3. Predicting Describe the results you expect to observe.

____

____

____

____

4. Inferring What can you infer about the probable locations of an electron in an atom from the above prediction?

____

____

____

____

5. Comparing and Contrasting Do you expect your results to be identical to those of other students, or similar to those of other students, or completely different from those of other students? Explain your answer.

____

____

____

____

____

Materials *(per group)*

game die
masking tape
graph paper
pencil
red pencil
metric ruler

Procedure

1. Cover all six sides of the die with masking tape. Mark one of the sides with one dot, four of the sides with two dots each, and the remaining side with three dots.
2. Select a square near the center of the graph paper and use a red pencil to color it red. This red square will represent the nucleus of a hydrogen atom with one electron.

Name ______________________ Class ________________ Date ____________

3. Toss the die. Use a regular pencil to color in a square according to the following rules:

   If the number 1 appears face up on the die, color in any square that is between 0 cm and 4 cm from the "nucleus."

   If the number 2 appears face up on the die, color in any square that is between 4 cm and 6 cm from the "nucleus."

   If the number 3 appears face up on the die, color in any square that is between 6 cm and 8 cm from the "nucleus."

4. Repeat Step 3, tossing the die and marking the graph for a total of 50 tosses. Record your results in the data table.

Observations

DATA TABLE

Distance from "Nucleus"	Number of Colored-in Squares
0–4 cm	
4–6 cm	
6–8 cm	

Analysis and Conclusions

1. **Observing** In which zone are most of the colored-in squares on your diagram?

   ____

   ____

2. **Using Models** What does each colored-in square on your diagram represent?

   ____

   ____

3. **Inferring** Based on your data, where would you be most likely to find an electron? Explain your answer.

   ____

   ____

   ____

Name ______________________ Class __________________ Date ____________

4. **Comparing and Contrasting** Compare your diagram to a classmate's. Are they identical? In what ways are they alike or different?

____

____

____

5. **Drawing Conclusions** Can the exact position of an electron in an atom be determined? What can you know about an electron's location?

____

____

____

6. **Predicting** Suppose you had tossed the die 100 times. How do you think your results would have compared with the results you obtained by tossing the die 50 times?

____

____

____

Go Further

Redesign the procedure in this investigation to model the behavior of the two electrons in a helium atom. Can the electrons be in the same location at the same time? Can they be in the same location at different times? Describe the modified procedure and the results you might expect.

Using Clues to Identify Elements

Background Information

Chemical elements can be classified according to their properties as metals, nonmetals, and metalloids. **Metals** are good conductors of heat and electricity. Many metals are malleable and ductile. **Nonmetals** are poor conductors of heat and electricity, and solid nonmetals tend to be brittle. **Metalloids** have properties between those of metals and nonmetals.

Elements in the same group on the periodic table have the same number of **valence electrons,** which are electrons in the highest occupied energy level of an atom. The number of an A group matches the number of valence electrons in atoms of each element in the group. For example, the Group 4A elements each have four valence electrons per atom. The exception to this pattern is the element helium, which is in Group 8A but has only two valence electrons.

Because elements in a group have the same number of valence electrons, they tend to have similar properties. The most reactive metals are the **alkali metals** in Group 1A on the far left side of the periodic table. The Group 2A elements are the **alkaline earth metals,** which are somewhat less reactive than the alkali metals. Groups of elements become less metallic in their properties from left to right across the periodic table. The most reactive nonmetals are the **halogens** in Group 7A. Group 8A contains the **noble gases,** which are colorless and odorless, and rarely react with other elements.

In this investigation, you will use a list of clues to identify 34 elements and place them in their correct locations in the periodic table.

Problem

Where do the elements described in the clues fit in the periodic table?

Pre-Lab Discussion

Read the entire investigation. Then, work with a partner to answer the following questions.

1. **Analyzing Data** How will the index cards be useful when you are reading the clues to the elements?

____

____

____

____

____

____

2. **Inferring** Do you have to know a specific, identifying property for each element in order to place all 34 elements in the partial periodic table? Explain your answer.

3. **Classifying** Are elements with similar properties in the same row or the same column of the periodic table?

4. **Analyzing Data** Explain how information about an element's physical state at room temperature will help you fill in the partial periodic table.

5. **Classifying** How would information about number of valence electrons be useful for placing elements in the periodic table?

6. **Analyzing Data** Why is it important to review the clues after you have read all of the clues once?

Name ______________________ Class ________________ Date ____________

Materials *(per group)*

25 index cards

copy of the periodic table from the textbook for reference

Procedure

1. Work in pairs. Examine the partial periodic table that follows the list of clues. Note that it contains spaces for the 34 elements in Periods 1 through 5 and Groups 1A through 8A. The locations of the metalloids are shaded.
2. For this investigation, these 34 elements have been randomly assigned a number from 1 to 34. (*Hint:* This number has no relation to the atomic number or mass of the element.) By using the list of clues, you will identify where each element belongs in the partial periodic table.
3. Read the clues in order. You will probably find it useful to summarize the information in each clue by using index cards, to which you can refer later as needed. Fill in the partial periodic table by placing each element's assigned number in the appropriate box. Use a pencil so that you can correct any mistakes.
4. Sometimes a single clue will enable you to identify an element and place its number in the correct box. In most cases, however, you will need to combine information from different clues in order to identify the element.
5. Reread the clues as many times as necessary. When you are certain that you have correctly identified all the elements referred to in a clue, set that index card aside.

List of Clues

1. Elements 2, 5, 18, 29, and 33 are colorless, odorless, unreactive gases. Of these gases, element 29 has the largest atomic mass.
2. Elements 13, 19, 23, and 34 have six valence electrons, and element 13 is a metalloid.
3. Elements 9, 14, 16, and 21 are highly reactive metals in the same group. Of these metals, element 16 is the least reactive.
4. Elements 1, 8, 11, 13, 14, 17, 24, and 29 are in the same period.
5. Elements 11, 26, 27, and 28 have three valence electrons.
6. Elements 1, 4, 6, and 30 are found in the same group. Element 6 is in chlorophyll molecules.
7. Elements 10, 22, 24, and 32 are in the same group. Element 22 is a liquid at room temperature.
8. Elements 2, 10, 15, and 34 are nonmetals in the same period.
9. Elements 7, 15, 17, and 25 are in the same group. Of these, only element 7 is a gas at room temperature.
10. Elements 12, 20, and 26 are metalloids. Elements 20 and 12 are in the same group.

Name ______________________ Class ______________________ Date ______________

11. Element 30 is important to maintain strong bones and teeth.
12. An atom of element 21 has one more proton than an atom of element 2.
13. Elements 3 is a nonmetal with one valence electron.
14. Element 27 is the most abundant metal in Earth's crust.
15. Element 31 is a solid at room temperature. Most of the compounds in your body contain this element.
16. Element 18 has two electrons.
17. Element 33 has a smaller atomic mass than element 5.
18. Element 32 is the most reactive nonmetal.
19. Element 20 and element 19 are combined in a compound found in glass.
20. Glass that contains element 26 does not shatter easily.
21. Element 19 is the most abundant element in Earth's crust.

Observations

Partial Periodic Table

	1A	2A	3A	4A	5A	6A	7A	8A
1								
2								
3								
4								
5								

Name ______________________ Class ______________ Date __________

Analysis and Conclusions

1. **Drawing Conclusions** Identify each element in the list of clues by matching its assigned number to the correct name of the element.

2. **Analyzing Data** Were you able to place some elements in the partial periodic table with just a single clue? Use examples to explain.

3. **Analyzing Data** Provide at least two examples of when you needed to use more than one clue to identify an element.

4. Applying Concepts Why were you able to use clues about atomic mass to place elements, even though the periodic table is organized by atomic number?

5. Comparing and Contrasting Which elements are not included in the partial periodic table? Compare the number of elements in the partial periodic table to the number of known elements.

Go Further

Now that you have identified the elements from the list of clues, write at least five additional clues based on information from Chapter 5.

Name ______________________ Class ________________ Date ____________

Comparing Chemical Properties Within a Group

Background Information

The properties of elements repeat in a regular pattern across the periods in the periodic table. From left to right across each period, elements tend to be less metallic and more nonmetallic. Elements in the same group in the table have similar properties because they have the same number of valence electrons. A valence electron is an electron that is in the highest occupied energy level of an atom. These electrons play a key role in chemical reactions. The properties of elements within a group are not identical because the valence electrons are in different energy levels.

The elements in Group 2A in the periodic table are known as alkaline earth metals. Many properties of alkaline earth metals change in a predictable way from top to bottom within the group. One of those properties is reactivity, or the tendency to combine chemically with other substances. The reactivity of an element can be demonstrated by how the element reacts or how its compounds react with other substances.

The formation of a precipitate in a solution is one clue that a chemical change has occurred. A precipitate is a solid that forms and separates from a liquid mixture. In this investigation, you will mix solutions of similar alkaline earth compounds with a set of test solutions and observe whether or not precipitates form. You will use the results to predict how the reactivity of the alkaline earth metals changes from top to bottom within Group 2A.

Problem

How does reactivity vary among the alkaline earth metals?

Pre-Lab Discussion

Read the entire investigation. Then, work with a partner to answer the following questions.

1. **Controlling Variables** Why is it important not to mix the test solution in one well with the solution in another well on your spot plate?

 ____

 ____

2. **Designing Experiments** Why is the order of the rows in the well plate the same as the order of elements in the periodic table?

 ____

 ____

Name ______________________ Class ________________ Date ____________

3. **Controlling Variables** What are the manipulated, responding, and controlled variables in this investigation?

____

____

4. **Predicting** Write a prediction of how the reactivity of the alkaline earth metals will change from the top of Group 2A to the bottom.

____

Materials *(per group)*

spot plate

sheet of notebook paper

dropper bottles containing solutions of the following compounds:

- magnesium nitrate
- barium nitrate
- calcium nitrate
- potassium carbonate
- potassium chromate
- potassium sulfate
- strontium nitrate

Safety

Put on safety goggles and a lab apron. Be careful to avoid breakage when working with glassware. Some chemicals used in this investigation are toxic. Always use special caution when working with laboratory chemicals, as they may irritate the skin or stain skin or clothing. Never touch or taste any chemical unless instructed to do so. Follow your teacher's instructions for disposing of used chemicals. Wash your hands thoroughly after carrying out this investigation. Note all safety alert symbols next to the steps in the Procedure and review the meaning of each symbol by referring to the Safety Symbols on page xiii.

Procedure

1. Place the spot plate in the center of a sheet of notebook paper, as shown in Figure 1. There should be four wells per column and three wells per row.
2. Along the side of the notebook paper next to each of the four rows of wells, write the names of the four alkaline earth metals that are present in each nitrate compound you are using. Write the names in the order shown in Figure 1. This is the order of these four elements in Group 2A.
3. Label the paper above each of the three columns of wells, as shown in Figure 1.

Name ______________________ Class ________________ Date ____________

4. Place 3 drops of potassium carbonate in each of the four wells under the label Potassium Carbonate. Place 3 drops of potassium sulfate in each of the four wells under the label Potassium Sulfate. Place 3 drops of potassium chromate in each of the four wells under the label Potassium Chromate. Make sure that each solution is placed in the wells of only column one. **CAUTION:** *Some chemicals used in this investigation are toxic. Be careful not to get the solutions on your skin.*

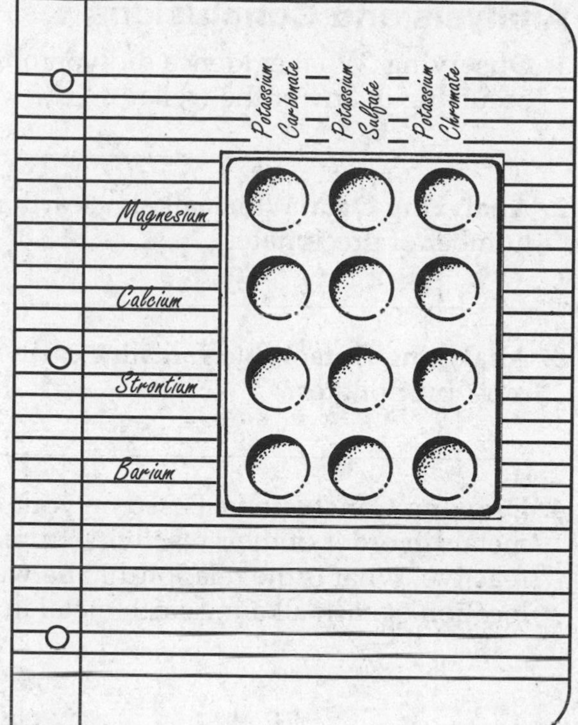

Figure 1

5. Place 3 drops of magnesium nitrate in each of the three wells in the row labeled Magnesium. Observe whether or not a precipitate forms in each well and record the results in the data table.
6. Place 3 drops of calcium nitrate in each of the three wells in the row labeled Calcium. Observe whether or not a precipitate forms in each well and record the results in the data table.
7. Place 3 drops of strontium nitrate in each of the three wells in the row labeled Strontium. Observe whether or not a precipitate forms in each well and record the results in the data table.
8. Place 3 drops of barium nitrate in each of the three wells in the row labeled Barium. Observe whether or not a precipitate forms in each well and record the results in the data table.
9. Follow your teacher's instructions for disposing of the chemicals on the spot plate. Wash the spot plate and your hands thoroughly with soap or detergent and warm water.

Observations

DATA TABLE

Alkaline Earth Metal	Carbonate	Sulfate	Chromate
Magnesium			
Calcium			
Strontium			
Barium			

Name ______________________ Class ______________ Date __________

Analysis and Conclusions

1. **Observing** What evidence did you observe of a chemical change occurring in any of the wells?

____

2. **Analyzing Data** Which alkaline earth metal formed the smallest number of precipitates?

____

3. **Analyzing Data** Which alkaline earth metal formed the most precipitates?

____

4. **Drawing Conclusions** Based on your data, list the alkaline earth metals in order of their reactivity, from most reactive to least reactive. What is the relationship between reactivity and the location of each alkaline earth metal in the periodic table?

____

____

____

5. **Evaluating and Revising** Did your data support or contradict your prediction?

____

6. **Predicting** Group 1A in the periodic table contains alkali metals. Based on your investigation of the Group 2A elements, which element in Group 1A, other than francium, would you predict to be most reactive? Least reactive?

____

7. **Predicting** Can the results for reactivity in this investigation be applied to the elements in Group 7A? Explain your prediction.

____

____

____

Go Further

If you had a solution containing a mixture of magnesium nitrate, strontium nitrate, and barium nitrate, how could you separate the mixture? (*Hint:* Review the information in the data table.)

Playing the Ionic Compounds Card Game

Background Information

Ionic compounds are composed of charged particles called **ions.** Positively charged ions are called **cations,** and negatively charged ions are called **anions.** Although ionic compounds are composed of ions, they are electrically neutral. The sum of the positive charges of the cations and the negative charges of the anions is zero. The formula of an ionic compound can be determined from the ratio of cations and anions needed to produce a total charge equal to zero. The symbol for the cation always appears first in the formula.

The names of ionic compounds are based on the names of their ions. For most cations, the name of the cation is the same name as the element name. However, many transition metals form more than one ion. For these ions, a Roman numeral is used to show the charge. For example, Fe^{2+} is iron(II) and Fe^{3+} is iron(III). Anions are named by combining part of the name of the element and the ending *–ide.* For example, the name for O^{2-} is oxide. A covalently bonded group of atoms that has a positive or negative charge is called a **polyatomic ion.** These ions have names that reflect their composition.

In this investigation, you will practice naming ionic compounds and writing their formulas by playing a card game.

Problem

How are the names and formulas of ionic compounds determined?

Pre-Lab Discussion

Read the entire investigation. Then, work with a partner to answer the following questions.

1. **Inferring** What is the object of the game?

____

____

____

____

2. **Classifying** How many cation symbol cards, cation name cards, anion symbol cards, and anion name cards are required for this card game?

____

____

____

____

Name ______________________ Class ________________ Date ____________

3. Inferring How many cards of each type does each player receive at the beginning of a round?

____

____

____

4. Inferring What happens after a player makes a correct match?

____

____

____

____

5. Making Judgments When does the game end?

____

____

Materials *(per group)*

100 unlined index cards

Procedure

1. Work in groups of four. Use the index cards to prepare four decks of playing cards. Examples of cards are shown in Figure 1.
   - **a. Cation symbol cards.** Prepare four cation symbol cards for each of the following cations. Write the symbol for each cation on the front of an index card. On the back of each card, write "Cation Symbol."

     Na^+ K^+ Mg^{2+} Ca^{2+} Al^{3+} Fe^{2+} Fe^{3+} Cu^+ Cu^{2+} Zn^{2+}
   - **b. Cation name cards.** Prepare one cation name card for each of the following cations. Write the name of each cation on the front of an index card. On the back of each card, write "Cation Name."

     sodium potassium magnesium calcium aluminum

     iron(II) iron(III) copper(I) copper(II) zinc
   - **c. Anion symbol cards.** Prepare four anion symbol cards for each of the following anions. Write the symbol for each anion on the front of an index card. On the back of each card, write "Anion Symbol."

     F^- Cl^- O^{2-} S^{2-} PO_4^{3-} CO_3^{2-} NO_3^- N^{3-} Br^- OH^-
   - **d. Anion name cards.** Prepare one anion name card for each of the following anions. Write the name for each anion on the front of an index card. On the back of each card, write "Anion Name."

     fluoride chloride oxide sulfide phosphate

     carbonate nitrate nitride bromide hydroxide

Name ______________________ Class ______________________ Date ______________________

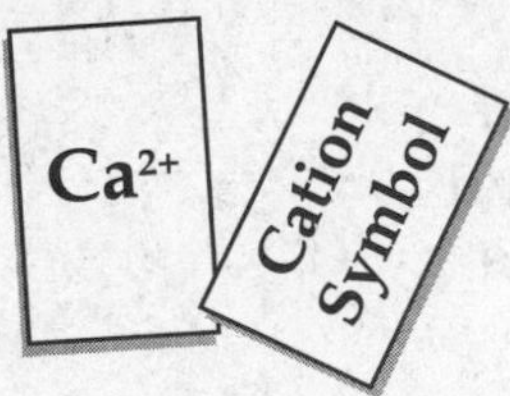

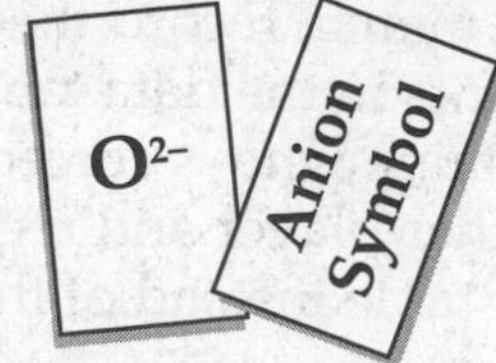

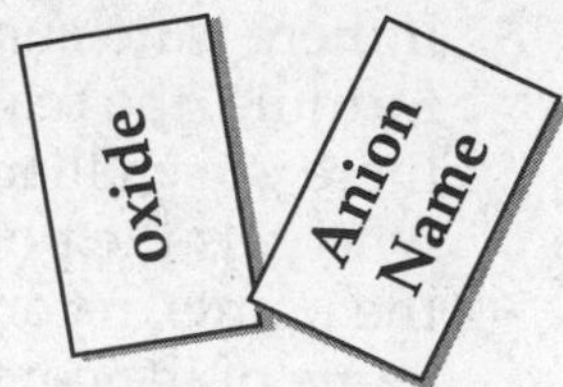

Figure 1

2. After you finish preparing the cards, shuffle each deck of cards separately and place the decks facedown on the table.
3. To determine who goes first, have each player draw a cation symbol card. The player who draws the ion with the highest charge goes first. If players draw the same charge, they should draw another card. Replace the cards and shuffle the cation symbol deck. Play continues clockwise.
4. To start the game, each player draws three cation symbol cards, three anion symbol cards, one cation name card, and one anion name card. Then, turn over one card from each deck of symbol cards to start a discard pile, as shown in Figure 2.

Figure 2

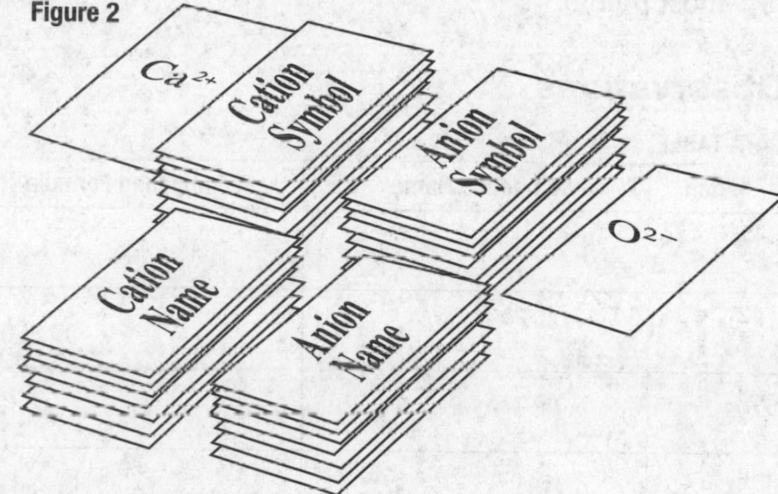

5. The object of the game is to gather the correct number and type of symbol cards to match the formula of the compound represented by the selected cation and anion name cards. As soon as you think you have a match, declare it and show your cards. If you are correct, you will receive one point for each ion in the compound. For example, you would receive three points for the ions in $MgCl_2$.
6. When you show your cards, any other player can challenge your match by providing the correct formula. If your formula is incorrect (the charges do not add up to zero) or if your formula does not match your name cards, the challenger gets the points.
7. During a player's turn, the player may do one of the following:
   - **a.** Draw a card from either the cation symbol deck or discard pile, or from the anion symbol deck or discard pile, and discard a cation or anion symbol card to the appropriate discard pile; or
   - **b.** Draw a new cation name card, anion name card, or both, and place the old name cards at the bottom of the appropriate decks.

   If you can make a match after drawing a card, you must declare it before discarding any cards. Once cards are discarded, the turn is over, and play continues.

8. If there is no challenge after you declare a match, record the formula, the name, and the number of points in the data table. If there is a challenge, the group must determine who is correct and who gets the points. If you challenge another player and receive the points, record "Challenge" in the data table instead of the name of the compound.
9. After you declare a match and the group determines who gets the points, draw new ion symbol cards and ion name cards to replace the ones you showed to make a match. Put the used ion symbol cards in the appropriate discard pile. Set the used name cards aside and out of play. At that point, your turn is over, and play continues.
10. If either the cation symbol cards or the anion symbol cards are all used, mix the appropriate discard pile, turn it over, and continue play. When either the cation name cards or the anion name cards are all used, the game is over. The winner is the player with the most points.

Observations

DATA TABLE

Match	Compound Name	Compound Formula	Points
1			
2			
3			
4			
5			
6			
7			
8			
9			
10			
		Total	

Name ______________________ Class ______________ Date ____________

Analysis and Conclusions

1. **Calculating** Describe how to determine the correct ratio of ions in a compound.

2. **Inferring** Explain why it is not possible to write a formula for a compound of sodium and calcium.

3. **Applying Concepts** Each of the chemical names below contains an error. Describe the nature of the error in each name.

   a. Potassium sulfur

   b. Oxide potassium

   c. Copper oxide

4. **Relating Cause and Effect** How many anions are required to balance one aluminum ion? Explain your answer.

____

____

____

5. **Drawing Conclusions** How are the name and formula of an ionic compound determined?

____

____

____

____

____

____

____

Go Further

In this investigation, you used the charges on ions to determine the formulas of compounds. How could you change this game so you could play it with covalent compounds? Design a card game that you could use to practice writing formulas and naming covalent compounds containing two elements.

Name ______________________ Class ____________________ Date ____________

Comparing Ionic and Molecular Compounds

Background Information

Ions in an ionic compound and molecules in a molecular compound are held together by forces of attraction called **chemical bonds.** An **ionic bond** is the force that holds positively charged cations and negatively charged anions together in a crystal lattice. Each cation is attracted to all the neighboring anions in the lattice. Each anion is attracted to all the neighboring cations in the lattice.

In molecules, atoms are held together by covalent bonds. In a **covalent bond,** two atoms share a pair of valence electrons. The atoms are held together by the attractions between the protons in each nucleus and the shared electrons. If one atom in a covalent bond has a greater attraction for electrons than the other atom does, the electrons are not shared equally between the atoms. The atom with the greater attraction has a partial negative charge, while the other atom has a partial positive charge. This type of covalent bond is called a **polar covalent bond.** When the electrons are shared equally between the atoms, the bond is called a **nonpolar covalent bond.** Whether a molecule is polar or nonpolar depends on the type of covalent bonds and the shape of the molecule.

In this investigation, you will use ease of melting to compare the strength of the ionic bonds in sodium chloride to the strength of intermolecular attractions in paraffin. Paraffin is a mixture of hydrocarbons, which are molecular compounds that contain only hydrogen and carbon. Then, you will compare the ability of the molecules in sugar and the molecules in paraffin to dissolve in water.

Problem

How do different forces of attraction affect the behavior of ionic compounds and molecular compounds?

Pre-Lab Discussion

Read the entire investigation. Then, work with a partner to answer the following questions.

1. **Inferring** How would you expect the strength of the forces that hold a solid together to affect the melting point of the solid?

____

____

____

Name ______________________ Class ______________________ Date ______________

2. **Predicting** A solid can dissolve in water if the particles in the solid are attracted to water molecules. Would you expect an ionic compound to dissolve easily in water? A compound with polar molecules? A compound with nonpolar molecules? Explain your answers. (*Hint:* Water molecules are strongly polar.)

3. **Controlling Variables** Identify the manipulated and responding variables in this investigation.

4. **Formulating Hypotheses** Record your hypothesis of whether the bonds that hold ions together in a crystal are stronger than the intermolecular attractions that hold molecules together in a solid.

5. **Evaluating** What results in this investigation would support your hypothesis?

Materials *(per group)*

sodium chloride
paraffin
3 spatulas
2 crucibles
ring stand with iron ring
clay triangle
Bunsen burner
tongs
2 test tubes with stoppers
glass-marking pencil
sugar
test-tube rack
clock or watch

Safety

Put on safety goggles and a lab apron. Be careful to avoid breakage when working with glassware. Tie back loose hair and clothing when working with flames. Do not reach over an open flame. Use extreme care when working with heated equipment or materials to avoid burns. Note all safety alert symbols next to the steps in the Procedure and review the meaning of each symbol by referring to the Safety Symbols on page xiii.

Name ______________________ Class ________________ Date __________

Procedure

1. Use a spatula to place a pea-sized quantity of sodium chloride in a crucible. Use a second spatula to place a pea-sized quantity of paraffin in a second crucible.
2. Use the ring stand, iron ring, and clay triangle to support the crucible of sodium chloride above a burner.
3. Light the burner and observe the contents of the crucible for 1 minute. Keep the flame away from the contents of the crucible. Record your observations in the data table. **CAUTION:** *Be careful when working with flames. Tie back loose hair and clothing.*
4. Use tongs to carefully remove the crucible from the flame. Gently place the crucible in a safe place on the lab table where you will not accidentally touch it as it cools. **CAUTION:** *Use extreme care when working with heated equipment or materials to avoid burns. Do not touch objects after they have been heated. Allow them to cool completely first.*

Figure 1

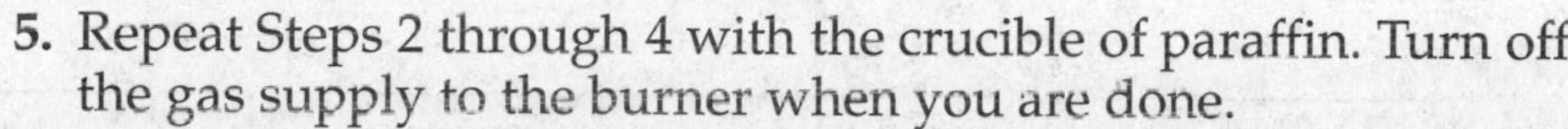

5. Repeat Steps 2 through 4 with the crucible of paraffin. Turn off the gas supply to the burner when you are done.
6. Label two test tubes *1* and *2* with the glass-marking pencil. Fill the test tubes halfway with water.
7. Use a new spatula to place a pea-sized quantity of sugar in test tube 1. Use the spatula that you used for paraffin in Step 1 to place a pea-sized quantity of paraffin in test tube 2.
8. Stopper the test tubes. Holding the stoppers firmly in place, shake each test tube to speed up the dissolving of the salt and paraffin.
9. Observe the contents of the test tubes and record your observations.

Observations

DATA TABLE

Solid Material	Melting	Dissolving in Water
Sodium chloride		
Paraffin		
Sugar		

Name ______________________ Class ________________ Date ____________

Analysis and Conclusions

1. **Inferring** Based on your data on melting, which forces are stronger—the ionic bonds in sodium chloride or the attractions between molecules in paraffin? Explain your answer.

2. **Inferring** Based on your data on dissolving in water, which material is more likely to contain polar molecules—sugar or paraffin? Explain your answer.

3. **Evaluating and Revising** Did your data support or contradict your hypothesis?

4. **Predicting** Which type of compound—ionic or molecular—would you expect to have a higher boiling point? Explain your answer.

Go Further

Suppose you had a sample of sodium chloride and paraffin mixed together. How could you separate the sodium chloride from the paraffin?

Name ______________________ Class ________________ Date ____________

Using Single-Replacement Reactions to Compare Reactivities

Background Information

In nature, elements can occur either free (uncombined with other elements) or chemically combined in a compound. The tendency of an element to combine with other substances is called the reactivity of that element. The more reactive an element is, the more likely it is to combine with other substances. In a **single-replacement reaction,** one element takes the place of another element in a compound. In general, more reactive elements replace less reactive elements. As a result of the reaction, the less reactive element is freed from the compound. Consider the following reaction.

$$Zn + CuSO_4 \rightarrow Cu + ZnSO_4$$

The more reactive zinc replaces copper and combines with the sulfate ion. The less reactive copper is released from the compound and becomes a free element.

When a metal is placed in hydrochloric acid (HCl), a single-replacement reaction can occur. If the metal is more reactive than the hydrogen in the acid, the metal will replace the hydrogen, and bubbles of hydrogen gas (H_2) will be produced. The more reactive a metal is, the more vigorously it will react with hydrochloric acid.

The alkali metals and alkaline earth metals have only one or two electrons in their highest energy level. By losing those electrons, these elements can easily acquire a stable electron configuration with a completely filled highest energy level. As a result, the alkali metals and alkaline earth metals tend to be highly reactive.

In this investigation, you will determine whether various metals undergo single-replacement reactions when placed in hydrochloric acid. Based on your observations of these reactions, you will then rank the metals by reactivity.

Problem

Which metals are most reactive?

Pre-Lab Discussion

Read the entire investigation. Then, work with a partner to answer the following questions.

1. **Predicting** If any of the metals react with hydrochloric acid, what kind of compound will be formed?

____

____

____

Name ______________________ Class ________________ Date ____________

2. **Inferring** How will your observations help you determine which metals are the most reactive? Explain your answer.

3. **Controlling Variables** Identify the manipulated, responding, and controlled variables in this investigation.

   a. Manipulated variable

   b. Responding variable

   c. Controlled variables

4. **Formulating Hypotheses** State a hypothesis about which metals are the most reactive.

5. **Predicting** Based on your hypothesis, predict which metal will react most vigorously with hydrochloric acid. Explain the reason for your prediction.

Name ______________________ Class ________________ Date ____________

Materials *(per group)*

glass-marking pencil
5 test tubes
test-tube rack
10-mL graduated cylinder
1 *M* hydrochloric acid
zinc (Zn)
copper (Cu)
aluminum (Al)
iron (Fe)
magnesium (Mg)

Safety

Put on safety goggles and a lab apron. Be careful to avoid breakage when working with glassware. Wear plastic disposable gloves when handling chemicals, as they may irritate the skin or stain skin or clothing. Never touch or taste any chemical unless instructed to do so. Follow your teacher's instructions for disposing of the used hydrochloric acid. Wash your hands with warm water and soap or detergent before leaving the laboratory. Note all safety alert symbols next to the steps in the Procedure and review the meaning of each symbol by referring to the Safety Symbols on page xiii.

Procedure

1. Use the glass-marking pencil to label each test tube with the symbol for each metal listed in Materials. Place the test tubes in a test-tube rack.
2. One at a time, place the appropriate metal in each test tube. Carefully pour 5 mL of hydrochloric acid into each of the five test tubes, using the graduated cylinder. **CAUTION:** *Put on gloves when working with hydrochloric acid. Handle hydrochloric acid with care. It is corrosive. If it spills on your skin, rinse it off with plenty of cold water and notify your teacher immediately.*
3. Observe what happens to the metal in each test tube and feel each test tube as the reaction proceeds. Record your observations in the data table.
4. When you have completed the investigation, follow your teacher's instructions for disposing of the used acid. Rinse the pieces of metal several times with water and put them into a container provided by your teacher. Do not put any metal in the sink.

Name ______________________ Class ______________ Date __________

Observations

DATA TABLE

Metal	Observations
Magnesium (Mg)	
Aluminum (Al)	
Iron (Fe)	
Copper (Cu)	
Zinc (Zn)	

Analysis and Conclusions

1. **Analyzing Data** Which of the metals that you tested in this investigation are more reactive than hydrogen? Explain your answer.

2. **Analyzing Data** Which of the metals that you tested in this investigation are less reactive than hydrogen? Explain your answer.

Name ______________________ Class ________________ Date ____________

3. Drawing Conclusions The rate at which hydrogen gas is produced as a result of these single-replacement reactions is an indication of the relative reactivity of the metals. List the metals in order of their reactivity from the most reactive to the least reactive.

____

____

____

____

4. Inferring Were these reactions endothermic or exothermic? Explain your answer.

____

____

____

____

____

5. Evaluating and Revising Did the results of the lab support or contradict your hypothesis?

____

____

____

____

____

6. Calculating Write a balanced chemical equation for the single-replacement reaction, if any, that occurred between the acid and each metal. Refer to Figure 1 for the charges of the ions involved.

a. Magnesium

____

b. Aluminum

____

c. Iron

____

d. Copper

____

e. Zinc

____

Element	Charge of Ion
H	1+
Cl	1–
Mg	2+
Al	3+
Fe	3+
Cu	2+
Zn	2+

Figure 1

7. Inferring What could you do to determine whether the gas produced as a result of these reactions is hydrogen?

8. Applying Concepts Nonmetals can also be involved in single-replacement reactions. If chlorine is more reactive than bromine, write a balanced chemical equation for the reaction between chlorine gas (Cl_2) and potassium bromide (KBr).

Go Further

Balance each of the following chemical equations. Then, classify each reaction as a synthesis, decomposition, or single-replacement reaction.

1. $Cu + AgNO_3 \rightarrow Ag + Cu(NO_3)_2$

2. $H_2 + O_2 \rightarrow H_2O$

3. $Al + ZnCl_2 \rightarrow Zn + AlCl_3$

4. $Al(OH)_3 \rightarrow Al_2O_3 + H_2O$

Recognizing a Synthesis Reaction

Background Information

In a **synthesis reaction,** two or more substances combine to form a single substance. The substances that combine can be elements, compounds, or both. The general equation for a synthesis reaction is

$$A + B \rightarrow AB$$

The symbols A and B represent two elements or compounds that combine to form the compound AB. For example, when a metal combines with oxygen from the air, a synthesis reaction occurs. A compound called a metal oxide is produced. The reaction can be described by the following word equation:

Metal + Oxygen → Metal oxide

In this investigation, you will heat copper metal in air. Then, you will examine the product to determine whether a synthesis reaction has occurred.

Problem

How can you know when a synthesis reaction has occurred?

Pre-Lab Discussion

Read the entire investigation. Then, work with a partner to answer the following questions.

1. **Calculating** If the balance indicated that the evaporating dish has a mass of 44.8 g and you want to have exactly 5.0 g of copper, what should the balance read with the copper in the evaporating dish?

____

____

2. **Inferring** Why is it necessary to spread the copper powder out in a thin layer in Step 5? (*Hint:* What substance do you expect to react with the copper?)

____

____

3. **Predicting** What evidence of a chemical change might you observe in this investigation?

____

____

4. **Predicting** What observation would be evidence of a synthesis reaction? Explain your answer.

____

____

Name ______________________ Class ________________ Date ____________

Materials *(per group)*

ring stand
iron ring
wire gauze
Bunsen burner
evaporating dish
triple-beam balance
scoop
copper powder
clock or watch
tongs

Safety

Put on safety goggles, plastic gloves, and a lab apron. Be careful when using matches. Use caution when handling breakable equipment. Tie back loose hair and clothing when working with flames. Do not reach over an open flame. Use extreme care when working with heated equipment or materials to avoid burns. Note all safety alert symbols next to the steps in the Procedure and review the meaning of each symbol by referring to the Safety Symbols on page xiii.

Procedure

1. Set up the ring stand, iron ring, and wire gauze as shown in Figure 1.
2. Place the Bunsen burner on the base of the ring stand. Do not light the burner yet. Adjust the position of the iron ring so that its center is directly over the burner and about 5 cm above the top of the burner.
3. Place the evaporating dish on the balance and find its mass to the nearest 0.1 g. Record this mass in the data table.
4. To measure 5.0 g of copper powder, add 5.0 g to the mass of the evaporating dish and move the riders on the balance to this number.

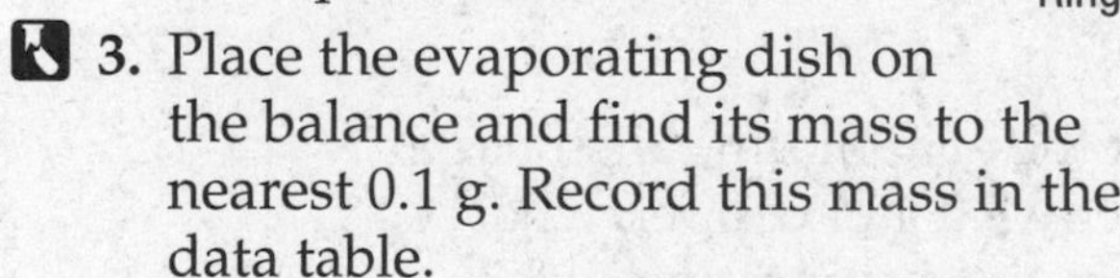

Figure 1

5. Using the scoop, slowly add copper powder to the evaporating dish until the pointer of the balance is centered. In the data table, record the mass of the copper powder and evaporating dish.
6. Place the evaporating dish containing the copper powder on the wire gauze. Use the scoop to spread out the copper powder in a thin layer in the bottom of the dish.
7. Light the Bunsen burner and heat the evaporating dish for 5 to 10 minutes until you observe a change in the color of the copper powder. **CAUTION:** *Tie back loose hair and clothing before working with flames. Do not reach over an open flame.*
8. Turn off the Bunsen burner and allow the evaporating dish to cool for 10 minutes. Use tongs to place the evaporating dish on the balance and find its mass. **CAUTION:** *The evaporating*

dish and its contents may still be hot. Handle the evaporating dish only with tongs. In the data table, record the mass of the evaporating dish and its contents.

9. Use the scoop to examine the product of the reaction. Observe its color or colors. Record your observations below the data table.

Observations

DATA TABLE

Measurement	Mass (g)
Mass of evaporating dish	
Mass of evaporating dish and copper powder	
Mass of copper powder	
Mass of evaporating dish and product after heating	
Mass of product	

Observations of Product

____

____

Analysis and Conclusions

1. **Observing** What did you observe as a result of heating the copper powder that might indicate that a chemical reaction took place?

____

2. **Inferring** Explain why there was a change in mass as a result of heating the copper powder in the evaporating dish.

____

3. **Classifying** What type of chemical reaction occurred?

____

4. **Inferring** Was this reaction endothermic or exothermic? Explain your answer.

____

5. **Calculating** Calculate the percent change in mass by using the following formula.

$$\text{Percent change in mass} = \frac{\text{Change in mass}}{\text{Mass of copper}} \times 100\%$$

____

6. **Drawing Conclusions** There are actually two different oxides of copper produced as a result of this reaction. They are copper(I) oxide and copper(II) oxide. If all the copper changed to copper(I)

oxide, the mass would change by 12 percent. If all the copper changed to copper(II) oxide, the mass would change by 25 percent. Based on the percent change in mass, what must have been produced as a result of the reaction?

____

7. **Calculating** Write a balanced chemical equation for the synthesis reactions that took place.

____

____

8. **Evaluating** Compare the percent change in mass that you calculated with those calculated by your classmates. What variables could account for differences between your results and those of your classmates?

____

____

____

9. **Controlling Variables** How could these variables be controlled so that the results obtained are more precise?

____

____

10. **Observing** Copper(II) oxide is black and copper(I) oxide is red. Do your observations support your answer to Question 7? Explain your answer.

____

Go Further

Caulking compound is used to make a watertight seal around bathtubs, sinks, and pipes. A synthesis reaction occurs when caulking compound is placed on a surface and exposed to the air. This reaction leads to hardening of the soft caulking compound. To investigate the role of water in this reaction, place a small amount of caulking compound on two small pieces of wood or cardboard. Place one of the pieces in a beaker and cover it with water. Leave the other piece exposed to the air. After 5 minutes, use a glass stirring rod to probe each sample of caulking compound and compare the firmness of the two samples. Record your observations. Repeat this observation every 5 minutes for 30 minutes or until one of the samples becomes firm and rubbery. Report your conclusions about the role of water in this synthesis reaction.

Comparing Antacids

Background Information

Acids are substances that produce hydronium ions (H_3O^+) when dissolved in water. **Bases** are substances that produce hydroxide ions (OH^-) when dissolved in water. The reaction between an acid and a base is called **neutralization.** Antacids are basic substances that are taken to neutralize excess stomach acid. Different brands of antacids may differ in a number of ways, including their chemical composition, the quantity of acid neutralized per dose, and the speed with which neutralization occurs.

An **indicator** is a substance that changes color in the presence of acids and bases. Indicators are used to show whether a solution is acidic or basic and to show when a neutralization reaction is complete.

In this investigation, you will use an indicator to compare the quantity of acid that several antacids neutralize. The amount of indicator that you will use is very small and will not affect the reaction that you are studying.

Problem

Which brand of antacid neutralizes the most acid per dose?

Pre-Lab Discussion

Read the entire investigation. Then, work with a partner to answer the following questions.

1. **Predicting** In Part A of this investigation, which sodium hydroxide solution do you predict will neutralize more acid? Explain your answer.

____

____

____

____

2. **Designing Experiments** In Part A of this investigation, how will you determine which sodium hydroxide solution neutralized more acid?

____

____

____

____

____

____

3. Formulating Hypotheses State a hypothesis that you could test in Part B of this investigation.

____

____

____

____

____

4. Designing Experiments Describe an experiment you could perform to test your hypothesis.

____

____

____

____

____

5. Controlling Variables What are the manipulated, responding, and controlled variables in the experiment that you described in your answer to Question 4?

____

____

____

____

____

Suggested Materials *(per group)*

glass-marking pencil
2 250-mL beakers
10-mL graduated cylinder
50-mL graduated cylinder
0.1 *M* hydrochloric acid (HCl) solution
dropper bottle of bromthymol blue solution
3 glass stirring rods
0.1 *M* sodium hydroxide (NaOH) solution
0.5 *M* NaOH solution
buret of 0.1 *M* NaOH solution on ring stand
3 different brands of antacid tablets
3 spoons
2 dropper pipets
Ask your teacher for any additional materials that you will need to carry out Part B of this investigation.

Name ______________________ Class ________________ Date ____________

Safety

Put on safety goggles, plastic gloves, and a lab apron. Be careful to avoid breakage when working with glassware. Never touch or taste any chemical unless instructed to do so. Always use caution when working with laboratory chemicals, as they may irritate the skin or stain skin or clothing. Wash your hands thoroughly after carrying out this investigation. Note all safety alert symbols next to the steps in the Procedure and review the meaning of each symbol by referring to the Safety Symbols on page xiii.

Design Your Experiment

Part A: Comparing the Neutralizing Power of Basic Solutions

1. Use a glass-marking pencil to label two 250-mL beakers 0.1 *M* NaOH and 0.5 *M* NaOH.
2. Use the 50-mL graduated cylinder to place 50 mL of 0.1 *M* HCl solution into each beaker.
3. Add 1 drop of the bromthymol blue solution to the beaker labeled 0.1 *M* NaOH and stir with a glass stirring rod. Count each drop as you continue to add bromthymol blue solution 1 drop at a time, until the solution becomes yellow. Add the same number of drops of bromthymol blue solution to the beaker labeled 0.5 *M* NaOH and stir with the same glass stirring rod.
4. Use the 10-mL graduated cylinder to add 5 mL of 0.1 *M* NaOH solution into the beaker labeled 0.1 *M* NaOH. Stir the solution with a clean glass stirring rod.
5. In the sink, rinse the 10-mL graduated cylinder thoroughly with water. Then, use the graduated cylinder to add 5 mL of 0.5 *M* NaOH solution into the beaker labeled 0.5 *M* NaOH. Stir the solution with a clean glass stirring rod. **CAUTION:** *Handle the 0.5* M *NaOH solution with care. It is poisonous and can burn skin and clothing.*
6. To compare the quantity of HCl remaining in each beaker, place the beaker labeled 0.5 *M* NaOH under the buret. Record the initial volume of the 0.1 *M* NaOH solution that is in the buret in Data Table 1.
7. In the sink, rinse all three glass stirring rods thoroughly with water. Stir the contents of the beaker labeled 0.5 *M* NaOH with a clean glass stirring rod as you slowly add 0.1 *M* NaOH solution from the buret to the beaker. Stop adding NaOH solution to the beaker as soon as the color of the solution in the beaker changes to blue. Observe the volume of solution remaining in the buret. Record this volume in Data Table 1.
8. Subtract the volume of NaOH solution remaining in the buret from the initial volume of the NaOH solution to determine the volume of NaOH solution that you added to the beaker. Record this volume in Data Table 1.

Name ______________________ Class ______________ Date ____________

9. Ask your teacher to refill your buret with 0.1 *M* NaOH solution. Repeat Steps 6 through 8 with the beaker labeled 0.1 *M* NaOH.

Part B: Using Indicators to Determine Antacid Strength

10. Design an experiment to compare the neutralizing power of three different brands of antacid tablets. Record the hypothesis that you will test.

____

____

____

____

____

11. Write a detailed plan of how you will carry out your experiment. You may choose to base your experiment on the method of comparing the neutralizing power of solutions that you used in Part A of this investigation. Construct Data Table 2 in which to record your observations in the space provided on page 82. If you need more space, attach additional sheets of paper.

____

____

____

____

____

____

____

____

____

____

____

____

____

____

____

____

Name ______________________ Class ________________ Date ____________

12. What are the manipulated, responding, and controlled variables in your experiment?

a. Manipulated variable

____

____

b. Responding variable

____

____

c. Controlled variables

____

____

____

13. What safety precautions will you need to take in your experiment?

____

____

____

____

14. List the possible results of your experiment and whether each possible result would support or contradict your hypothesis.

____

____

____

____

____

____

____

15. Show your written experimental plan to your teacher. When your teacher approves your plan, carry out your experiment and record your observations in your data table.

Name ______________________ Class ________________ Date ____________

Observations

DATA TABLE 1

Beaker	Initial Volume of NaOH Solution in Buret (mL)	Final Volume of NaOH Solution in Buret (mL)	Volume of NaOH Solution Used (mL)
0.1 *M* NaOH			
0.5 *M* NaOH			

DATA TABLE 2

If you need more space, attach an additional sheet of paper.

Name ____________ Class ____________ Date ____________

Analysis and Conclusions

1. **Inferring** What can you infer from the volume of NaOH solution that you added to each beaker in Steps 7 through 9?

2. **Analyzing Data** Based on the results of Part A of this investigation, which NaOH solution neutralized more acid in Steps 4 and 5 of Part A? Explain your answer.

3. **Analyzing Data** Which antacid tablet neutralized the most acid? Which tablet neutralized the least acid? Explain your answers.

4. **Evaluating and Revising** Did your data support or contradict your hypothesis? Explain your answer.

5. Observing How did the antacid tablets differ from the NaOH solutions you used in Part A of this investigation? How did these differences affect the way you tested the tablets?

6. Drawing Conclusions What chemical properties other than the quantity of acid that it neutralized might make one brand of antacid tablet better than another?

Go Further

Safety officers at chemical factories must plan for the possibility that a large quantity of a dangerous acid might be spilled in a work area. Use resources in the library or on the Internet to research what methods and materials are used to safely clean up acid spills. Use your knowledge of neutralization reactions to explain how these emergency procedures work

Comparing Solubilities and Rates of Dissolving

Background Information

When one substance dissolves in another, the mixture is called a solution. The substance that dissolves is the **solute.** A substance that dissolves other substances is called a **solvent.** The rate at which a solid solute dissolves depends on several factors including temperature, stirring, and the surface area of the solute. **Solubility** is the maximum amount of a solute that can dissolve in a given amount of a solvent at a certain temperature. The solubility of different substances varies, but it is always the same for a given substance at a given temperature.

In this investigation, you will determine the effect of surface area on the rate at which table salt (sodium chloride, NaCl) dissolves in water. You will also investigate how temperature affects the solubility of ammonium chloride (NH_4Cl) in water.

Problem

How do surface area and temperature affect the rate of dissolving and solubility?

Pre-Lab Discussion

Read the entire investigation. Then, work with a partner to answer the following questions.

1. **Controlling Variables** In Part A, what is the manipulated variable that you will use to investigate the rate of dissolving?

   ____

2. **Predicting** In Part A, what do you predict will be the effect of the manipulated variable on the rate of dissolving?

   ____

3. **Predicting** In Part B, what do you predict will be the effect of the manipulated variable on solubility?

   ____

Materials *(per group)*

rock salt (sodium chloride, NaCl)
table salt (sodium chloride, NaCl)
paper towel
hand lens
3 150-mL beakers
triple-beam balance
2 scoops
100-mL graduated cylinder
clock or watch
3 glass stirring rods
thermometer
ammonium chloride (NH_4Cl)
small spoon
hot plate
graph paper

Name ______________________ Class ________________ Date ____________

Safety 

Put on safety goggles, plastic gloves, and a lab apron. Be careful to avoid breakage when working with glassware. Use extreme care when working with heated materials to avoid burns. Never touch or taste any chemical unless instructed to do so. Wash your hands thoroughly after carrying out this investigation. Note all safety alert symbols next to the steps in the Procedure and review the meaning of each symbol by referring to the Safety Symbols on page xiii.

Procedure

Part A: The Effect of Surface Area on Rate of Dissolving

1. Place a few grains of rock salt and a few grains of table salt on a paper towel. Observe the rock salt and table salt. Then, use a hand lens to compare the particles of rock salt and the particles of table salt. Record which salt has the smaller particles in Data Table 1.
2. Place a beaker on the balance. Measure and record the mass of the beaker.
3. Use the scoop to place a sample of rock salt in the beaker. Measure the mass of the beaker and salt. Add or remove rock salt from the beaker if necessary until the mass of the beaker and salt is 5 to 10 grams more than the mass of the beaker alone. Record the mass of the beaker and salt.
4. Repeat Steps 2 and 3 with a second beaker and a sample of table salt. Be sure that the mass of table salt in the beaker does not differ from the mass of the rock salt by more than 0.1 g.
5. Use a graduated cylinder to add 75 mL of room-temperature water to each beaker. Note the time. Observe the solutions for 2 minutes. After 2 minutes, look for any signs of dissolving. Record your observations.
6. Place a glass stirring rod in each beaker. Note the time. Working with a partner, stir the water gently in each beaker. Be sure to stir both samples at the same time and at the same slow rate. Note the time when each sample completely dissolves. Record the time it took for each salt sample to dissolve completely.

Part B: The Effect of Temperature on Solubility

7. To investigate solubility, put 50 mL of room-temperature water into a clean beaker. Use a thermometer to measure the temperature of the water. Record this temperature in Data Table 2. Remove the thermometer from the beaker.

8. Add one spoonful of ammonium chloride to the water in the beaker. Stir vigorously with a clean glass stirring rod until no more of the solid will dissolve. Make sure that you allow enough time for the solid to dissolve. **CAUTION:** *Be careful handling ammonium chloride and its solutions, which are poisonous.*

9. Repeat Step 8 until no more ammonium chloride will dissolve. Note the number of spoonfuls of ammonium chloride that you added. Be sure to allow enough time for each spoonful of ammonium chloride to dissolve before adding more. Record the number of spoonfuls that dissolved in Data Table 2.

10. Place the beaker of ammonium chloride solution on a hot plate. Place the thermometer in the beaker. Turn the hot plate to the medium-low setting and warm the solution to 40°C. **CAUTION:** *Be careful handling the hot plate and hot solutions. They can cause burns.*

11. Remove the thermometer from the beaker. Add more spoonfuls of ammonium chloride to the beaker. Stir the solution and use the thermometer to check the temperature of the solution after you add each spoonful. Note the total number of spoonfuls of ammonium chloride that you added. Be sure to allow enough time for each spoonful of ammonium chloride to dissolve before adding more. Use the heat setting of the hot plate to keep the temperature constant as you add ammonium chloride to the beaker.

12. Record the total number of spoonfuls that have dissolved.

13. Turn up the hot plate to warm the solution to 60°C. Then, repeat Steps 11 and 12 with the solution at this temperature.

14. Turn up the hot plate to warm the solution to 80°C. Then, repeat Steps 11 and 12 with the solution at this temperature.

15. When you have recorded all of your data, turn off the hot plate and allow the solution to cool. Follow your teacher's instructions for disposing of the used chemicals. Wash your hands thoroughly with warm water and soap or detergent before leaving the laboratory.

16. On a sheet of graph paper, make a graph of the solubility of ammonium chloride versus temperature. Plot temperature on the horizontal axis and solubility (in spoonfuls per 50 mL water) on the vertical axis.

Observations

DATA TABLE 1

Type of Sodium Chloride	Particle Size	Mass of Beaker (g)	Mass of Beaker and Salt (g)	Mass of Salt (g)	Appearance of Mixture After 2 Minutes Without Stirring	Time to Dissolve (seconds)
Rock salt						
Table salt						

Name ______________________ Class ______________ Date ___________

DATA TABLE 2

Temperature (°C)	Number of Spoonfuls of Ammonium Chloride Dissolved
18–20	
40	
60	
80	

Analysis and Conclusions

1. **Inferring** How did stirring affect the rate at which the salt dissolved? Explain how you think stirring caused this effect.

2. **Inferring** Why do you think the different types of salt dissolved at different rates?

3. **Predicting** Predict what effect, if any, you think the size of salt grains would have on their solubility. Explain your answer.

4. **Using Graphs** Based on your graph and your observations in Part B, what do you think the solubility of ammonium chloride (in spoonfuls per 50 mL water) would be at 10°C? At 70°C? At 100°C?

Go Further

Design an experiment to determine the effect of temperature on the rate of dissolving of a different solid in water. Write a detailed plan of your experiment. Your plan should state a hypothesis, identify variables, and describe the procedures and safety precautions that you will use. Show your plan to your teacher. When your teacher approves your plan, carry out your experiment and report your results and conclusions.

Testing for Nutrients in Foods

Background Information

Nutrients are those substances in food that are necessary for health. There are three main classes of organic nutrients. The first class, **carbohydrates,** consists of sugars and starches, which are polymers of the sugar glucose. The second class, lipids, includes fats and oils. The third class consists of **proteins,** which are polymers of amino acids. Because the compounds in each class of nutrients contain different functional groups, a different chemical test can be used to detect each type of nutrient.

For carbohydrates, there are two tests, one to detect sugars and one to detect starches. A mixture called Benedict's solution changes color when it is heated with many types of sugars, and a solution of iodine changes color in the presence of starch. A solution of copper sulfate, called biuret reagent, changes color when it reacts with proteins. A bright red dye called Sudan IV dissolves in lipids, but not in water. If a material has the ability to dissolve Sudan IV dye, this is a sign that the material contains lipids.

In this investigation, you will observe the reaction of each of these test materials with samples of glucose (a sugar), starch, vegetable oil, and powdered gelatin (protein). Then, you will design an experiment using each of the test materials to determine which classes of organic nutrients are present in several foods.

Problem

Which foods contain sugars, starches, lipids, and proteins?

Pre-Lab Discussion

Read the entire investigation. Then, work with a partner to answer the following questions.

1. **Controlling Variables** Why is a test tube of water included in the Procedure for Part A of this investigation? Explain your answer.

____

____

____

2. **Predicting** In Part A of this investigation, which food substance(s) do you expect to react with each test material?

   a. Benedict's solution

   ____

   b. Iodine solution

   ____

c. Sudan IV dye

d. Biuret reagent

3. **Controlling Variables** Identify the manipulated, responding, and controlled variables in Part A of this investigation.

   a. Manipulated variables

   b. Responding variables

   c. Controlled variables

4. **Predicting** Which nutrients do you think are present in each food that you will test in Part B of this investigation?

   a. Orange juice

   b. Potato

   c. Whole milk

   d. Skim milk

   e. Margarine

   f. Egg yolk

   g. Egg white

Name ______________________ Class ______________ Date ____________

5. **Designing Experiments** Describe a set of procedures you could use in Part B to test your predictions.

Materials *(per group)*

500-mL beaker
hot plate
paper towel
glass-marking pencil
5 test tubes
test-tube rack
4 spatulas
glucose
cornstarch
powdered gelatin
2 dropper pipets
vegetable oil
3 10-mL graduated cylinders
Benedict's solution
tongs
clock or watch
iodine solution
Sudan IV dye
5 stoppers for test tubes
biuret reagent
orange juice
minced potato
whole milk
skim milk
margarine
egg yolk
egg white

Safety

Put on safety goggles and a lab apron. Wear plastic disposable gloves when handling chemicals, as they may irritate the skin or stain skin or clothing. Be careful to avoid breakage when working with glassware. Use extreme care when working with heated equipment or materials to avoid burns. Keep Sudan IV dye away from any open flame. Observe proper laboratory procedures when using electrical equipment. Never touch or taste any chemical unless instructed to do so. Wash your hands thoroughly after carrying out this investigation. Note all safety alert symbols next to the steps in the Procedure and review the meaning of each symbol by referring to the Safety Symbols on page xiii.

Design Your Experiment

Part A: Observing Chemical Tests for Nutrients

1. Fill a 500-mL beaker about one-fourth of the way with water. Place the beaker on the hot plate. Turn the hot plate to a high setting and bring the water to a boil. **CAUTION:** *Be careful using the hot plate and handling boiling water and hot glassware.*
2. On a sheet of paper towel, write *glucose, cornstarch, gelatin,* and *vegetable oil* near different corners of the towel.
3. Use a glass-marking pencil to label five test tubes 1 through 5 and place them in the test-tube rack. Using a separate clean spatula for each substance and just enough of each substance to cover the end of the spatula, place glucose in test tube 1, cornstarch in test tube 2, and gelatin in test tube 3. Use a dropper pipet to place 4 drops of vegetable oil in test tube 4. Store the spatulas and pipet in the appropriate places on the paper towel when they are not in use.
4. Use a graduated cylinder to add 3 mL of water to each test tube, including test tube 5.
5. Fill each of the test tubes halfway with Benedict's solution.
6. Use tongs to place the test tubes into the beaker of boiling water. Leave the test tubes in the boiling water for 5 minutes.
7. After 5 minutes have passed, use tongs to return each test tube to the test-tube rack. Observe any changes in the appearance of the contents of each test tube. Record your observations in Data Table 1.
8. Thoroughly wash the five test tubes and discard the contents in the sink. Carefully dry the test tubes and place them back in the test-tube rack.
9. Repeat Steps 3 and 4.
10. Use a dropper pipet to add 1 or 2 drops of iodine solution to each test tube. Note whether the iodine remains brown or if it changes to another color. Record your observations in Data Table 1.
11. Again, wash and dry the test tubes, and repeat Steps 3 and 4.
12. Use a clean spatula to add a few grains of Sudan IV dye to each test tube. **CAUTION:** *Do not get any dye on your skin or clothing. Keep the dye away from any open flames.*

13. Place a stopper firmly into each test tube and shake the test tubes gently. Observe whether the dye has been absorbed by any material in the test tube. Record your observations in Data Table 1. **CAUTION:** *Make sure that the test tubes are securely closed to avoid spilling.*

14. Wash and dry the test tubes, and repeat Steps 3 and 4. Use a clean dropper pipet to add 3 drops of biuret reagent to each test tube. Observe any changes in the appearance of the contents of each test tube. Record your observations in Data Table 1. **CAUTION:** *Biuret reagent is poisonous and can burn and stain skin and clothing.*

Part B: Using Chemical Tests to Identify Nutrients

15. Design an experiment to test the predictions you made in Pre-Lab Discussion Question 4. Write a detailed plan of how you will carry out your experiment. Use your knowledge of chemical tests for organic nutrients from Part A of this investigation to help you plan your procedures. Construct Data Table 2 in which to record your observations in the space provided on page 94.

16. What are the manipulated, responding, and controlled variables in your experiment?
    a. Manipulated variables
    b. Responding variables
    c. Controlled variables

17. What safety precautions will you need to take?

18. Show your written experimental plan to your teacher. When your teacher approves your plan, carry out your experiment and record your observations.

Name ______________ Class ______________ Date ______________

Observations

DATA TABLE 1

Test Tube	Food	Benedict's Solution	Iodine Solution	Sudan IV Dye	Biuret Reagent
1	Sugar				
2	Cornstarch				
3	Gelatin				
4	Vegetable oil				
5	Water				

DATA TABLE 2

If you need more space, attach additional sheets of paper.

Name ______________________ Class ________________ Date ____________

Analysis and Conclusions

1. **Observing** Which food(s) reacted with Benedict's solution in Part B?

2. **Observing** Which food(s) reacted with iodine solution?

3. **Analyzing Data** What change did you observe in the Sudan IV dye test? Which foods caused this change?

4. **Analyzing Data** What color change did you observe for the biuret solution test? Which foods caused this change?

5. **Comparing and Contrasting** Based on your data from Part B, what is the major difference between whole milk and skim milk?

6. **Comparing and Contrasting** Which nutrient did you find in the egg yolk that you did not find in the egg white?

7. Evaluating and Revising Which of your predictions did your data support?

____

____

____

____

____

____

____

____

8. Drawing Conclusions On a diet consisting almost entirely of milk, human babies grow rapidly and maintain good health. Use your data to explain how this is possible.

____

____

____

____

____

Go Further

Benedict's solution does not react with all sugars. Design an experiment to compare the reactions of Benedict's solution with various sugars. After your teacher approves your experimental plan, obtain samples of several sugars and perform your experiment. Then, use a biology or chemistry textbook to determine the molecular structures of the sugars you used in your experiment. Compare your data to these structures. Formulate a hypothesis about the relationship between the molecular structure of a sugar and its ability to react with Benedict's solution.

Name ______________________ Class ________________ Date ____________

Cross-Linked Polymers

Background Information

A **polymer** is a large molecule that forms when smaller molecules called monomers are linked together through covalent bonds. In some polymers, all of the monomer molecules are identical. Other polymers contain more than one type of monomer. Under certain conditions, two polymer molecules can be joined at different locations along the molecule by covalent bonds called cross-links. These links can also form between two sections of a single polymer molecule. The existence of cross-links can make the polymer more elastic (able to return to its original shape after being pushed or pulled) and stronger (harder to tear apart).

Some cross-linked polymers form a type of colloid called a gel when they are dispersed in a liquid such as water. Gels have a loose, irregular structure, which prevents the liquid from flowing. In a water-based gel, the amount of water also affects the physical properties of the gel. Adding water to a gel makes it more like a liquid in its properties. Reducing the amount of water makes the gel more like a solid.

In this investigation, you will observe the properties of cross-linked protein polymers in gelatin.

Figure 1

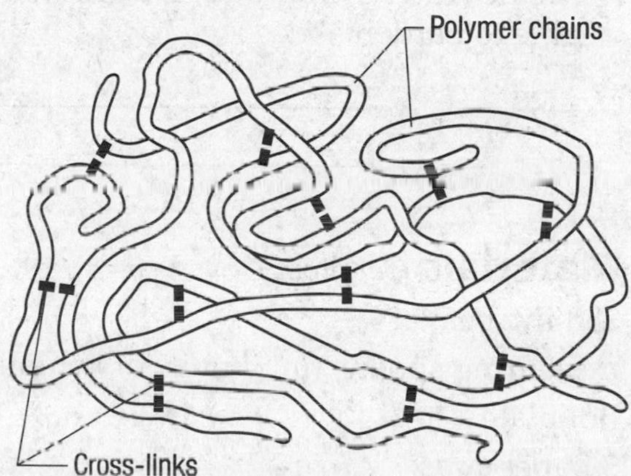

Problem

How does cross-linking affect the physical properties of polymers?

Pre-Lab Discussion

Read the entire investigation. Then, work with a partner to answer the following questions.

1. **Formulating Hypotheses** State a hypothesis about how increasing the amount of gelatin added to a given volume of water will affect the amount of cross-linking in the resulting polymer.

____

____

____

2. **Observing** How can you test the gelatin to determine the extent of cross-linking that has occurred?

____

____

Name ____________________ Class ____________________ Date ____________

3. **Controlling Variables** Identify the manipulated, responding, and controlled variables.

   a. Manipulated variable

   ____

   b. Responding variable

   ____

   c. Controlled variables

   ____

4. **Inferring** Wood glue, like gelatin, consists of proteins extracted from the bones and tissues of animals, which are mixed with water. As the water evaporates, the glue hardens. Explain what causes the glue to harden.

   ____

   ____

Materials *(per group)*

250-mL beaker
measuring spoons (in SI units of volume)
hot plate
3 paper cups
20 mL (4 teaspoons) sugar-free gelatin mix
3 wooden splints

Safety

Put on safety goggles and a lab apron. Be careful to avoid breakage when working with glassware. Never touch or taste any chemical unless instructed to do so. Use extreme care when working with heated equipment or materials to avoid burns. Observe proper laboratory procedures when using electrical equipment. Note all safety alert symbols next to the steps in the Procedure and review the meaning of each symbol by referring to the Safety Symbols on page xiii.

Procedure

Day 1

1. Label the three paper cups with your name.

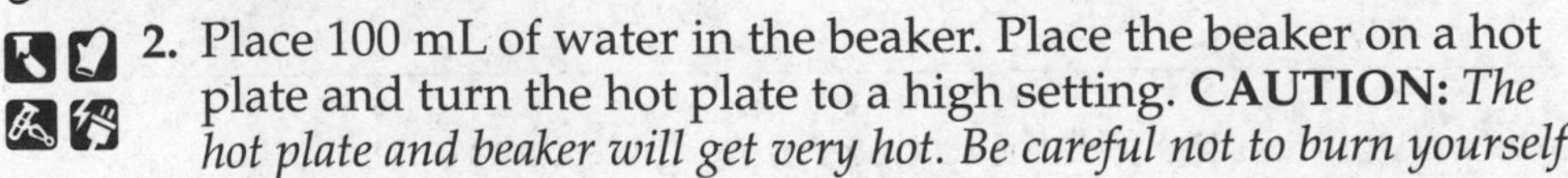

2. Place 100 mL of water in the beaker. Place the beaker on a hot plate and turn the hot plate to a high setting. **CAUTION:** *The hot plate and beaker will get very hot. Be careful not to burn yourself.*
3. When the water boils, reduce the setting to low. Using the measuring spoons, carefully remove 30 mL (2 tablespoons) of hot water and place it in one of the paper cups. **CAUTION:** *Use heat-resistant gloves when removing hot water from the beaker.*

Name ______________________ Class __________________ Date __________

4. Add 2.4 mL (0.5 teaspoon) of gelatin to the paper cup. Stir the gelatin with one of the wooden splints until the gelatin is mixed completely in the water. **CAUTION:** *Do not taste the gelatin.*
5. Repeat Steps 2 and 3, placing 4.9 mL (1.0 teaspoon) of gelatin in the second cup and 9.8 mL (2.0 teaspoons) of gelatin in the third cup. Turn off the hot plate and set the paper cups aside to cool.
6. Observe the gelatin. Record your observations in the data table. Leave the gelatin exposed to air in an area where it will remain undisturbed overnight.

Day 2

7. Tear the paper cup away from the 2.4-mL gelatin sample.
8. Observe the gelatin disk. To investigate its elasticity and strength, try to twist it, squash it, and pull it apart. Try to change the polymer's shape slowly, and then rapidly. Record your observations in the data table.
9. Repeat Steps 7 and 8 with the other two gelatin samples.

Observations

DATA TABLE

Gelatin Volume (in 30 mL water)	Sample Properties: Day 1	Sample Properties: Day 2
2.4 mL (0.5 teaspoon)		
4.9 mL (1.0 teaspoon)		
9.8 mL (2.0 teaspoons)		

Name ______________________ Class ______________ Date ___________

Analysis and Conclusions

1. **Observing** How did the polymer gels change when you left them out overnight?

____

2. **Inferring** Which gelatin sample do you think contained more cross-links? Explain your answer.

____

____

3. **Evaluating and Revising** Did the results of this investigation support or contradict your hypothesis? Explain your answer.

____

____

____

Go Further

Flour made from grains such as wheat contains proteins called gliadin and glutelin. When dough (water mixed with the flour) is kneaded, these protein molecules are stretched, and cross-linked bonds form between them. Use resources in the library or on the Internet to find out how this cross-linking in bread dough takes place. Then, use the information you find to design an experiment to test how too little or too much kneading affects the dough. Show your teacher a written plan for your experiment. When your teacher approves your plan, carry out your experiment and report the results.

Modeling Radioactive Decay

Background Information

Radioactive material decays by emitting **alpha particles, beta particles,** or **gamma rays.** During the process of nuclear decay, a radioisotope spontaneously changes into a different element. The time it takes for one-half of a sample of a radioisotope to decay into another element is called **half-life.** The half-lives of various radioisotopes vary from less than a second to billions of years.

A capacitor is a device that can store a large quantity of electric charge and then slowly release that charge. The process of releasing charge is called discharging. The ability of a capacitor to store charge can be measured in units called microfarads. Like a radioisotope, a discharging capacitor has a half-life. Unlike radioactive materials, capacitors do not give off nuclear radiation. As a result, a discharging capacitor can be used as a safe model of radioactive decay.

In this investigation, you will determine the half-lives of two capacitors. Then, you will use your observations to explain the difference between the decay of two radioactive elements.

Problem

How can a model help describe the decay of radioactive isotopes?

Pre-Lab Discussion

Read the entire investigation. Then, work with a partner to answer the following questions.

1. **Using Analogies** What property of a capacitor makes it useful for modeling the decay of a radioactive isotope?

____

____

____

____

____

2. **Designing Experiments** How will you observe the discharge of the capacitors?

____

____

____

____

____

3. **Predicting** The rating of each capacitor (4600 or 6000 microfarads) indicates its ability to store charge. Which capacitor do you expect to have the longer half-life?

____

____

____

4. **Designing Experiments** You will use the power source to charge the capacitors. Why do you think you will need to disconnect the power source from each capacitor before you discharge the capacitor?

____

____

____

5. **Controlling Variables** Identify the manipulated, responding, and controlled variables in this investigation.

   a. Manipulated variable

   ____

   ____

   b. Responding variable

   ____

   ____

   c. Controlled variables

   ____

   ____

Materials *(per group)*

4 alligator clips
5 insulated wires
2 capacitors (4600 and 6000 microfarads)
DC voltmeter
DC power source
switch
clock or watch with second hand
graph paper
metric ruler

Name ______________________ Class ______________________ Date ______________________

Safety

Put on safety goggles. Observe proper laboratory procedures when using electrical equipment. Keep all electrical equipment away from water. Do not apply more voltage to the capacitors than their safe operating voltage. Note all safety alert symbols next to the steps in the Procedure and review the meaning of each symbol by referring to the Safety Symbols on page xiii.

Procedure

1. Work in groups of three. Use alligator clips and insulated wires to connect the 4600-microfarad capacitor, voltmeter, power source, and switch as shown in Figure 1. To avoid damaging the capacitor, make sure that the positive terminal of the capacitor is connected to the positive terminal of the power source and that the negative terminal of the capacitor is connected to the negative terminal of the power source. **CAUTION:** *Be very careful when using electricity. Do not close the switch yet. Before continuing with Step 2, have your teacher check your setup.*
2. Carefully examine the scale on the voltmeter. Because you will have to read the voltage very quickly, determine what each division on the voltmeter scale represents.
3. Close the switch and read the voltage. Do not start timing yet. Record this voltage in the data table next to 0 seconds.
4. One member of your group will be the timer. This person will watch the clock and alert the others in the group to each 10-second interval. A second group member, the reader, will watch and read the voltmeter and call out the voltage when the timer announces each 10-second interval. A third group member will be the recorder. This person will record the voltages in the data table.
5. Start timing the 10-second intervals as you open the switch. After 10 seconds, the timer should call out "10 seconds," while the reader tells what the voltage is. **Note:** *The reader should try to anticipate each 10-second interval. Otherwise, it may take more than 10 seconds to decide what the reading is.*

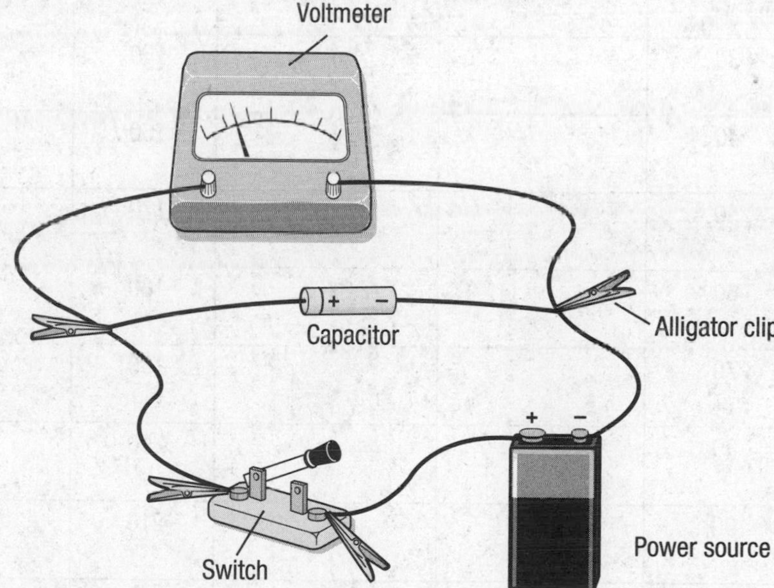

Figure 1

6. Continue to record the voltage for 230 seconds. If the voltage becomes too small to measure before that time, you may stop at that point. If necessary, you may continue the data table on another sheet of paper.
7. Replace the 4600-microfarad capacitor with the 6000-microfarad capacitor.
8. Repeat Steps 1 through 6 with the 6000-microfarad capacitor.

Observations

DATA TABLE

Time (seconds)	Voltage (volts)		Time (seconds)	Voltage (volts)	
	4600-Microfarad Capacitor	6000-Microfarad Capacitor		4600-Microfarad Capacitor	6000-Microfarad Capacitor
0			120		
10			130		
20			140		
30			150		
40			160		
50			170		
60			180		
70			190		
80			200		
90			210		
100			220		
110			230		

Analysis and Conclusions

1. **Using Graphs** On a sheet of graph paper, construct a graph of your data. Plot time on the horizontal axis and voltage on the vertical axis. Draw a smooth curve that comes as close as possible to each of your data points for the 4600-microfarad capacitor. Draw a second smooth curve for the data points for the 6000-microfarad capacitor. Label each curve with the rating of the capacitor it represents.

Name ______________________ Class __________________ Date ____________

2. **Analyzing Data** Use your graph to find the half-life of the 4600-microfarad capacitor. To do this, calculate half of the voltage across this capacitor at 0 seconds. For example, if the voltage at 0 seconds was 10 volts, half of the voltage is 5 volts. Then, locate this voltage on the vertical axis. Use the metric ruler to draw a horizontal line from this voltage to the curve for the 4600-microfarad capacitor. Mark the point where this line intersects the curve. Then, draw a vertical line from this point down to the horizontal axis. The half-life is the time at which the vertical line intersects the horizontal axis. Record the half-life of the 4600-microfarad capacitor below.

   Half-life of 4600-microfarad capacitor: ______________ seconds

3. **Analyzing Data** Use the procedure you used to answer Question 2 to determine the half-life of the 6000-microfarad capacitor.

   Half-life of 6000 microfarad capacitor: ______________ seconds

4. **Evaluating** Did your data support or contradict your prediction?

   ____

   ____

   ____

5. **Analyzing Data** How long did the 4600-microfarad capacitor take to reach one-fourth of its original voltage?

   ____

6. **Calculating** If the voltage across the 4600-microfarad capacitor was 9.0 volts at 0 seconds, how many half-lives would be needed for the voltage to fall to 0.1 volts? How many seconds would that take?

   ____

   ____

   ____

7. **Calculating** If the voltage across the 6000-microfarad capacitor was 9.0 volts at 0 seconds, how many half-lives would be needed for the voltage to fall to 0.1 volts? How many seconds would that take?

   ____

   ____

   ____

8. **Comparing and Contrasting** Which capacitor would take longer to fall to a voltage that is too low for the voltmeter to measure? Explain your answer.

   ____

   ____

   ____

9. Using Models Carbon-14 has a half-life of 5730 years. Uranium-238 has a half-life of 4.47×10^9 years. A radioisotope can be used to date an object only if enough of the radioisotope remains in the object to measure. Use your observations of the two capacitors to explain why carbon-14 can be used to date objects as old as 50,000 years, but uranium-238 can be used to date the objects that ar millions of years old.

Go Further

Use resources in the library or on the Internet to research how a technique called fission-track dating can be used to estimate the age of an object.

Detecting Nuclear Radiation

Background Information

A cloud chamber is a device that can be used to observe **radioactivity.** In the chamber, vapor of a substance such as alcohol is cooled to a low temperature. A particle of high energy passing through the chamber ionizes the molecules that the particle strikes in its path. Alcohol vapor condenses around the ions, producing a thin white trail. Each white trail reveals the path of a radioactive particle.

There are many sources of nuclear radiation. Cosmic rays, or high-energy particles from space, are one common source of nuclear radiation. Many rocks and building materials also produce small amounts of nuclear radiation. You can use a cloud chamber to determine whether background sources or radioactive samples produce measurable levels of radiation in your environment.

In this investigation, you will build a cloud chamber and use it to determine whether you are usually exposed to nuclear radiation.

Problem

Are you exposed to nuclear radiation in your daily life?

Pre-Lab Discussion

Read the entire investigation. Then, work with a partner to answer the following questions.

1. **Formulating Hypotheses** State a hypothesis about whether you are usually exposed to nuclear radiation.

____

____

2. **Controlling Variables** Identify the manipulated, responding, and controlled variables in this investigation.

   a. Manipulated variable

   ____

   b. Responding variable

   ____

   c. Controlled variables

   ____

3. **Predicting** Based on your hypothesis, predict what you will observe in Step 7.

____

____

Name ______________________ Class ______________ Date __________

4. **Predicting** Predict how your observations will differ in Steps 7 and 10. Explain the reasons for your prediction.

____

____

____

5. **Inferring** Why is dry ice used in this lab?

____

____

Materials *(per group)*

black felt
scissors
large glass jar with screw-on lid
thick blotting paper
fast-drying glue
dropper pipet
isopropyl alcohol
dry ice
plastic tray
clock or watch
sealed alpha-radiation source
powerful flashlight
small wooden block

Safety

Put on safety goggles and a lab apron. Be careful to avoid breakage when working with glassware. Wear plastic disposable gloves when handling chemicals, as they may irritate the skin or stain skin or clothing. Never touch or taste any chemical unless instructed to do so. Keep alcohol away from any open flame. Be careful when handling sharp instruments. Be careful using dry ice. Never allow dry ice to touch your skin. Be careful with the alpha-radiation source. Alpha particles cannot pass through skin, but the source of the particles can be dangerous if swallowed or inhaled. Wash your hands thoroughly after carrying out this investigation. Note all safety alert symbols next to the steps in the Procedure and review the meaning of each symbol by referring to the Safety Symbols on page xiii.

Procedure

1. To construct a cloud chamber, use scissors to cut a circle of black felt slightly smaller than the inside diameter of the glass jar. **CAUTION:** *Be careful when using scissors.*
2. Place the felt circle in the bottom of the jar, as shown in Figure 1.
3. Cut a circle of thick blotting paper slightly smaller than the inside of the lid of the jar. Use fast-drying glue to stick the blotting paper to the bottom of the lid.
4. Use the dropper pipet to apply isopropyl alcohol to the blotting paper until it is saturated, but not so wet that alcohol drips from it. Let any excess alcohol drain into the sink. **CAUTION:** *Be careful handling isopropyl alcohol. It is poisonous.*
5. Screw the lid onto the jar.

Name ______________________ Class ________________ Date ____________

6. Place the jar onto a large piece of dry ice that your teacher has placed into the tray. **CAUTION:** *Do not touch the dry ice. It can damage your skin.*

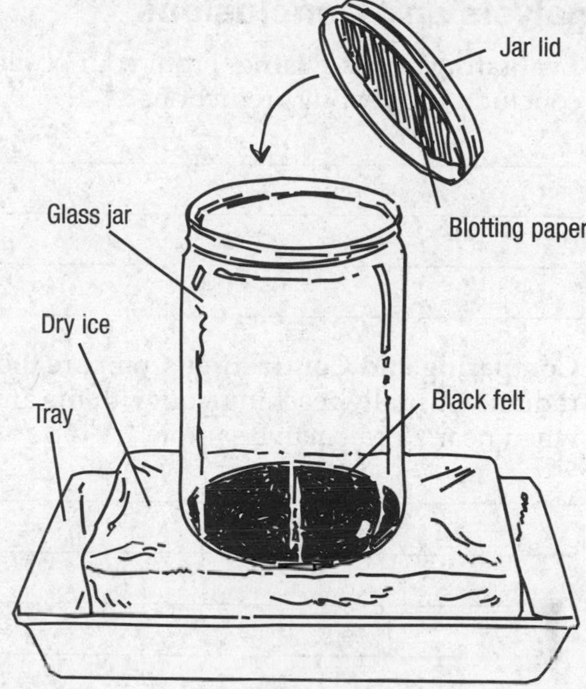

Figure 1

7. Working in a room that is partially darkened, direct the beam of the flashlight through the side of the jar. Observe the cloud chamber for the next 5 minutes. Count the number of white trails you observe. Record your observations in the data table.

8. Unscrew the lid of the jar, leaving the jar in place on the dry ice. Put the wooden block on the felt at the bottom of the jar. If the blotting paper in the lid has begun to dry out, use the dropper pipet to place a few more drops of alcohol onto it. Obtain an alpha-radiation source from your teacher. Place the radiation source on top of the block. **CAUTION:** *Do not touch the radioactive material inside the alpha source.*

9. Screw on the lid of the jar again.

10. Direct the flashlight beam into the jar and watch what happens for the next 5 minutes. If possible, count the number of white trails you observe. Record your observations in the data table.

11. Return the radiation source to your teacher. Wash your hands thoroughly with warm water and soap or detergent before leaving the laboratory.

Observations

DATA TABLE

Source of Nuclear Radiation	Number of White Trails
Background	
Background plus alpha source	

Name ____________________ Class ______________ Date ____________

Analysis and Conclusions

1. **Evaluating and Revising** From your observations, what can you conclude about your predictions?

____

____

____

____

2. **Comparing and Contrasting** Compare the amount of nuclear radiation usually reaching you with the amount you would receive when near a radioactive sample.

____

____

____

____

3. **Evaluating and Revising** From your observations, what can you conclude about your hypothesis?

____

____

____

____

4. **Making Judgments** Based on your observations, how would you advise someone who wanted to protect people's health by completely eliminating exposure to nuclear radiation?

____

____

____

____

Go Further

Suppose that you had a source of both alpha and beta radiation in a cloud chamber. What could you do to make the paths of the two kinds of particles different so that you could tell them apart? Explain your answer. (*Hint:* Recall that alpha and beta particles are oppositely charged.)

Measuring Distance and Displacement

Background Information

Vectors have many uses. For example, you can use vectors to describe the distance an object travels and the displacement that results from an object's movement. Before you can make use of vectors, you must first select a frame of reference.

To use vectors to describe an object's position or movement on a flat surface, you must first define a frame of reference that includes the origin—a specific point that does not move. Two imaginary lines, or axes, that pass through the origin at right angles are then chosen, as shown in Figure 1. These two lines are the *x*-axis and the *y*-axis. Using the axes, you can describe the position of an object in terms of its *x*- and *y*-coordinates, for example, the point (4, 8) on a graph. Note that the coordinates of the origin are (0, 0).

Figure 1 shows that you can also define a vector to describe an object's position by drawing an arrow from the origin to the object's position. The object's coordinates (7, 2) determine the length and direction of the vector. Figure 2 shows that any vector in the frame of reference can be broken down into *x*- and *y*-components. Therefore, any vector is also the **resultant vector** of its own *x*- and *y*-components. Resultant vectors are also used to represent the result of vector addition.

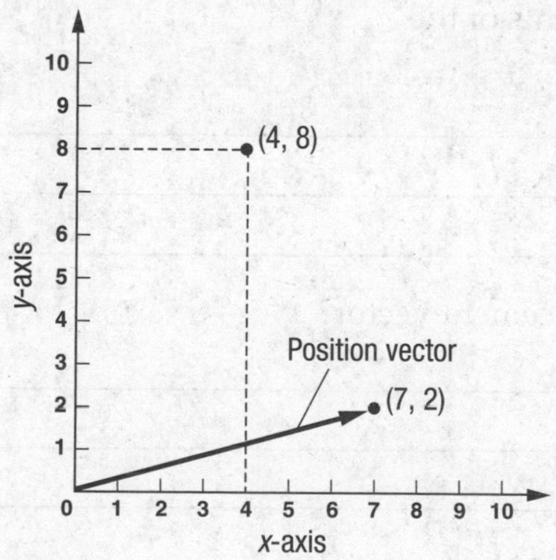

Figure 1

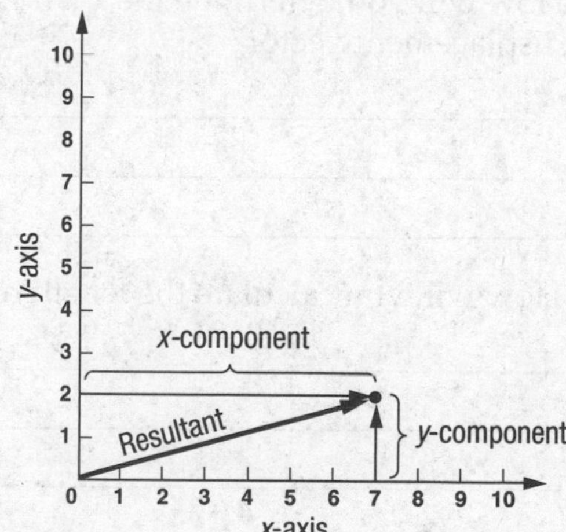

Figure 2

You can use a similar method to define a vector describing an object's displacement. To do this, draw a vector from the object's starting point to its ending point. Figure 3 shows the x- and y-coordinates of an object's starting and ending points. Note that the x- and y-components of the displacement vector are simply the difference between the x- and y-coordinates of the starting and ending points.

In this investigation, you will compare two methods of determining the length of a displacement vector.

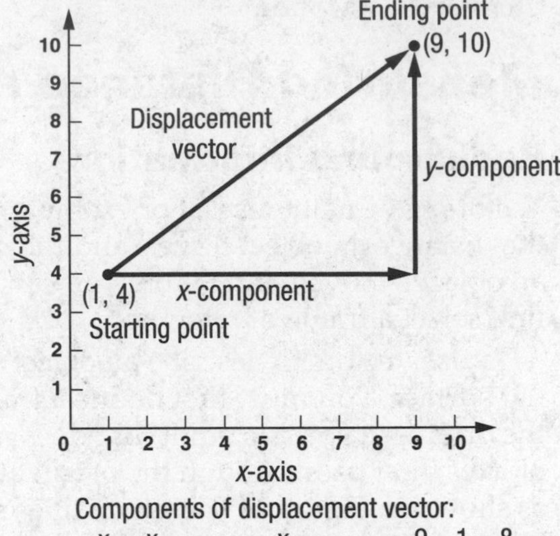

Components of displacement vector:

$x = x_{\text{ending point}} - x_{\text{starting point}} = 9 - 1 = 8$

$y = y_{\text{ending point}} - y_{\text{starting point}} = 10 - 4 = 6$

Figure 3

Problem

How can vectors be used to determine displacement?

Pre-Lab Discussion

Read the entire investigation. Then, work with a partner to answer the following questions.

1. How will you determine the x- and y-coordinates of each position?

____

____

2. How will you determine the x- and y-components of the displacement vector?

____

____

____

3. How will you calculate the length of the displacement vector?

____

____

____

4. How will you measure the length of the displacement vector?

____

____

____

Name ______________________ Class ______________ Date ____________

Materials *(per group)*

masking tape
meter stick
calculator
string

Safety 

Put on safety goggles. Use caution to avoid bumping into people or objects when moving around the room. Note all safety alert symbols next to the steps in the Procedure and review the meaning of each symbol by referring to the Safety Symbols on page xiii.

Procedure

1. Work with a classmate. Mark a dot on a small piece of masking tape. Mark the origin of your frame of reference by sticking a piece of masking tape on the floor, away from furniture and other obstacles.
2. Use the width of the classroom as the *x*-direction and the length of the classroom as the *y*-direction. Attach a 2-meter strip of tape to the floor, running from the origin in the *x* direction. This is the *x*-axis. Attach a second 2-meter strip of tape to the floor, running from the origin in the *y* direction. This is the *y*-axis. Note that the *x*- and *y*-axes should be at right angles to each other.
3. Select a point 1 to 4 meters from the origin as your starting point. Mark this point by sticking a piece of masking tape on the floor and marking a dot on it. Label this piece of tape *Start*.
4. Walk from the starting point to another point 1 to 4 meters from the origin. Mark this point by sticking a piece of masking tape on the floor and marking a dot on it. Label this piece of tape *End*.
5. Use a meter stick to measure the *x*-coordinate of the starting point to the nearest centimeter, as shown in Figure 4. Be careful to measure parallel to the *x*-axis. Record your measurement in the data table.
6. Repeat Step 5, measuring parallel to the *y*-axis, to determine the *y*-coordinate of the starting point. Record your measurement in the data table.

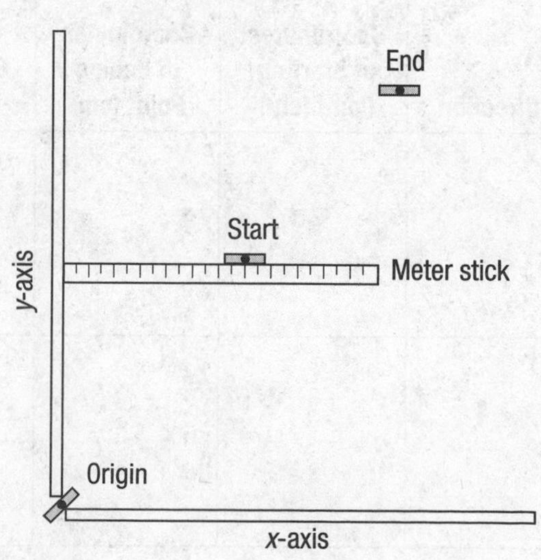

Figure 4

7. Measure and record the x- and y-coordinates of the ending point in the same way that you determined the coordinates of the starting point.
8. Determine the x-component of the displacement vector by subtracting the x-coordinate of the starting point from the x-coordinate of the ending point. Record this value in the data table as the vector component in the x-direction.
9. Repeat Step 8 with the y-coordinates of the starting and ending points to calculate the y-component of the displacement vector. Record this value in the data table as the vector component in the y-direction.
10. Calculate and record the square of the vector component in the x-direction. Calculate and record the square of the vector component in the y-direction.
11. Use the following formula to calculate the length of the displacement vector

$$L = \sqrt{x^2 + y^2}$$

where L is the length of the displacement vector, and x and y are the x- and y-components of the displacement vector. Record this value in the data table as the vector length of the displacement vector.
12. Working with your partner, stretch a string from the starting point to the ending point. While holding the string in this position, mark the string at both points. Use a meter stick to measure the distance between the two marks on the string. Record this measurement in the data table as the measured vector length of the displacement vector.

Observations

DATA TABLE

Direction	Coordinates of Starting Point (cm)	Coordinates of Ending Point (cm)	Displacement Vector			
			Vector Component (cm)	Square of Vector Component	Vector Length (cm)	
					Calculated	Measured
x						
y						

Name ______________________ Class ________________ Date ____________

Analysis and Conclusions

1. **Measuring** What tool can you use to measure the distance moved by an object?

2. **Measuring** How can you measure the distance an object has moved?

3. **Measuring** How can you measure the magnitude of the displacement of an object?

4. **Calculating** How can you calculate the displacement of an object?

5. **Controlling Variables** How could using a large book as the displaced object produce significant error in your results?

6. **Comparing and Contrasting** How did the calculated length of the displacement vector compare with the measured length of the displacement vector?

7. **Inferring** Describe a condition in which it would be impossible to actually measure a displacement.

8. **Comparing and Contrasting** How does the distance moved by an object between its starting point and ending point compare to the displacement vector between the same points?

Go Further

In this investigation, you determined the distance between two points by measuring and calculating the displacement vector. How could you determine displacement by using a graph? Write a procedure you would follow to answer this question. Have your teacher approve your procedure before you carry out the investigation. How does the displacement determined by this graphing method compare with the actual measurement of the displacement?

Name ______________________ Class ______________ Date ___________

Investigating Free Fall

Background Information

Free fall is the movement of an object toward Earth because of gravity. An object that is in free fall experiences acceleration. **Acceleration** is the rate at which velocity changes. Acceleration occurs when there is a change in speed, change in direction, or both. During free fall, speed increases at a constant rate. But what happens when an object also moves horizontally as it falls? The curved path that results is known as projectile motion—a topic you will cover in more detail in Chapter 12. Do you think an object's horizontal motion will affect its fall?

In this investigation, you will compare the fall of two identical objects from the same height. The first object will fall straight down. The second object will be given an initial horizontal velocity at the start of its fall. You will determine how the horizontal motion of the second object affects the time it takes to fall.

Problem

What effect does horizontal motion have on the time an object takes to fall?

Pre-Lab Discussion

Read the entire investigation. Then, work with a partner to answer the following questions

1. **Controlling Variables** Identify the manipulated, responding, and controlled variables in this investigation.

   a. Manipulated variable

   ____

   ____

   b. Responding variable

   ____

   ____

   c. Controlled variables

   ____

   ____

2. **Formulating Hypotheses** State a hypothesis about the effect of horizontal motion on the time an object takes to fall.

   ____

   ____

Name ______________________ Class ________________ Date ____________

3. **Predicting** Make a prediction about the result of this investigation. Will one object fall more quickly than the other, or will both objects hit the floor at the same time?

4. **Controlling Variables** Why are you told to let one object fall through a hole in the box, instead of rolling the object off the edge of the table?

5. **Calculating** How will you determine the average time for the five trials?

6. **Measuring** Why do you think you will need a stopwatch that can measure tenths of a second?

Materials *(per group)*

2 small spherical objects
stopwatch (that can measure tenths of a second)
meter stick
masking tape

Safety

Put on safety goggles. Keep your hands and feet out of the path of falling objects. Note all safety alert symbols next to the steps in the Procedure and review the meaning of each symbol by referring to the Safety Symbols on page xiii.

Name ______________________ Class ______________ Date ______________

Procedure

Part A: Timing Free Fall

 1. Work with a classmate. Hold the object over the floor so that its bottom is in line with the top of the table, as shown in Figure 1. Have your classmate check that the object is being held at the correct height.

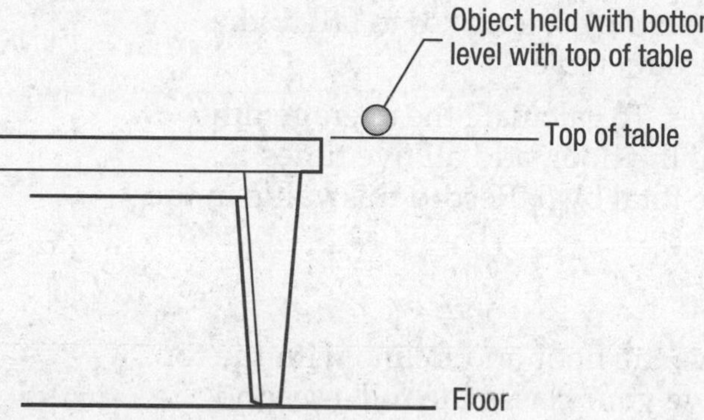

Figure 1

 2. Position your classmate so that he or she can have a clear view of the object and the floor below. Have your classmate be prepared to start the stopwatch.

3. Count down from five and release the object when you reach zero. Have your classmate begin the stopwatch as soon as he or she sees you release the object. Your classmate will use the stopwatch to measure the time it takes the object to hit the floor. Record this time in the data table.

4. Repeat Step 3 four more times. To calculate the average time that the sphere takes to reach the floor, add all five times together, then divide the total by 5. Record this value in the data table.

5. Using the meter stick, measure and place a piece of masking tape on the floor 1 meter from the point directly under the edge of the tabletop, as shown in Figure 2.

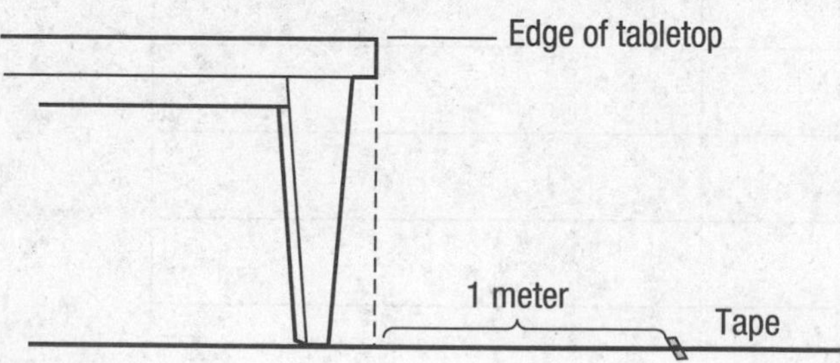

Figure 2

6. Place the object to be dropped near the edge of the tabletop. Push the object off the table with just enough force so that it lands on or close to the tape. **CAUTION:** *To avoid hurting anyone, be careful not to push the object too hard.* Practice pushing the object off the table until you can make it land on or close to the tape nearly every time.
7. Repeat Step 6 one more time and have your classmate use the stopwatch to measure the time the object takes to fall to the floor. Record this time in the data table.
8. Repeat Step 7 four more times. To calculate the average time that the object takes to fall to the floor, add all five times together and then divide the total by 5. Record this value in the data table.

Part B: Comparing Free Fall

9. Hold one of the objects above the floor and in line with the top of the table, as in Step 1. Have your classmate roll a second object toward the edge of the table. When you see the rolling object fall off the edge of the table, release the object you are holding. Watch and listen to observe whether one object hits the floor before the other.
10. Repeat Step 9 four more times. Record your observations in the space provided for results of Part B below the data table.

Observations

DATA TABLE

Trial	Vertical Fall Time (seconds)	Fall With Horizontal Motion Time (seconds)
1		
2		
3		
4		
5		
TOTAL		
Average		

Results of Part B

____

____

____

____

Analysis and Conclusions

1. **Calculating** What was the average time required for the object dropped straight down to hit the floor?

2. **Calculating** What was the average time the object with the initial horizontal velocity took to hit the floor?

3. **Observing** In Part B, did one sphere hit the floor before the other or did both spheres land at the same time?

4. **Evaluating and Revising** Did your data support or contradict your hypothesis? Explain your answer.

Go Further

The greater an object's mass, the stronger is the force of gravity on the object. Does this mean that more massive objects fall more quickly than less massive objects? Design an experiment to answer this question. Write a detailed plan for your experiment. Describe the procedures you will use and identify all the variables involved. Show your plan to your teacher. If your teacher approves, carry out your experiment.

Using a Pendulum to Measure the Acceleration Due to Force of Gravity

Background Information

A freely falling object accelerates at a rate that depends on the force of gravity. Near the surface of Earth, acceleration due to gravity (g) is equal to approximately 9.8 m/s^2. There are several ways to measure acceleration due to gravity. In this investigation, you will use a method that makes use of a pendulum. A pendulum consists of a weight, also known as a bob, that swings back and forth from a rope or string. Because the fixed end of the string is tied in place, it exerts a centripetal force that pulls the falling weight into a circular path. The time required for a pendulum to complete a back-and-forth swing is called the period of the pendulum. In Part A of this investigation, you will determine whether the period of a pendulum depends on the angle from which the bob is released.

Because the friction forces acting on the pendulum are neglible, it can be assumed that the pendulum is acted on by a single force—the force of gravity. A simple equation relating the acceleration due to gravity, the length of the pendulum, and the period of the pendulum can be written. In Part B of this investigation, you will design and carry out an experiment in which you will use a pendulum and this equation to determine the value of g.

Problem

How can you use a pendulum to determine the acceleration due to gravity?

Pre-Lab Discussion

Read the entire investigation. Then, work with a partner to answer the following questions.

1. **Designing Experiments** In Part A of this investigation, how will you determine the period of the pendulum?

____

____

____

____

2. **Predicting** In Part A of this investigation, how will the angle from which the pendulum is released affect the period of the pendulum?

____

____

____

3. **Formulating Hypotheses** State a hypothesis that you could test in Part B of this investigation.

____

____

____

4. **Designing Experiments** Describe an experiment that you could perform to test your hypothesis.

____

____

____

____

____

5. **Controlling Variables** Identify the manipulated, responding, and controlled variables in the experiment described in Question 4.

____

____

____

____

6. **Evaluating** What experimental result would support your hypothesis? What result would contradict your hypothesis?

____

____

____

____

____

____

____

Materials *(per group)*

ring stand
2 books
clamp
metal rod, approximately 30 cm long
2-m fishing line
meter stick
100-g mass
protractor
stopwatch
graph paper

Ask your teacher to provide you with any additional materials that you will need to carry out Part B of this investigation.

Name ______________ Class ______________ Date ______________

Safety

Wear safety goggles when performing this investigation. Note all safety alert symbols next to the steps in the Procedure and review the meaning of each symbol by referring to the Safety Symbols on page xiii.

Procedure

Part A: Determining If the Angle of Release Affects the Period of a Pendulum

1. Place the ring stand near the edge of a table, as shown in Figure 1. Place two textbooks on the base of the ring stand to prevent it from falling over. Use the clamp to attach the metal rod to the ring stand so that it extends beyond the edge of the table.
2. Tie one end of the fishing line to the portion of the metal rod that extends over the table. Tie the 100-g mass to the other end of the fishing line so that the center of the mass is 1.0 m below the metal rod, as shown in Figure 1.

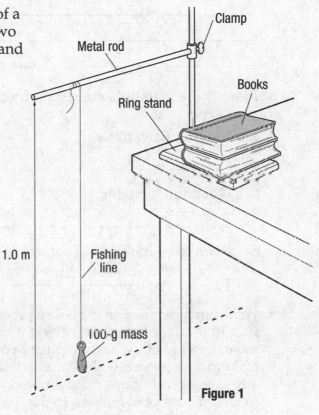

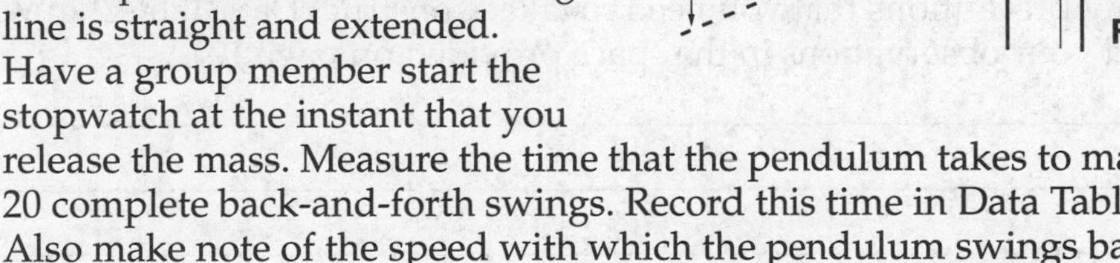

Figure 1

3. Using the protractor to measure the angle, position the mass at an angle of 10 degrees. **Note:** *When the mass hangs straight down, the angle is 0 degrees.* Hold the mass in this position so that the fishing line is straight and extended. Have a group member start the stopwatch at the instant that you release the mass. Measure the time that the pendulum takes to make 20 complete back-and-forth swings. Record this time in Data Table 1. Also make note of the speed with which the pendulum swings back and forth.
4. Repeat Step 3 two more times, first releasing the mass at a 20-degree angle and then a 30-degree angle. For each trial, record in Data Table 1 the time the pendulum takes to complete 20 back-and-forth swings.
5. Calculate the period of the pendulum by dividing the time the pendulum takes to make 20 complete swings from each of the three positions by 20. Record these values in the appropriate places in Data Table 1.
6. Make a graph of your data. Plot the angle (10, 20, and 30 degrees) on the horizontal axis (x -axis) and the period of the pendulum on the vertical axis (y -axis). Draw a straight line through the data points.

Part B: Design Your Own Investigation

7. Plan an experiment that will make use of a pendulum to determine the acceleration due to gravity (g). The acceleration due to gravity of the pendulum bob can be calculated by dividing the length of the pendulum (L) by the period of the pendulum (T) squared.

$$g = \frac{39.5L}{T^2}$$

Record the hypothesis that you will test.

8. Identify the manipulated, responding, and controlled variables in your experiment.

a. Manipulated variable

b. Responding variable

c. Controlled variables

9. Write out a detailed step-by-step procedure that you will use. Your procedure should produce data that will test your hypothesis. As you plan your experiment, think about what equipment you will need, what measurements you will make, and how you will record and display your data (tables, graphs). Include any safety precautions that you need to take. Construct Data Table 2 in which to record your observations in the space provided on page 127.

Name ______________________ Class ______________ Date __________

Safety Precautions

____

____

____

____

____

10. Submit your written experimental plan to your teacher. When your teacher has approved your plan, carry out your experiment and record your observations in Data Table 2.

Observations

DATA TABLE 1

Starting Position (degrees)	Time for 20 Swings (seconds)	Period (seconds)
10		
20		
30		

DATA TABLE 2

If you need more space, attach additional sheets of paper.

Name ______________________ Class ________________ Date __________

Analysis and Conclusions

1. **Observing** In Part A of this investigation, how did the angle from which you released the pendulum affect the maximum speed of the pendulum's motion?

2. **Analyzing Data** What did your results in Part A indicate about the relationship between the period of the pendulum and the position from which you released the pendulum?

3. **Evaluating and Revising** Did your results in Part B support or contradict your hypothesis? Explain your answer.

4. **Evaluating and Revising** Use the equation below to determine the experimental error for each of the calculated values for g. Record these error values in Data Table 2.

$$\text{Experimental error} = \left(\frac{\text{Experimental value} - \text{Accepted value}}{\text{Accepted value}}\right) \times 100\%$$

Why might your calculated values of g differ from the accepted value?

Go Further

Predict how the mass of a pendulum affects the period of the pendulum and the calculated value of g. Design an experiment to test your predictions. Show your teacher a detailed description of your experimental plan. When your teacher approves, carry out your experiment and report your results.

Testing Galileo's Hypothesis

Background Information

In 1638, Galileo Galilei published a book that described the motion of freely falling objects. In this book, Galileo hypothesized that freely falling objects accelerate at a constant rate. However, Galileo could not test his hypothesis directly because the precise and accurate instruments needed to measure time and distance did not exist. To solve this problem, he designed an experiment to test his hypothesis indirectly by carefully measuring the time and distance of balls rolling down ramps. When a ball rolls down a ramp with a small incline, it accelerates more slowly than it does during free fall.

In this investigation, you will determine whether a steel ball accelerates at a constant rate as it rolls down ramps of varying lengths. Then, you will determine how the steepness of a ramp affects the acceleration of the ball.

Problem

How do the length and steepness of a ramp affect the rate of acceleration of an object rolling down the ramp?

Pre-Lab Discussion

Read the entire investigation. Then, work with a partner to answer the following questions.

1. **Formulating Hypotheses** State a hypothesis about whether the gravitational force on an object changes as it rolls down a ramp.

____

2. **Predicting** Based on your hypothesis, predict how the ball will accelerate as it rolls down the ramp. Explain your answer.

____

____

____

3. **Controlling Variables** Identify the manipulated, responding, and controlled variables in this experiment.

   a. Manipulated variables ______________________

   b. Responding variable ______________________

   c. Controlled variable ______________________

4. **Predicting** How do you expect the steepness of the ramp to affect the acceleration of the ball?

____

Name ______________________ Class ______________ Date ____________

Materials *(per group)*

1.5-m board
2 books
meter stick
steel ball, approximately 4 cm in diameter
stopwatch
calculator

Safety

Wear safety goggles. Handle the board carefully to avoid splinters. Note all safety alert symbols next to the steps in the Procedure and review the meaning of each symbol by referring to the Safety Symbols on page xiii.

Procedure

Part A: Determining Acceleration

1. Work with a partner. Put one of the books on the floor. Place one end of the board on the book to form a ramp. Then, place the meter stick on the board with its zero end at the bottom of the ramp, as shown in Figure 1. Mark a line at distances of 0.5 m and 1.0 m from the end of the board. Move the meter stick so that its zero is aligned at the 1.0 m mark you just made on the board and mark a line at a distance of 1.5 m from the end of the board. Refer to Data Table 1, which you will use to compile data obtained in Steps 2 and 8 of Part A.

Figure 1

2. Position the steel ball at the mark located 1.5 m from the bottom of the ramp. Have your partner start the stopwatch at the instant you release the ball. Have your partner stop the stopwatch when the ball reaches the bottom of the ramp. **CAUTION:** *Stop the ball when it reaches the bottom of the ramp.* Record the time of Trial 1 for a distance of 1.5 m in the data table.

3. Repeat Step 2 four more times. Record the times of Trials 2 to 5 for a distance of 1.5 m.

4. Position the steel ball at the mark located 1.0 m from the bottom of the ramp. Release the ball and time the ball as it rolls down the ramp, as in Step 2. Record the time of Trial 1 for a distance of 1.0 m.

5. Repeat Step 4 four more times. Record the times of Trials 2 to 5 for a distance of 1.0 m.

6. Position the steel ball at the mark located 0.5 m from the bottom of the ramp. Release the ball and time its roll down the ramp as before. Record the time of Trial 1 for a distance of 0.5 m.

7. Repeat Step 6 four more times. Record the times of Trials 2 to 5 for a distance of 0.5 m.
8. Calculate and record the average time for each distance. To do this, add the five times together and divide the total by 5.

Part B: Determining If the Steepness of the Ramp Affects the Ball's Acceleration

9. Place another book under the elevated end of the board to make the ramp steeper.
10. Repeat Steps 2 through 8. Record your measurements and calculations in Data Table 2.
11. It can be shown that for an object starting from rest and accelerating at a constant rate, the acceleration is equal to $2D/T^2$, where D is the distance and T is the time of travel. Use the values of D and T in Data Tables 1 and 2 to calculate the acceleration of the ball for each distance and ramp height. Record the results in Data Table 3.

Observations

DATA TABLE 1

Ramp Supported by One Book			
Trial	Distance = 1.5 m Time (s)	Distance = 1.0 m Time (s)	Distance = 0.5 m Time (s)
1			
2			
3			
4			
5			
TOTAL			
Average			

DATA TABLE 2

Ramp Supported by Two Books			
Trial	Distance = 1.5 m Time (s)	Distance = 1.0 m Time (s)	Distance = 0.5 m Time (s)
1			
2			
3			
4			
5			
TOTAL			
Average			

Name ______________________ Class ________________ Date __________

DATA TABLE 3

Height of Ramp	Distance = 1.5 m	Distance = 1.0 m	Distance = 0.5 m
	Acceleration (m/s²) = $2D/T^2$		
1 book	0.23	0.21	0.23
2 books	0.41	0.45	0.39

Analysis and Conclusions

1. **Analyzing Data** Compare the accelerations that you calculated for the three distances in Part A. Did your data agree with your prediction? Explain your answer.

___

___

___

2. **Evaluating and Revising** Did your data support your hypothesis? Explain your answer.

___

___

3. **Analyzing Data** How did the steepness of the ramp affect the rate of acceleration?

___

___

4. **Inferring** Why would it be much more difficult to perform this experiment with a very steep ramp or with a freely falling object?

___

___

5. **Evaluating and Revising** How could this experiment be improved to produce more accurate data?

___

___

Go Further

How would changing the mass of the steel ball rolling down the ramp affect the results of this experiment? Design an experiment to answer this question. Write a detailed plan for your experiment. Your plan should state the hypothesis to be tested, identify variables, and describe the procedures and safety precautions you will take. Show your plan to your teacher. When your teacher approves your plan, carry out your experiment and report your results.

Investigating Sinking and Floating

Background Information

When an object is placed in a fluid, the force of gravity causes part or all of the object to sink below the upper surface of the fluid. At the same time, the fluid exerts an upward push, or **buoyant force,** on the object. The part of the object below the surface displaces the fluid. The size of the buoyant force is equal to the weight of the fluid that the object displaces. Fluids exert a buoyant force on all objects, regardless of whether the objects sink or float.

Consider an object submerged in a fluid. If the object has the same density as the fluid, then the weight of the object will be equal to the weight of an equal volume of fluid. In that case, the buoyant force will be equal to the weight of the object. As a result, the object will remain at any depth where it is placed. If the object is less dense than the fluid, the buoyant force on the object will be greater than the weight of the object. In this case, the object will rise to the surface and float. If the object is more dense than the fluid, the buoyant force on the object will be less than the weight of the object, and the object will sink.

This principle explains why a grain of sand sinks in water, whereas a basketball that has a much greater weight can float. Sand is denser than water. Therefore, the weight of the sand grain is greater than the buoyant force it receives from the water. The buoyant force acting on the basketball is greater than the weight of the basketball. As a result, the basketball floats.

In this investigation, you will predict which objects will float in water. Then, you will perform experiments to test your predictions.

Problem

What happens to the ability of an object to float as its mass and volume change?

Pre-Lab Discussion

Read the entire investigation. Then, work with a partner to answer the following questions.

1. **Controlling Variables** Identify the manipulated, responding, and controlled variables in this investigation.

   a. Manipulated variables

   ____

   ____

   b. Responding variables

   ____

   ____

Name ______________________ Class __________________ Date ___________

c. Controlled variables

____

____

2. **Predicting** Predict how adding BBs to the canister will affect the following variables.

   a. The level of the canister in the water

   ____

   ____

   ____

   b. The level of the water in the beaker

   ____

   ____

   ____

3. **Predicting** The bottle you will use in Steps 10 through 13 is larger than the canister. Which container do you predict will float at a lower level (more deeply) in the water? Explain your answer.

____

____

____

____

____

4. **Applying Concepts** What factors determine whether an object sinks or floats in water?

____

____

____

____

____

Materials *(per group)*

film canister
masking tape
metric ruler
250-mL beaker
BBs
paper towels
triple-beam balance
plastic bottle

Name ____________________ Class ______________ Date ____________

Safety

Put on safety goggles. Be careful to avoid breakage when working with glassware. Wipe up any spilled water immediately to avoid slips and falls. Note all safety alert symbols next to the steps in the Procedure and review the meaning of each symbol by referring to the Safety Symbols on page xiii.

Procedure

1. Attach a strip of masking tape to the side of the film canister, extending from the bottom to the top of the canister. Starting from the bottom of the canister, use the metric ruler and a pencil to accurately mark 0.5-cm intervals on the side of the canister, as shown in Figure 1.

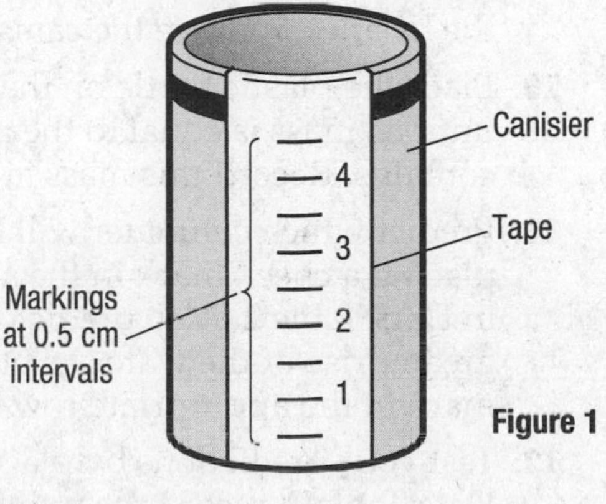

Figure 1

2. Repeat Step 1, using the plastic bottle.
3. Fill the beaker approximately three-fourths full with water. Place 20 BBs in the canister. Place the canister in the beaker with its open end pointed upward. Add or remove BBs from the canister, one at a time, until approximately half of the canister floats below the surface of the water. **Note:** *To remove BBs, take the canister out of the beaker. To add BBs, leave the canister in the beaker while carefully placing the BBs in the canister.* Count the BBs as you add or remove them from the canister. In the first row of Data Table 1, record the number of BBs in the canister. Remember to include the first 20 BBs that you added.
4. Use the metric ruler to measure the level of the water in the beaker from the tabletop to the surface of the water. Record this measurement in Data Table 1. Also determine the level of the canister in the water and record this measurement in Data Table 1.

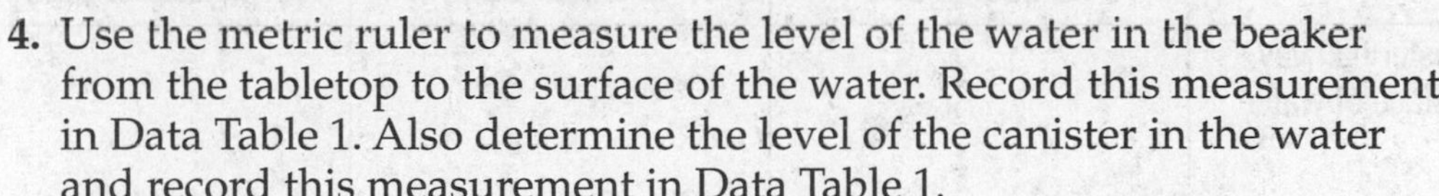

5. Predict how the level of the canister in the water and the level of the water in the beaker will change if you remove 10 BBs from the canister. Record your prediction as Prediction 1 in Data Table 1.
6. Now test your prediction. Take the canister out of the beaker, first tapping it gently against the inside of the beaker to minimize any water loss from the beaker. Remove 10 BBs from the canister and carefully place the canister back in the beaker. In Data Table 1, record the number of BBs in the canister, the level of the canister in the water, and the level of the water in the beaker.
7. Replace the 10 BBs that you removed from the canister. Predict how the level of the canister and the level of the water will change if you add 10 more BBs to the canister. Record your prediction as Prediction 2 in Data Table 1.

8. Test your prediction by carefully adding 10 BBs to the canister. In Data Table 1, record the number of BBs in the canister, the level of the canister in the water, and the level of the water in the beaker.
9. Carefully remove the canister of BBs from the beaker, while minimizing any water loss from the beaker. Use paper towels to dry the outside of the canister. Use the triple-beam balance to determine the mass of the canister and BBs. Record this mass in Data Table 2. Without changing the positions of the riders on the balance, remove the canister and set it aside.
10. Place the plastic bottle on the balance. Add BBs to the bottle until its mass is equal to the mass of the canister and the BBs it contains. Record this mass in Data Table 2.
11. Predict which container will float more deeply in the water by placing a check mark in the appropriate row below Prediction 3 in Data Table 2. Also predict which container will cause the greater rise of the water level in the beaker by placing a check mark in the appropriate row below Prediction 4 in Data Table 2.
12. Test your predictions by placing the canister into the beaker. In Data Table 2, record the number of BBs in the canister, the level of the canister, and the level of the water. Carefully remove the canister.
13. Repeat Step 12, using the plastic bottle.

Observations

DATA TABLE 1

Action	Number of BBs	Level of Canister in Water (cm)	Level of Water in Beaker (cm)
Float canister halfway below surface of water			
Remove 10 BBs			
Add 10 BBs			

Prediction 1 ______________________________

Prediction 2 ______________________________

Name ______________________ Class ______________________ Date ______________

DATA TABLE 2

Container	Mass of Container and BBs (g)	Prediction 3 (Identify the container that will float more deeply in water.)	Level of Container in Water (cm)	Prediction 4 (Identify which container will cause the greater rise of the water level in the beaker.)	Level of Water in Beaker (cm)
Canister					
Bottle					

Analysis and Conclusions

1. **Analyzing Data** How did the number of BBs in the canister affect the level at which the canister floated in the water?

____

____

2. **Evaluating and Revising** Did your observations support your predictions of how the number of BBs in the canister would affect the level of the canister in the water and the level of the water in the beaker? Explain your answer.

____

____

____

____

3. **Comparing and Contrasting** Compare the volume of the canister containing the BBs to the volume of water that the canister displaced. Which was greater?

____

____

4. **Predicting** Assume that the canister is made of a material that is less dense than water. What would happen if you filled the canister with water and then placed it in the beaker of water? Explain your answer.

____

____

5. **Drawing Conclusions** Explain why the canister and the bottle floated at different levels in the water.

6. **Comparing and Contrasting** Compare the water level when the canister was floating in the beaker to the water level when the plastic bottle was floating in the beaker in Steps 12 and 13. Explain your result.

7. **Applying Concepts** Suppose a boat is in a swimming pool. You are sitting in the boat and holding a rock. You drop the rock into the pool. The rock sinks to the bottom without splashing any water out of the pool. Using what you learned in this investigation, explain whether the water level in the pool will be higher, lower, or the same after you drop the rock into the pool.

Go Further

Use your knowledge of forces and buoyancy to predict the result of the experiment described below. Then, with your teacher's approval and supervision, carry out the experiment to test your prediction.

A beaker of water is sitting on a balance. The balance indicates the mass of the beaker of water. Taking great care not to touch the sides of the beaker, you dip your finger into the water. Does the reading on the balance change? If it does, will it increase or decrease?

Investigating Siphons

Background Information

A siphon is a tube filled with liquid that connects two containers. Liquid can flow through the siphon from one container to the other. The direction of this flow depends on forces that act on the liquid. One of these forces is gravity. If one of the containers is higher than the other, the force of gravity will cause liquid to flow down through the siphon from the higher container into the lower one.

Fluid pressure due to fluid depth also affects the flow through a siphon. **Pressure** is the amount of force per unit area. All liquids exert pressure against their containers. The deeper a liquid is, the greater the pressure it can exert. The pressure exerted on the bottom of a beaker is due to the weight of the fluid above it. Therefore, fluid pressure due to fluid depth is also related to the force of gravity. If the two containers have different levels of liquid, the liquid will flow through the siphon from the container with greater fluid depth (and pressure) to the container with less fluid depth (and pressure).

In this investigation, you will predict how water will flow through a siphon. Then, you will perform an experiment to test your prediction.

Problem

How does water flow through a siphon?

Pre-Lab Discussion

Read the entire investigation. Then, work with a partner to answer the following questions.

1. **Formulating Hypotheses** State a hypothesis about how water flows through a siphon.

____

____

____

____

2. **Predicting** Based on your hypothesis, predict how the water will flow through a siphon that connects each of the following pairs of identical beakers.

   a. Both beakers contain equal volumes of water, but one beaker is at a higher elevation than the other.

   ____

   ____

b. Both beakers are at the same height, but one beaker contains more water than the other.

____

____

c. Both beakers are at the same height and contain equal volumes of water.

____

____

3. Controlling Variables Identify the manipulated, responding, and controlled variables in this investigation.

a. Manipulated variables

____

____

b. Responding variables

____

____

c. Controlled variables

____

____

Materials *(per group)*

2 600-mL beakers
ring stand
iron ring
wire gauze
utility clamp
40 cm flexible tubing
clock or watch

Safety

Put on safety goggles and a lab apron. Be careful to avoid breakage when working with glassware. Wipe up any spilled water immediately to avoid slips and falls. Note all safety alert symbols next to the steps in the Procedure and review the meaning of each symbol by referring to the Safety Symbols on page xiii.

Procedure

1. Add approximately 275 mL of water to each beaker.
2. Position an iron ring and a wire gauze low on the ring stand, as shown in Figure 1. Use a utility clamp to secure one of the beakers on the wire gauze, as shown. Place the second beaker next to the ring stand.

Name ______________________ Class ________________ Date __________

3. In the data table, record your prediction of what will happen to the water in the beakers when a siphon is used to connect the beakers. Predict whether you expect water to flow through the siphon. If you predict that water will flow through the siphon, which direction do you expect the water to flow?

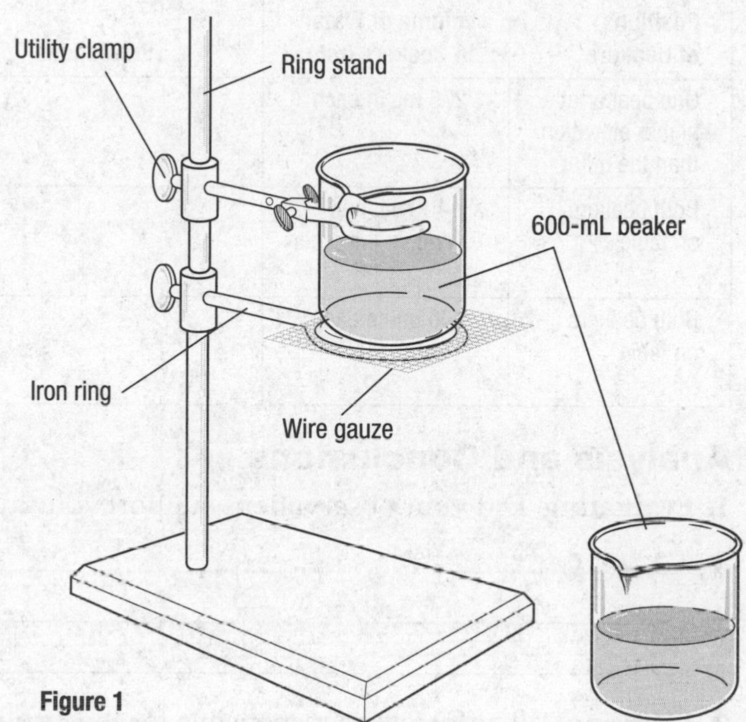

Figure 1

4. Place the flexible tubing in the sink. Hold one end of the tubing under the faucet and allow water to run through the tubing. When water begins to flow out the lower end of the tubing, use your finger to block the lower end. When the entire length of the tubing has filled with water, use another finger to cover the upper end. Be sure that no air remains in the tubing. Do not allow the water to flow out of the tubing.
5. Keeping the ends of the tubing covered, place one end of the tubing in the bottom of each beaker. Remove your finger from the ends of the tube only after both ends of the tube are submerged. Observe the beakers for 1 minute. Note any changes in the water level in the beakers. Record your observations in the data table.
6. Remove the elevated beaker from the ring stand. Add or remove water from each beaker so that one beaker contains 400 mL of water and the other contains 100 mL of water. Place both beakers on the tabletop. Repeat Steps 3 through 5.
7. Add or remove water from each beaker so that each beaker contains 300 mL of water. Place both beakers on the tabletop. Repeat Steps 3 through 5.

Name ______________________ Class ________________ Date __________

Observations

DATA TABLE

Positions of Beakers	Volume of Water in Beakers (mL)	Predictions	Observations
One beaker at a higher elevation than the other	275 mL in each		
Both beakers on table	400 mL and 100 mL in the other		
Both beakers on table	300 mL in each		

Analysis and Conclusions

1. **Evaluating** Did your observations support your hypothesis?

____

____

____

2. **Inferring** What force was responsible for the result you observed in Step 5?

____

3. **Inferring** What was responsible for the result you observed in Step 6?

____

____

4. **Predicting** Explain what you would have to do in order to move the water from the lower beaker to the upper beaker in the setup you used in Step 5.

____

____

____

5. **Predicting** Suppose two beakers sitting side by side are filled to the same depth, but one beaker is wider than the other. What would you expect to observe when the beakers are connected by a siphon? Explain your answer.

____

____

____

Name ______________________ Class ________________ Date ____________

Go Further

How do you think the diameter of the tubing you used in this investigation affected the rate at which water flowed between the beakers? Design an experiment to answer this question. Write a detailed plan for your experiment. Your plan should state the hypothesis to be tested, identify the manipulated, responding, and controlled variables, and describe the procedures and safety precautions you will use. You will need to find a way to measure the rate at which water flows through a siphon. Show your plan to your teacher. When your teacher approves your plan, carry out your experiment, and report your results and conclusions.

Comparing the Mechanical Advantage of Levers

Background Information

A **lever** consists of a rigid bar that is free to rotate around a fixed point. The fixed point on the bar rotates around the **fulcrum.** Like all machines, a lever changes the size of a force that is applied to it, the direction of a force applied to it, or both. The force exerted on a lever is the **input force.** The distance between the fulcrum and the point where the input force acts is the **input arm.** The force that the lever exerts on the load is the **output force.** The distance between the fulcrum and the output force is the **output arm.** Note that the output force may be larger or smaller than the input force, depending on the type of lever.

There are three types of levers, called first-class, second-class, and third-class levers. The three classes differ in the relative positions of the fulcrum and the input and output forces. A **first-class lever,** such as a seesaw, has its fulcrum between the input and output forces. In a second-class lever, such as a wheelbarrow, the output force, is between the input force and the fulcrum. A third-class lever, such as a broom, has its input force between the fulcrum and the output force.

The **mechanical advantage** of any machine is the number of times that the machine multiplies the input force. The **actual mechanical advantage** (AMA) of a lever is equal to the output force divided by the input force.

$$\text{AMA} = \frac{\text{Output force}}{\text{Input force}}$$

In this investigation, you will determine and compare the actual mechanical advantage of first-class and second-class levers. Then, you will design and carry out an investigation to determine the mechanical advantage of a third-class lever.

Problem

How do the mechanical advantages of first-class, second-class, and third-class levers differ?

Pre-Lab Discussion

Read the entire investigation. Then, work with a partner to answer the following questions.

1. **Designing Experiments** Why are you told in Step 1 to record the weight of the 500-g mass as the output force for every first-class and second-class lever that you will use in this investigation?

____

____

Name ______________________ Class ______________________ Date ______________

2. **Calculating** How will you calculate the actual mechanical advantage (AMA) of the levers in this investigation?

___

___

3. **Predicting** What factors do you predict will affect the actual mechanical advantage of the levers in this investigation?

___

___

4. **Controlling Variables** Identify the manipulated, responding, and controlled variables in this investigation.

   a. Manipulated variables

   ___

   b. Responding variables

   ___

   c. Controlled variable

   ___

5. **Predicting** Which class of levers do you expect to have the greatest actual mechanical advantage? Explain your answer.

___

___

___

___

___

___

6. **Formulating Hypotheses** State a hypothesis that you could test in Part C of this investigation.

___

___

Materials *(per group)*

500-g mass with hook
spring scale
wedge-shaped block of wood, about 10 cm high
meter stick
string
scissors
loop of wire

Name ______________________ Class ______________________ Date ______________

Safety

Put on safety goggles. To prevent injury from falling objects, do not wear sandals or open-toed shoes. Wear only closed-toed shoes in the laboratory. Note all safety alert symbols next to the steps in the Procedure and review the meaning of each symbol by referring to the Safety Symbols on page xiii.

Procedure

Part A: Determining the AMA of First-Class Levers

1. Work with a classmate. Hang the 500-g mass from the spring scale. Read the weight of the mass on the spring scale. Record this weight as the output force in each row of Data Table 1.
2. To make a first-class lever, place the wedge-shaped block of wood on the table to serve as a fulcrum. Place the 50-cm mark of the meter stick on the fulcrum so that the 100-cm end of the meter stick extends beyond the edge of the table, as shown in Figure 1. Use string to tie the 500-g mass to the meter stick at the 10-cm mark. This mass serves as the load that the lever will lift.
3. Place the wire loop around the meter stick at the 90-cm mark, 40 cm away from the fulcrum. Hang the spring scale from the wire loop.

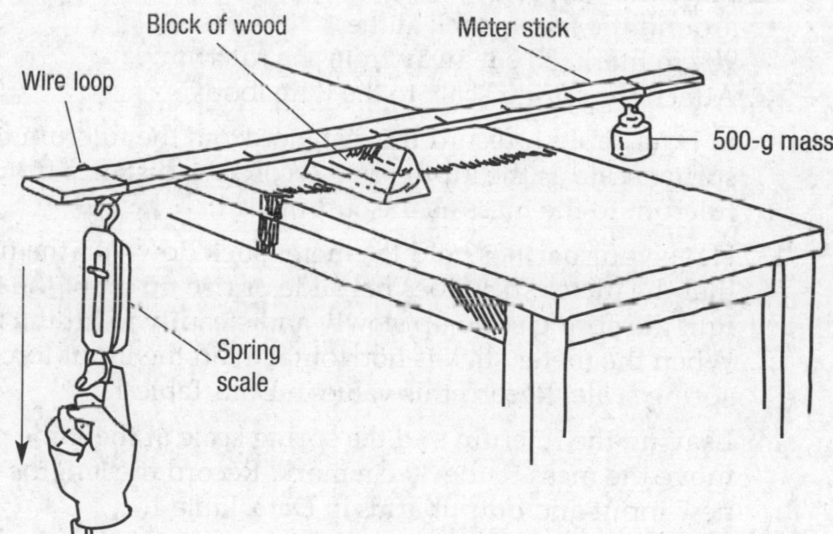

Figure 1

4. In the first row of Data Table 1, record the distance from the fulcrum to the spring scale as the input arm. Record the distance from the fulcrum to the mass as the output arm.
5. Pull the spring scale down slowly and steadily to lift the mass. When the meter stick is horizontal, read the input force on the spring scale. Record this value in Data Table 1.
6. Leaving the mass and the spring scale at the same positions, move the fulcrum to the 30-cm mark. Record the lengths of the new input and output arms in Data Table 1.
7. Repeat Step 5.
8. Repeat Steps 6 and 7, but this time, move the fulcrum to the 20-cm mark.
9. Calculate the mechanical advantage of the first-class lever in all the positions you tested. Record these values in Data Table 1.

Name ______________________ Class ______________ Date __________

Part B: Determining the AMA of Second-Class Levers

10. To make a second-class lever, place the 10-cm mark of the meter stick on the fulcrum as shown in Figure 2. Tie the mass to the meter stick at the 50-cm mark.

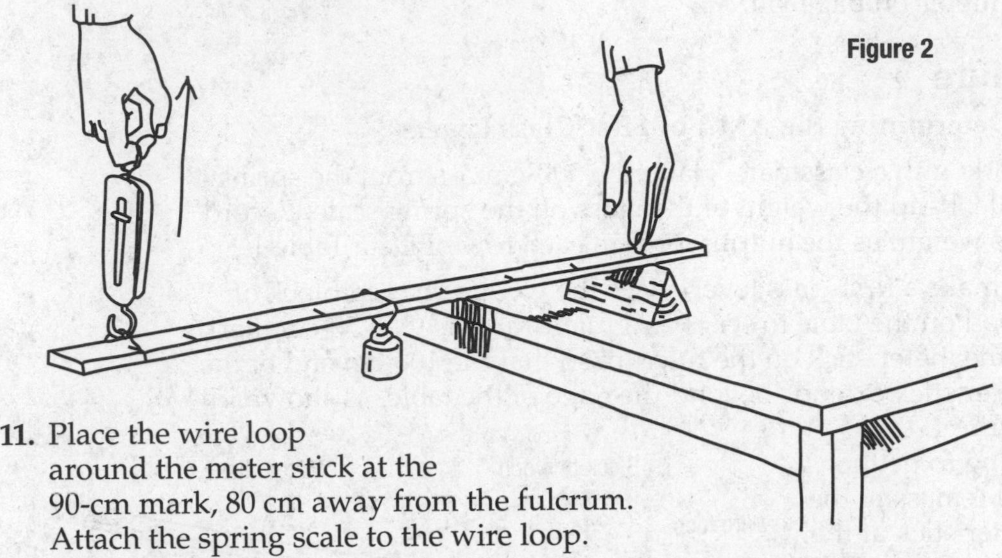

Figure 2

11. Place the wire loop around the meter stick at the 90-cm mark, 80 cm away from the fulcrum. Attach the spring scale to the wire loop.
12. In Data Table 1, record the distance from the fulcrum to the spring scale as the input arm. Record the distance from the fulcrum to the mass as the output arm.
13. Have your partner hold the meter stick down on the fulcrum so that the meter stick does not slide or rise up off of the fulcrum. Pull the spring scale up slowly and steadily to lift the mass. When the meter stick is horizontal, read the input force on the spring scale. Record this value in Data Table 1.
14. Leaving the fulcrum and the spring scale at the same positions, move the mass to the 30-cm mark. Record the lengths of the new input and output arms in Data Table 1.
15. Repeat Step 13.
16. Repeat Steps 14 and 15, but this time, move the mass to the 20-cm mark.
17. Calculate the actual mechanical advantage of the second-class lever in all the positions you tested. Record these values in Data Table 1.

Part C: Design Your Own Investigation

⚠ 18. Design an investigation to determine the actual mechanical advantage of a third-class lever. Record the hypothesis that you will test.

Hypothesis

____

____

19. In the lines below, write a detailed plan of how you will carry out your investigation. You may choose to base your investigation on the method of determining the actual mechanical advantage of a lever that you used in Parts A and B. Construct Data Table 2 in which to record your observations in the space provided on page 150.

20. What are the manipulated, responding, and controlled variables in your investigation?

a. Manipulated variable

b. Responding variable

c. Controlled variables

21. What safety precautions will you need to take in your investigation?

Name ______________________ Class __________________ Date __________

22. List the possible results of your investigation. State whether each possible result would support or contradict your hypothesis.

____

____

____

____

____

23. Show your plan to your teacher. When your teacher approves your plan, carry out your investigation and record your observations in your data table.

Observations

DATA TABLE 1: Parts A and B

Fulcrum Position (cm)	Output Arm (cm)	Input Arm (cm)	Output Force (N)	Input Force (N)	Actual Mechanical Advantage
First-Class Lever					
50					
30					
20					
Second-Class Lever					
10					
10					
10					

DATA TABLE 2: Part C

If you need more space, attach additional sheets of paper.

Name ______________________ Class ________________ Date ____________

Analysis and Conclusions

1. **Analyzing Data** How did moving the fulcrum of the first-class lever closer to the output force affect the actual mechanical advantage?

2. **Comparing and Contrasting** Did changing the lengths of the input and output arms affect the actual mechanical advantage of all three classes of levers in the same way? Explain your answer.

3. **Evaluating and Revising** In Part C of this investigation, did your data support or contradict your hypothesis? Explain your answer.

4. **Drawing Conclusions** Based on the mechanical advantages that you calculated for each class of lever, how do third-class levers differ from the other two types? How could a third-class lever be useful?

5. **Drawing Conclusions** What could you do to any lever to increase its actual mechanical advantage?

Go Further

Suppose you need to use a nutcracker to crack an especially tough nut. You have the choice of two similar nutcrackers that each have two handles connected at one end. One nutcracker has longer handles than the other one. Which class of lever are the nutcrackers? How can you tell? Which nutcracker would you use? Where would you place the nut relative to the arms? Explain your answer in terms of actual mechanical advantage.

Comparing Pulleys

Background Information

One of the most common uses of machines is to increase a force. The force that you exert on a machine is the **input force.** The force that the machine exerts is the **output force.** You can compare the ability of machines to increase input force by determining their actual mechanical advantages. Actual mechanical advantage (AMA) is calculated by dividing the output force by the input force.

$$\text{AMA} = \frac{\text{Output force}}{\text{Input force}}$$

Pulleys are simple machines that are used to lift objects. A pulley consists of a rope wrapped around a wheel. The simplest kind of pulley is a grooved wheel around which a rope is pulled. Pulleys can be used to change the direction of an input force. For example, a pulley attached, or fixed, to the top of a flagpole allows you to raise the flag up by pulling down.

A combination of fixed and movable pulleys is called a pulley system, or block-and-tackle. A pulley system is used to multiply input force so that heavy objects can be lifted. Pulley systems are commonly seen around construction sites.

In this investigation, you will determine the actual mechanical advantage of several different pulleys and pulley systems.

Problem

How do pulleys help to raise objects?

Pre-Lab Discussion

Read the entire investigation. Then, work with a partner to answer the following questions.

1. **Observing** What is the output force in this investigation?

____

2. **Inferring** Why will you record the same output force for all the pulleys in this investigation?

____

____

____

3. **Calculating** How will you calculate the actual mechanical advantage of the pulleys in this investigation?

____

____

4. **Predicting** How do you expect the actual mechanical advantage to change as more pulleys are added to the pulley system?

____

Materials *(per group)*

2 single pulleys
2 double pulleys
1-m nylon fishing line
ring stand
iron ring
10-N spring scale
1-kg mass

Safety

Put on safety goggles. Do not wear open-toed shoes or sandals in the laboratory. Note all safety alert symbols next to the steps in the Procedure and review the meaning of each symbol by referring to the Safety Symbols on page xiii.

Procedure

1. Find the weight of the 1-kg mass by hanging it from the spring scale. Record this weight in the data table as the output force for all of the pulley arrangements.
2. Set up a single fixed pulley, as shown in Figure 1. **CAUTION:** *Make sure that the ring is over the base of the ring stand to reduce the chance that the equipment will tip over.* Pull down on the spring scale to lift the mass. As you do this, observe the reading on the spring scale. Record this value in the data table as the input force.
3. Set up a single movable pulley, as shown in Figure 2. Lift the mass by pulling up on the spring scale. As you do this, observe the reading on the spring scale. Record this value in the data table as the input force.
4. Set up the pulley systems, as shown in Figure 3. For each pulley system, observe the reading on the spring scale as you pull it to lift the mass. Record the value in the data table as the input force for the pulley system.

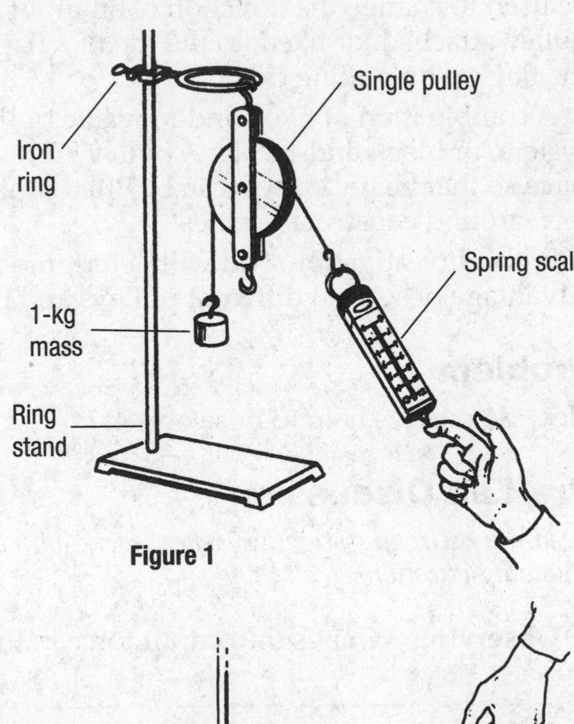

Figure 1

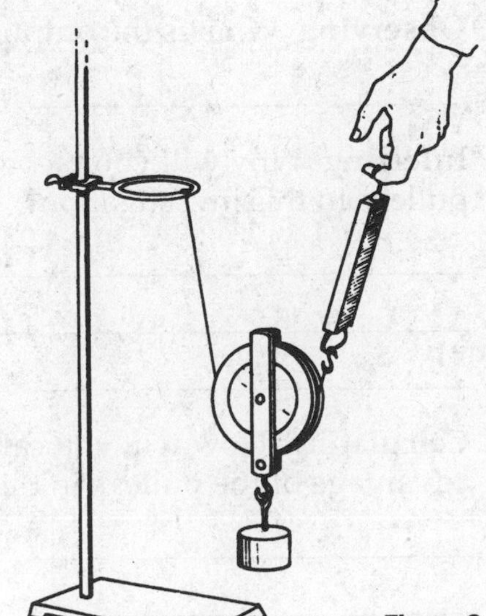
Figure 2

Figure 3

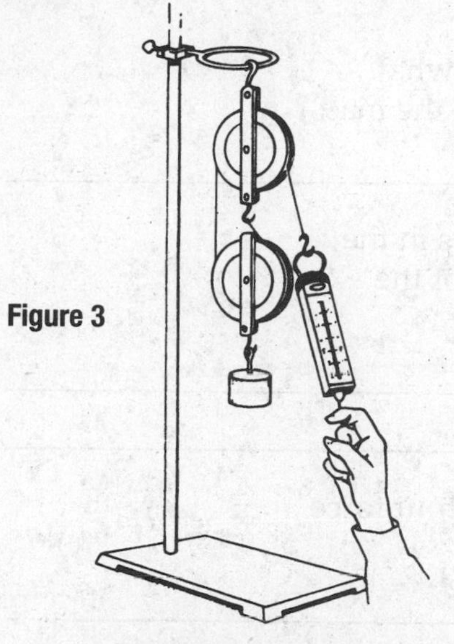
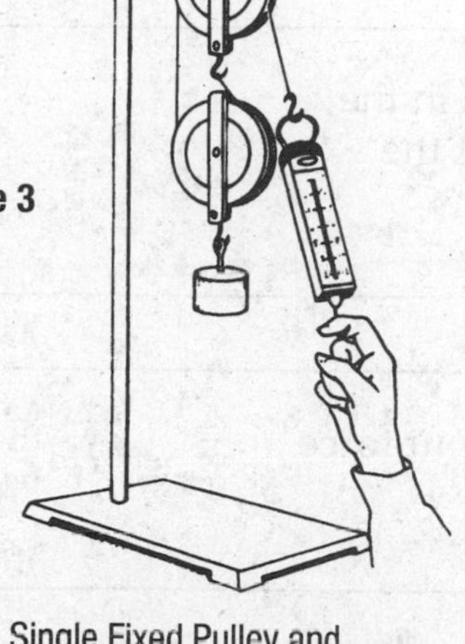

Single Fixed Pulley and Single Movable Pulley

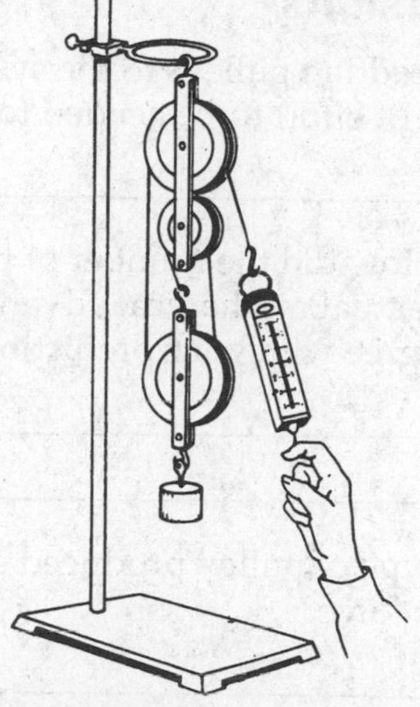

Double Fixed Pulley and Single Movable Pulley

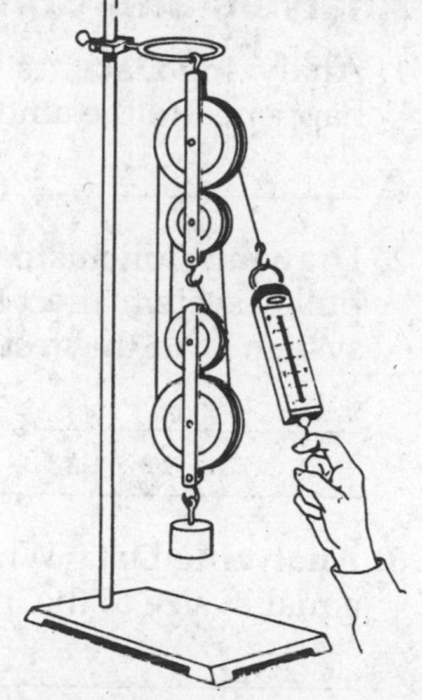

Double Fixed Pulley and Double Movable Pulley

5. Calculate the actual mechanical advantage for each pulley system. To do this, divide the output force by the input force. Record the actual mechanical advantage of each pulley system in the data table.

Observations

DATA TABLE

Pulleys	Output Force (newtons)	Input Force (newtons)	Actual Mechanical Advantage
Single fixed			
Single movable			
Single fixed and single movable			
Double fixed and single movable			
Double fixed and double movable			

Name ______________________ Class ________________ Date __________

Analysis and Conclusions

1. **Analyzing Data** As you added pulleys to the system, what happened to the amount of effort force needed to raise the mass?

____

2. **Drawing Conclusions** How did the number of pulleys in the pulley system affect the actual mechanical advantage of the system? Did this result agree with your prediction?

____

____

3. **Analyzing Data** What type of pulley produced an output force equal in size to the input force?

____

4. **Inferring** What is the practical use of a pulley that does not change the size of the input force?

____

5. **Inferring** When using any simple machine, you never "get something for nothing." Although a pulley system reduces the amount of input force needed to lift a mass, it does so at a cost. What must be increased as the amount of input force is decreased?

____

Go Further

In this investigation, you calculated actual mechanical advantage by dividing the output force by the input force. How could you use distances moved by the output and input forces to calculate actual mechanical advantage? Design an experiment to answer this question. Write a detailed plan for your experiment. Your plan should state the hypothesis to be tested, identify the manipulated, responding, and controlled variables, and describe the procedures and safety precautions that you will use. Show your plan to your teacher. When your teacher approves your plan, carry out your experiment and report your results and conclusions. Compare your data with the data you obtained in this investigation. Is one method better for determining mechanical advantage?

Name ____________________ Class ____________________ Date ____________

Determining the Effect of Mass on Kinetic Energy

Background Information

You wouldn't be afraid to stop a marble rolling down an incline, but if a bowling ball was rolling down the same incline, you'd probably move out of the way. Both objects are rolling because of Earth's gravity, yet the bowling ball has much more energy. The **potential energy** (PE) of an object being pulled by gravity is the product of its mass (m), the acceleration due to gravity (g), and its height (h).

$$PE = mgh$$

Think of a marble and a bowling ball rolling down the same slope from the same starting point. In the absence of friction, they move at the same speed, but they have different amounts of energy. It is a lot easier to see this difference when the potential energy is converted to **kinetic energy** as the object begins to move. As the marble and the bowling ball accelerate to the same speed (v) under the force of gravity, the only difference in their kinetic energies (KE) is due to mass.

$$KE = \frac{1}{2}mv^2$$

In this investigation, you will accelerate four different masses to the same speed. Then, you will compare their kinetic energies.

Problem

How is the energy of a moving object influenced by its mass?

Pre-Lab Discussion

Read the entire investigation. Then, work with a partner to answer the following questions.

1. **Controlling Variables** Identify the manipulated, responding, and controlled variables in this investigation.

   a. Manipulated variable

   ____

   ____

   b. Responding variable

   ____

   ____

   c. Controlled variables

   ____

   ____

Name ______________________ Class ______________ Date __________

2. Applying Concepts How will the mass of the rolling bottle affect its speed when it collides with the plastic cup? (*Hint:* The bottle accelerates much like a falling body.)

____

____

____

____

3. Predicting How do you expect the mass of the bottle to affect the distance the cup moves?

____

____

____

____

4. Applying Concepts How is work related to the distance that the cup moves?

____

____

____

____

5. Formulating Hypotheses State a hypothesis about how the kinetic energy of the rolling bottle affects the amount of work done on the cup and the distance the cup moves.

____

____

____

____

Materials *(per group)*

2 textbooks
flat board
masking tape
250-mL beaker
balance
plastic bottle that holds about 500–600 mL, with screw cap
plastic cup or margarine container
paper towel
meter stick

Name ______________________ Class ______________ Date __________

Safety 

Put on safety goggles. Handle the board carefully to avoid splinters. Note all safety alert symbols next to the steps in the Procedure and review the meaning of each symbol by referring to the Safety Symbols on page xiii.

Procedure

1. Stack the two textbooks. Place one end of the board on the stack of books to form a ramp, as shown in Figure 1. Tape the ramp in place so it cannot move.

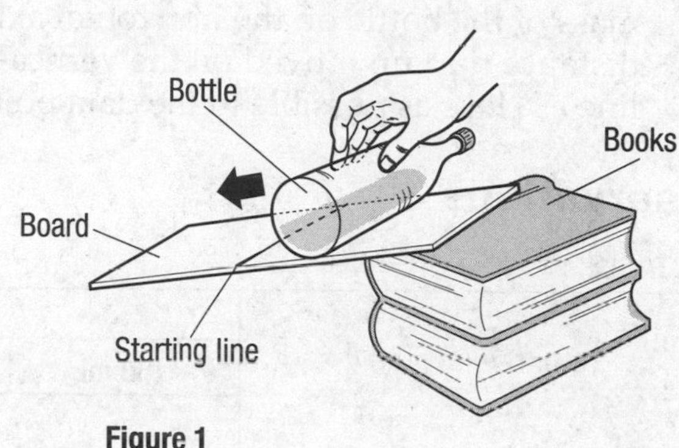

Figure 1

2. Attach a piece of masking tape across the ramp 15 cm from the bottom of the ramp. Use a pencil to mark the starting point on the masking tape. The bottle will be released from this point in each trial.
3. Using the beaker, carefully pour 100 mL of water into the bottle. Close the bottle tightly and dry the outside of the bottle with the paper towel. Wipe up any spills immediately.
4. Using the balance, measure the total mass of the bottle of water and record it in the data table.
5. Place a small piece of masking tape on the floor in line with the center of the ramp at a distance of 20 cm from the base of the ramp. This is the starting position for the cup in each trial.
6. Place the empty cup at its starting point, with its closest point to the ramp touching the piece of masking tape.
7. Hold the bottle of water lying across the ramp at the starting point, as shown in Figure 1. Allow it to roll down the ramp and collide with the cup. When both the bottle and the cup have stopped moving, use the meter stick to measure the distance the cup moved from its starting point. Record the result (to the nearest centimeter) in the appropriate place in the data table.
8. Repeat Steps 6 and 7 until you have made and recorded five measurements.
9. Using the beaker, add 100 mL of water to the bottle and close it tightly. Measure and record the new mass of the bottle.
10. Repeat Steps 6 and 7 to make five measurements using the new mass.
11. Again, add 100 mL of water to the bottle and close it tightly. Measure and record the new mass.
12. Repeat Steps 6 and 7 to make five additional measurements.

13. Add 100 mL of water to the bottle as before (for a total of 400 mL) and close it tightly. Measure and record the new mass.
14. Repeat Steps 6 and 7 to make five additional measurements.
15. Calculate the average distance that the cup moved for each bottle mass by adding the five distances and dividing by 5. Record your results to the nearest centimeter in the data table.
16. On the grid provided, construct a graph of your data with the mass of the bottle on the horizontal axis and the average distance the cup moved on the vertical axis. Draw a straight line as close as possible to the data points.

Observations

DATA TABLE

	Volume of Water			
	100 mL	200 mL	300 mL	400 mL
	Mass of Bottle and Water (g)			
Distance Moved by Cup (cm)				
Trial 1				
Trial 2				
Trial 3				
Trial 4				
Trial 5				
Total Distance (cm)				
Average Distance (cm)				

Name ______________________ Class ______________________ Date ______________

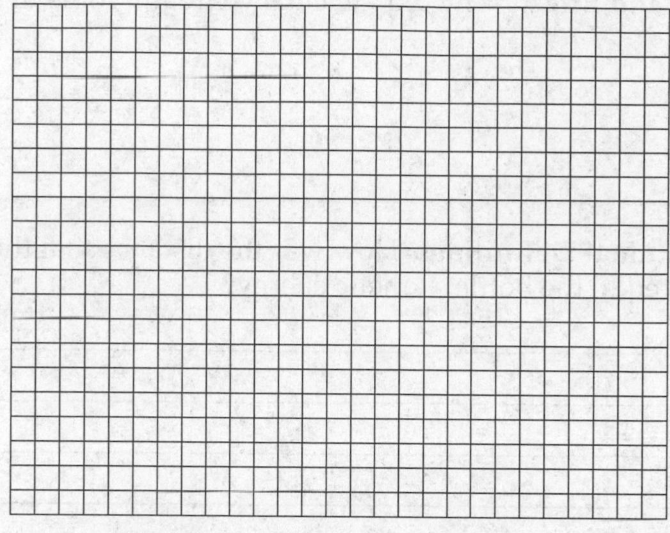

Analysis and Conclusions

1. **Controlling Variables** What procedure was followed to make sure that the bottle would be moving at the same speed each time it collided with the cup? Does this method work? Explain your answer.

2. **Inferring** Why is it important that the bottle have approximately the same speed each time it collides with the cup in order to measure the effect of mass on energy?

3. **Analyzing Data** As the mass of the bottle increased, what happened to the distance that the bottle moved the cup?

4. Relating Cause and Effect Why did the cup eventually come to a complete stop?

5. Forming Operational Definitions How was the distance that the cup moved related to the bottle's kinetic energy?

6. Evaluating and Revising Did your experimental results agree with your hypothesis about how the kinetic energy of the bottle affects the amount of work done on the cup? Explain your answer.

7. Applying Concepts This investigation assumes that the rolling bottle experiences only a small frictional force. How accurate is this assumption? Could this assumption affect the results of the investigation? Explain your answer.

Go Further

In this investigation, you examined the relationship between the mass of a rolling bottle and its kinetic energy. Design a procedure to measure how the height of a ramp affects the kinetic energy of a bottle rolling down the ramp. Have your teacher approve your procedure before you carry out the investigation. Propose an explanation for what you find.

Name ______________________ Class ______________ Date __________

Determining the Kinetic Energy of a Pendulum

Introduction

Energy of motion is called **kinetic energy** (KE). An object's kinetic energy depends on its mass (m) and speed (v).

$$KE = \frac{1}{2}mv^2$$

Energy of position is potential energy (PE), and it depends on mass, the acceleration due to gravity (g), and the height (h) of the object.

$$PE = mgh$$

The sum of an object's kinetic and potential energies is called its **mechanical energy.**

If you have seen a grandfather clock, you are probably familiar with a pendulum, which consists of a weight that swings back and forth on a rope or string. As the weight, or bob, moves through its arc, its mechanical energy is constantly converted between potential energy and kinetic energy. The kinetic energy increases as the potential energy decreases, and vice versa. If there were no friction, the mechanical energy of the pendulum would remain constant, and the pendulum would continue to swing back and forth, reaching the same height each time. Friction causes the height of a pendulum's swing to slowly decrease until the pendulum eventually stops.

In this investigation, you will perform an experiment to determine when a swinging pendulum has the largest amount of kinetic energy.

Problem

When does a swinging pendulum have the most kinetic energy?

Pre-Lab Discussion

Read the entire investigation. Then, work with a partner to answer the following questions.

1. **Controlling Variables** Identify the manipulated, responding, and controlled variables in this investigation.

   a. Manipulated variable

   ____

   b. Responding variable

   ____

   c. Controlled variables

   ____

   ____

Name ______________________ Class __________________ Date ______________

2. **Predicting** At what point in its arc do you expect the bob to have the most kinetic energy? At what point will it have the least kinetic energy? Explain your answers.

____

____

3. **Predicting** At what point in its arc do you expect the bob to have the most potential energy? At what point will it have the least potential energy? Explain your answers.

____

____

4. **Predicting** Will the block be moved farthest when the bob has the greatest potential energy or the greatest kinetic energy? Explain your answer.

____

____

5. **Formulating Hypotheses** State a hypothesis that this investigation can be used to test.

____

____

Materials *(per group)*

1-m string
fishing weight
flat, smooth board
4 identical bricks, approximately 8 cm in height
masking tape
lightweight wooden block
meter stick

Safety

Put on safety goggles. Be careful to stay out of the way of the swinging pendulum bob. Note all safety alert symbols next to the steps in the Procedure and review the meaning of each symbol by referring to the Safety Symbols on page xiii.

Procedure

1. Work with a classmate. Make a pendulum by tying the piece of string to the fishing weight. Hang the pendulum over the edge of a desk or table so that the weight, or bob, just clears a board placed on the floor beneath it. Tape the upper end of the string to the top of the desk or table, as shown in Figure 1.
2. Pull the bob slightly to the side and place a wooden block on the edge of the board, as shown, directly in the path of the pendulum's swing. Hold the bob in place next to the block while your lab partner measures the height of the bob above the floor. Record this value in the data table as the height of the bob at impact.

3. Pull the bob up and to the side until it reaches a height of 30 cm above the floor. Release the bob, allowing it to swing down and strike the wooden block. In the data table, measure and record the distance that the block moved along the board.
4. Replace the block on the edge of the board and repeat Step 3 two more times, releasing the bob from the same point as in the first trial.
5. Place a brick beneath each end of the board. Move the board and bricks sideways so that the bob, when released, will just clear the near end of the board.

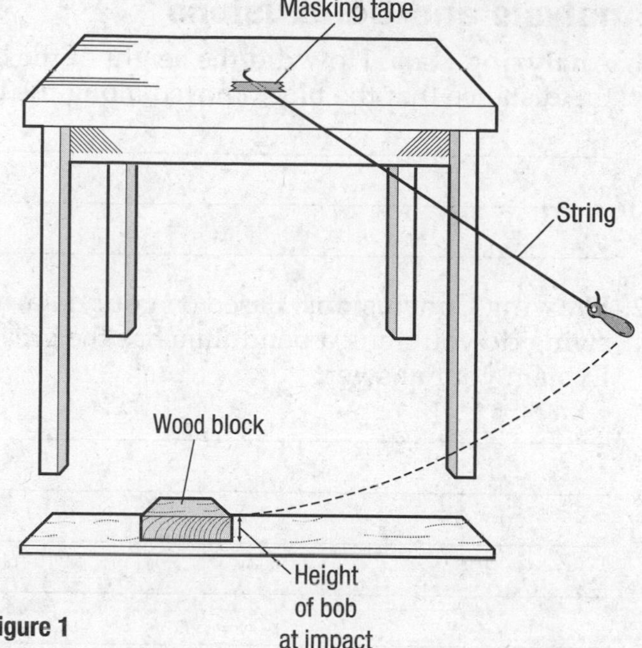

Figure 1

6. Place the block on the end of the board as before. Place the bob next to the block and have your partner measure its height above the floor. In the data table, record this as the height of the bob at impact.
7. Raise the bob 30 cm off the floor, as you did in Step 3. Release the bob and again measure and record in the data table the distance that the block moved along the board after impact.
8. Replace the block and repeat Step 7 two more times, releasing the bob from the same point as before.
9. Repeat Steps 5 through 8, this time adding a second brick under each end of the board and moving the board still closer to the release point.
10. Calculate the average distance that the block moved from each position. To do this, add the three distances you recorded and divide the total by 3. In the data table, record the average distances.

Observations

DATA TABLE

Number of Bricks Supporting the Board	Height of Bob at Impact (cm)	Distance Block Moved Along Board (cm)			
		Trial 1	Trial 2	Trial 3	Average
0					
2					
4					

Analysis and Conclusions

1. **Analyzing Data** How did the height of the bob at impact affect the distance that the block moved along the board?

2. **Drawing Conclusions** Based on your data, at what point in its swing do you think a pendulum has the greatest kinetic energy? Explain your answer.

3. **Evaluating and Revising** Did your data support or contradict your hypothesis? Explain your answer.

4. **Applying Concepts** Because of weathering, a rock on the edge of a cliff may become loose and fall. In terms of kinetic and potential energy, how is the rock at the edge of the cliff similar to a pendulum at the top of its arc?

Go Further

Draw five pictures, in sequence, showing a ball that has been thrown straight upward. Draw it going up (two pictures), at its highest point (one picture), and coming down (two pictures). In each picture, indicate which quantity, KE or PE, is greater. Also, indicate for each picture whether each kind of energy is in the process of increasing, decreasing, or staying the same.

Thermal Conduction and Surface Area

Background Information

The quantity of energy transferred by heat from a body depends on a number of physical properties of the body and its surroundings. For a given substance, the rate at which thermal energy is transferred by conduction depends on temperature difference, cross-sectional area, and a thermal conductivity constant that is unique to the substance. By choosing one of these properties as a manipulated variable and making the other properties controlled variables, the effect of the manipulated variable on thermal conduction can be determined experimentally.

In this investigation, you will study the rates of cooling of three containers of water of equal volume but different surface area.

Problem

How does heat loss depend on surface area?

Pre-Lab Discussion

Read the entire investigation. Then, work with a partner to answer the following questions.

1. **Formulating Hypotheses** How would you expect the rate of thermal energy transfer from the water to depend on the water's surface area? What is your reason for this expectation?

____

____

____

____

2. **Controlling Variables** Identify the manipulated, responding, and controlled variables in this investigation.

   a. Manipulated variable

   ____

   ____

   b. Responding variable

   ____

   ____

   c. Controlled variables

   ____

   ____

Name ______________________ Class ______________ Date ____________

3. **Designing Experiments** Why should plastic containers be used for holding the hot water during the experiment? Why should the containers and the graduated cylinder be warmed first with hot water?

4. **Using Tables and Graphs** How can you tell which graph indicates the greatest rate of thermal energy transfer?

Materials *(per group)*

3 cylindrical plastic containers with different surface diameters
metric ruler
hot tap water
3 Celsius thermometers
100-mL graduated cylinder
grease pencil
clock or watch
graph paper
3 colored pencils
1000-mL beaker (optional)
hot plate (optional)

Safety

Put on safety goggles and a lab apron. Be careful to avoid breakage when working with glassware. Use extreme care when working with heated equipment or materials to avoid burns. Observe proper laboratory procedures when using electrical equipment. Note all safety alert symbols next to the steps in the Procedure and review the meaning of each symbol by referring to the Safety Symbols on page xiii.

Procedure

1. Label the plastic containers *A*, *B*, and *C*, using the grease pencil. Label the container with the smallest diameter *A* and the one with the largest diameter *C*.

Name ______________________ Class ________________ Date ____________

2. Use the ruler to measure the diameter of each container and record this information in Data Table 1. Calculate the cross-sectional surface area, using the formula *Area* = (*Diameter*/2)$^2\pi$. Record these values in Data Table 1.

3. Run hot tap water until the water temperature reaches a constant value, about 50°C. Test the water temperature by holding a thermometer bulb in the stream of water. If you do not have a source of hot water, heat 600 mL of water in a beaker on a hot plate. Let the water reach a temperature of 50°C. **CAUTION:** *Use heat-resistant gloves. Be careful not to burn yourself or to break the thermometer or beaker. If using a hot plate, be careful to avoid burns and electrical shock.* Wipe up any spilled water immediately.

4. Warm the labeled containers by filling each of them with about 50 mL of hot water. Also fill the graduated cylinder to warm it. After a few minutes, pour out the water in the containers and the graduated cylinder. Refill the warm graduated cylinder with 100 mL of hot water. Quickly pour the water into container A. Repeat this process, pouring 100 mL of hot water into each of the other two containers.

5. Use the three thermometers to immediately measure the temperature of the water in the containers. Record the maximum temperature values in the second, third, and fourth columns of Data Table 2. The three beginning temperatures should be very similar. Look at a clock or watch and make a note of the time. Record the time in the "Time" column of Data Table 2. **CAUTION:** *Take care not to hit the thermometers against the sides of the containers.*

6. After 1 minute, record the time and the water temperature in each container. Continue to record the temperatures every minute for 15 minutes. Do not stir the water.

7. On a sheet of graph paper, make a graph of the information in Data Table 2. Plot the number of minutes from the start of the experiment on the horizontal axis (x-axis) and water temperature on the vertical axis (y-axis). Use a different-colored pencil for the data for each container. Draw curved lines to connect the data points for each container.

Name ______________________ Class ________________ Date ____________

Observations

DATA TABLE 1

	Diameter (cm)	Surface area (cm^2)
Container A		
Container B		
Container C		

DATA TABLE 2

Time (min)	Temperature of Water in Container A (°C)	Temperature of Water in Container B (°C)	Temperature of Water in Container C (°C)
0			
1			
2			
3			
4			
5			
6			
7			
8			
9			
10			
11			
12			
13			
14			
15			

Name ______________________ Class ______________ Date __________

Analysis and Conclusions

1. **Observing** In general, what happened to the temperature of the water in the containers? Describe the three curves on your graph.

2. **Observing** From which container of water was thermal energy transferred the fastest? On what evidence do you base your answer?

3. **Applying Concepts** What happened to the thermal energy that was in the water? Where did it go?

4. **Predicting** What would have happened, in terms of thermal energy transfer, if the water temperature had originally been 10.0°C? Explain your reasoning.

5. **Drawing Conclusions** Based on your findings in this investigation, make a general statement relating thermal energy transfer to surface area. How does this statement compare to the hypothesis you made before the investigation?

6. **Making Generalizations** Two lakes have exactly the same amount of water in them. The surrounding environment is at the same temperature. You can presume the ground beneath each lake is a thermal insulator. Which lake would lose thermal energy at a faster rate—one that was large and shallow or one that was small and deep? Explain your answer.

Go Further

Plan an investigation to determine how containers made of different materials affect heat loss. Indicate how the containers would differ from the containers used in the current experiment. Show your plan to your teacher. When your teacher approves your plan, carry out your experiment and report your results.

Boiling Water in a Paper Cup

Background Information

When a paper cup of water is heated over a flame, the transfer of the thermal energy occurs in three ways—conduction, convection, and radiation. Conduction occurs when there is contact between two materials. In the case of a paper cup containing water, conduction occurs from the paper cup to the water, and through the water itself. Convection occurs when a volume of heated liquid or gas moves from one place to another. When heating water in a paper cup, convection takes place in the air between the burner flame and the bottom of the paper cup, and in the water inside the cup. Radiation conveys energy by electromagnetic waves from a body at a temperature greater than that of its surroundings. In this investigation, the flame transfers thermal energy by radiation.

Because water has a high specific heat, a small amount of water can absorb a fairly large amount of energy without undergoing a large temperature change. An even greater amount of energy must be absorbed by water for it to undergo the phase change from liquid to gas. The temperature at which water boils at sea level is 100°C, and it remains at this temperature until all of the liquid water has boiled. The paper cup would start to burn if the temperature reached 233°C.

In this investigation, you will attempt to boil water in a paper cup over the flame of a Bunsen burner.

Problem

Will the water in a paper cup boil before the cup ignites?

Pre-Lab Discussion

Read the entire investigation. Then, work with a partner to answer the following questions.

1. **Predicting** Predict the result of boiling water through a paper cup. Explain why you believe your prediction is true.

____

____

____

____

____

____

____

____

____

____

Name ______________________ Class ______________ Date __________

2. **Applying Concepts** When water boils, its temperature remains constant. Why doesn't this contradict the law of conservation of energy?

3. **Designing Experiments** Why do you want to be sure that the paper cup does not have a wax coating?

4. **Making Generalizations** Use your prediction to explain why wet wood does not burn.

Materials *(per group)*

paper cup (without wax coating)
ring stand
support ring
wire gauze
thermometer
thermometer clamp
metal pie tin
Bunsen burner
matches

Safety

Put on safety goggles and a lab apron. Tie back loose hair and clothing when working with flames. Do not reach over an open flame. Be careful when using matches. Use extreme care when working with heated equipment or materials to avoid burns. Make sure that fire suppressant equipment is available. Note all safety alert symbols next to the steps in the Procedure and review the meaning of each symbol by referring to the Safety Symbols on page xiii.

Procedure

1. Set up the equipment as shown in Figure 1. There should be approximately 15 cm between the top of the Bunsen burner and the bottom of the wire gauze.

2. Remove the paper cup. Fill three-fourths of the cup with water and carefully place it back on the center of the wire gauze. Use a thermometer clamp to make sure that the thermometer is suspended in the water so that it does not touch the bottom of the cup.
3. In the data table, record the initial temperature of the water.
4. Light the Bunsen burner and adjust the flame so that it does not touch the bottom of the wire gauze. **CAUTION:** *Be sure that the flame never touches the wire gauze directly.*
5. Observe the experiment from the time you start heating the cup of water. What happens before the water boils? What happens to the cup as the water boils? Record your observations next to the data table. **CAUTION:** *Be careful when working with boiling water.*
6. In the data table, record the water temperature every 2 minutes.

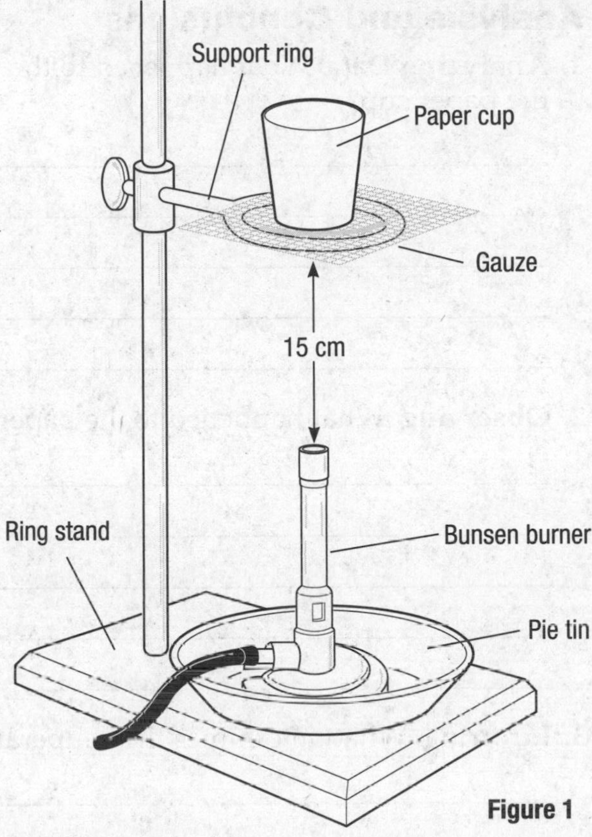

Figure 1

7. When the water occupies about one-fourth of the cup's volume, turn off the burner and let the water and the cup cool. **CAUTION:** *Do not handle equipment until it has cooled.*

Observations

DATA TABLE

Time (minutes)	Water Temperature (°C)
0	
2	
4	
6	
8	
10	
12	
14	
16	
18	
20	

Name ______________________ Class ________________ Date ____________

Analysis and Conclusions

1. **Analyzing Data** What happened to the temperature of the water in the paper cup?

2. **Observing** What happened to the paper cup?

3. **Inferring** What determines the temperature of the paper cup?

4. **Drawing Conclusions** Did your observations support or contradict your prediction? Explain your answer.

Go Further

For an additional investigation, determine whether the wire gauze between the flame and the cup prevented the cup from igniting.

Name ______________________ Class ________________ Date ____________

Measuring the Speed of Sound

Background Information

An echo is reflected sound that can be heard separately from the original sound that produced it. The original sound is heard for about 0.10 second. You will hear an echo clearly if you are far enough away so that it takes more than 0.10 second for the sound to travel to the reflecting surface and back to you. To calculate the speed of sound, you must find your distance from the reflecting surface when you are just far enough away so that you do not hear an echo. It will take 0.10 second for the sound to travel this distance and back.

Sound travels at different speeds through different materials. Temperature also affects how rapidly sound is transmitted. Sound will travel faster in warm air than in cold air. However, the speed of sound in air does not depend upon the frequency of the sound. If it did, you would not be able to listen to music because the high-pitched sounds would arrive at your ear at a different time than the low-pitched sounds would.

The speed of light is much greater than the speed of sound. You will use this principle to calculate the speed of sound. You will perform an experiment similar to one performed by French scientists in 1738. They set up a cannon on a hill and timed the interval between the flash and the sound. Since they knew the distance and the time, they could calculate the speed of sound.

In Part A of this investigation, you will create echoes and measure the distance between you and a reflecting surface in order to determine the speed of sound. Then, in Part B, you will calculate the speed of sound in air by measuring the time between seeing an event and hearing the event.

Problem

What is the speed of sound in air?

Pre-Lab Discussion

Read the entire investigation. Then, work with a partner to answer the following questions.

1. **Comparing and Contrasting** Which method for measuring the speed of sound in air do you think will produce more accurate results—the method used in Part A or the method in Part B? Explain your answer.

____

____

____

____

2. **Controlling Variables** Identify the manipulated and responding variables for both Parts A and B.

3. **Evaluating** The speed of sound in dry air at a temperature of 20°C is 342 m/s. What sources of error might account for obtaining a different value than this?

4. **Controlling Variables** How can the variables that introduce error in the results be controlled?

5. **Designing Experiments** How might you vary the design of the investigation in Part B to test if the speed of sound in air is independent of frequency?

Name ______________________ Class ________________ Date ____________

Materials *(per group)*

2 wooden blocks, each about 20 cm long
metric tape measure or meter stick
drum
stopwatch (that can measure hundredths of a second)
measuring rope, marked off in meters, or a bicycle with a metric odometer

Safety

Be careful when handling sharp instruments such as a tape measure. Note all safety alert symbols next to the steps in the Procedure and review the meaning of each symbol by referring to the Safety Symbols on page xiii.

Procedure

Part A: Estimating the Speed of Sound from Echoes

1. In an auditorium or outdoors near a high wall, use a metric tape measure or meter stick to measure a distance of 25 meters from the wall.
2. Stand facing the wall and clap the two wooden blocks together. Listen for an echo. If you can hear one, move closer to the wall by about 1 meter, and repeat. Keep moving closer, 1 meter at a time, until you can no longer hear a separate echo.
3. Measure and record the distance between you and the wall.

Part B: Determining the Speed of Sound From the Delay Between Seeing and Hearing an Event

4. This experiment must be conducted outdoors. Select an area such as an open field or a long, lightly traveled road. Record your observations of the weather conditions.
5. With the measuring rope (or a bicycle equipped with a metric odometer), measure a distance of 100 meters in a straight line.
6. One student should stand at each end of this measured distance, as shown in Figure 1.
7. One student should create a loud, short noise by striking the drum.

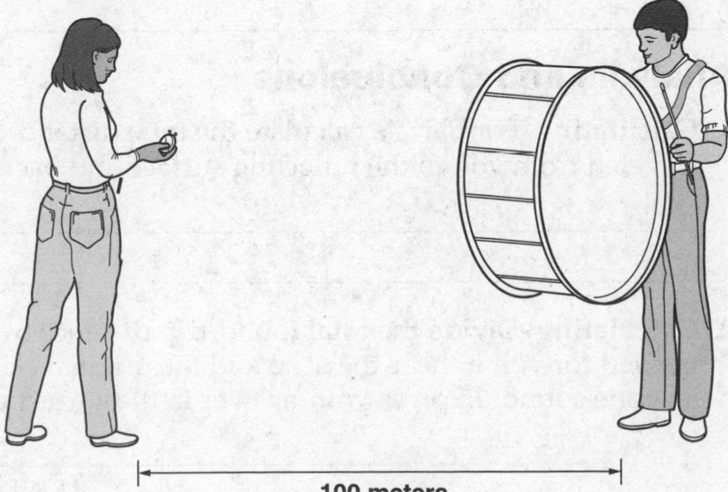

Figure 1

8. The other student should start the stopwatch precisely when he or she sees the drum being struck. The student should stop the watch precisely when he or she hears the noise.
9. Repeat Steps 8 and 9 three more times. Record the times to a hundredth of a second in the data table.
10. The two students should change places with each other and repeat the experiment. This will help to eliminate any effect the wind might have on the speed at which the sound waves travel. Record your results in the data table.

Observations

Part A

1. What did you observe when you made the sound at a distance of 25 meters from the reflecting surface?

____

____

2. At what distance were you no longer able to hear an echo?

____

Part B

DATA TABLE

Trial	Time (first student with stopwatch) (s)	Time (second student with stopwatch) (s)
1		
2		
3		
4		

Analysis and Conclusions

1. **Calculating** For Part A, calculate the total distance the sound traveled from you to the reflecting surface and back again.

____

____

2. **Calculating** Divide the total round-trip distance by the time, 0.10 s, needed for you to hear the echo and the original clapping sound as just one sound. Express your answer in the correct units.

____

____

Name ______________________ Class ______________ Date ____________

3. Inferring What type of surface would not have reflected sound back to you? Why?

____

____

____

____

4. Controlling Variables For Part B, what were the weather conditions in which you measured the speed of sound? Do you think the speed would have been different under different conditions?

____

____

____

____

____

____

5. Calculating Average the eight time values in the data table. Calculate the speed of sound by dividing the distance by the average time.

____

____

____

6. Analyzing Data What factors might have caused variations in the results of your eight trials?

____

____

____

7. Comparing and Contrasting Compare the values for the speed of sound in air calculated in Part A and in Part B. Account for both the differences and similarities in the results.

____

____

____

____

____

____

____

8. **Applying Concepts** Explain how you can determine the distance from you that lightning strikes if you know the speed of sound and have a stopwatch.

9. **Applying Concepts** When fireworks burst in the sky, will you hear the explosion or see the color first? Explain your answer.

10. **Applying Concepts** Sound usually travels faster in liquids than in gases, and faster in some solids than in liquids. Explain why a worker who puts one ear against a long steel pipe would hear two sounds if another worker struck the pipe only once at some distance away.

Go Further

Suspend an alarm clock inside a bell jar from which air can be evacuated by a vacuum pump. Observe what happens to the sound of the bell or alarm as the air is sucked out. Observe the speed of sound through other materials such as water or iron. Before conducting any experiments, submit your procedure to your teacher for approval.

Sounds in Solids

Background Information

Sound is a **longitudinal wave.** As sound travels through a substance, the particles vibrate back and forth parallel to the movement of the sound wave. When the particles vibrate, regions form where they are close together (**compression**) and where they are far apart (**rarefaction**). The sound wave consists of compressions and rarefactions spreading through a substance.

Sound must travel through a **medium.** Sound cannot travel through a vacuum because there are no particles to transmit the pattern of compressions and rarefactions. To transmit sound, the medium must vibrate. The term *vibrate* implies back-and-forth movement. If the particles move forth without moving back again, there is no vibration. Once particles begin forward motion, their inertia would continue to carry them forward unless some force brought them back again. A medium that has strong forces of attraction between the particles tends to be **elastic** because the particles spring back to their original positions after a sound wave passes.

A medium in which the particles are close together so that the vibration in one particle could easily pass to its neighboring particles tends to have greater elasticity than a medium in which the particles are far apart. The particles in metals are arranged very close together in an orderly pattern. This makes the metal rigid. It is very difficult to force the particles closer together. Therefore, a metal is not easily compressed or deformed. A piece of plastic, such as a plastic straw, bends easily. A material is elastic if it is rigid and hard to deform. Metal tends to be more elastic than plastic.

In this investigation, you will compare wood, cardboard, and metal for elasticity to discover how well each transmits sound.

Problem

How well do various materials transmit sound?

Pre-Lab Discussion

Read the entire investigation. Then, work with a partner to answer the following questions.

1. **Comparing and Contrasting** A spring is placed on a tabletop, and one end is held in a fixed position. Two strings are tied to the spring on coils about 1 cm apart, as shown in Figure 1. Then, the spring is given a shove at the left end, causing a wave to travel through it toward the right.

   a. Describe the movement of either string as the wave passes by.

   ____

   ____

Name ______________________ Class ______________ Date ____________

b. What happens to the distance between the two strings as the wave travels along the spring? Explain your answer.

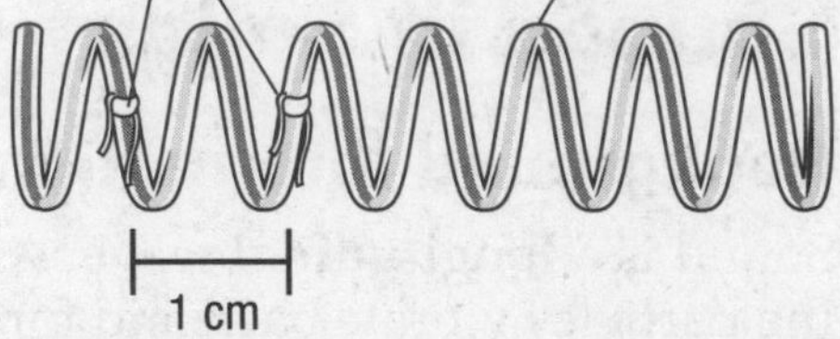

Strings Spring

1 cm

Figure 1

2. Using Models How is the behavior of the spring in Question 1 similar to that of a sound wave?

3. Using Models Suppose that you made a coil out of cotton and tried to send a wave down the cotton coil in the same way as described in Question 1 with a spring. What would happen? Explain your answer. Use the word *elastic* or *elasticity* in your explanation.

4. Inferring Which substance is probably the most elastic—wood, cardboard, or metal? Which is probably the least elastic? How would you test your prediction?

5. Predicting Rank wood, cardboard, and metal from highest to lowest for their ability to conduct sound. Explain your answer.

Materials *(per group)*

clock or watch with second hand (either should produce a ticking sound)
wooden meter stick
metal rod, 1 m long, (iron, steel, or aluminum)
cardboard sheet, 1 m long

Name ______________________ Class ______________________ Date ______________________

Safety

Put on safety goggles. Be careful when handling sharp instruments. Note all safety alert symbols next to the steps in the Procedure and review the meaning of each symbol by referring to the Safety Symbols on page xiii.

Procedure

1. Work with a partner. Check the elasticity of a meter stick by laying it flat on your lab table with about a third of its length hanging over the edge. One student holds the meter stick down on the lab table, and the other flicks the free end to see how easily it bends and how much it vibrates.
2. Repeat Step 1 with a metal rod and a piece of cardboard. Based on your observations, rank the three objects from the most elastic to the least elastic. The harder an object is to bend and the more vigorously it snaps back to its original shape, the more elastic the material is. In the data table, use the numbers 1 to 3 to rank elasticity, with 1 being the most elastic.
3. Hold a ticking watch or clock to your ear. Note the ticking.
4. Hold a wooden meter stick so that one end is pressed gently against your ear. Have your partner hold the watch against the far end of the meter stick. Note whether you can hear any ticking. **CAUTION:** *Use great care when placing the meter sticks and rods near the ear. Pushing these objects against the ear could result in injury.*

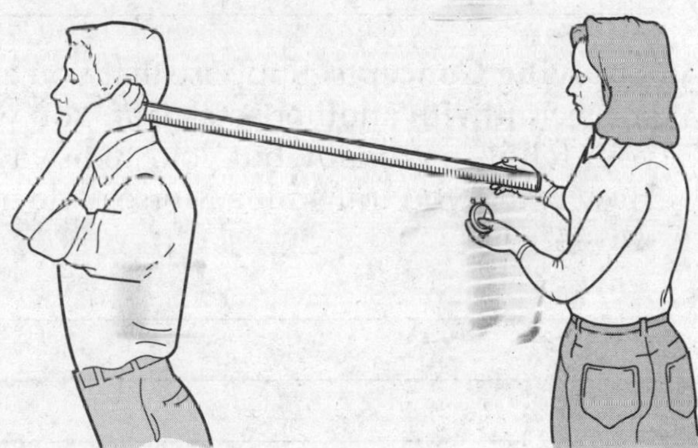

Figure 2

5. Repeat Step 5, substituting the metal rod for the meter stick. Note any observations.
6. Repeat Step 5, substituting a piece of cardboard for the meter stick. Note any observations.
7. Change roles with your partner and repeat Steps 3 through 7. Discuss your observations with your partner and record them, again using the numbers 1 (best) to 3 (poorest) to rank how well each medium conducts sound.

Observations

DATA TABLE

Medium	Elasticity (1 = most elastic)	Sound Conduction (1 = best conductor)
Meter stick		
Metal rod		
Cardboard		

Name ______________________ Class ______________ Date ____________

Analysis and Conclusions

1. **Forming Operational Definitions** What property of sound did you observe to determine if the medium was a good conductor?

____

2. **Comparing and Contrasting** Compare wood, metal, and cardboard as sound transmitters, based on your observations. How do these compare with your prediction?

____

____

____

____

3. **Making Generalizations** Based on your observations, what is the relationship between elasticity and the ability to conduct sound?

____

____

____

4. **Applying Concepts** Suppose that you are floating outside a spacecraft with another astronaut. You wish to say something to your fellow astronaut, but your two-way radio is not working. How could you transmit a Morse code message by using sound waves?

____

____

____

____

____

Go Further

Does elasticity affect the speed of a wave as well as the loudness (intensity) of the sound? Design an experiment to answer this question. Be sure to describe the responding and manipulated variables. Show your plan to your teacher. When your teacher approves your plan, carry out your experiment and report your results and conclusions.

Predicting Spectra

Background Information

Some materials are **transparent** to nearly all frequencies of visible light. This means that these materials transmit most of the light that strikes them. For example, window glass is transparent to nearly all frequencies of visible light. Most materials, however, transmit some frequencies and absorb others. These materials can appear colored.

If you observe the spectrum of light before and after it passes through a material, you can determine which frequencies the material absorbs. You can view the spectrum of light through a prism or an instrument known as a spectroscope. These instruments separate white light into its colors, a process called **dispersion.**

In this investigation, you will predict and observe how the spectrum of white light changes as the light passes through several solutions of different colors. Then, you will use your observations to explain how the color of a material is related to the wavelengths of light that it absorbs.

Problem

How is the color of a solution related to the wavelengths of light that it absorbs?

Pre-Lab Discussion

Read the entire investigation. Then, work with a partner to answer the following questions.

1. **Predicting** Imagine observing a white light through a piece of blue glass.

   a. What color would the light appear to be?

   ____

   b. What color of light would the glass transmit?

   ____

   ____

   c. What colors of light would the glass absorb?

   ____

   ____

2. **Predicting** Describe the spectrum you would see if you passed white light through a piece of blue glass.

   ____

   ____

Name ______________________ Class ________________ Date ____________

3. **Controlling Variables** Identify the manipulated, responding, and controlled variables in this investigation.
   a. Manipulated variable ______________________
   b. Responding variable ______________________
   c. Controlled variables ______________________
4. **Formulating Hypotheses** State a hypothesis about how the spectrum of white light changes as the light passes through a colored solution.

____

Materials *(per group)*

lamp and incandescent bulb
spectroscope
colored pencils
stoppered test tube of chlorophyll solution
stoppered test tube of phenolphthalein-sodium hydroxide solution
stoppered test tube of potassium permanganate solution

Safety

Put on safety goggles, a lab apron, and plastic gloves. Be careful to avoid breakage when working with glassware. Observe proper laboratory procedures when using electrical equipment. Never touch or taste any chemical unless instructed to do so. The chemicals used in this investigation are toxic and corrosive. Do not open any of the test tubes. Note all safety alert symbols next to the steps in the Procedure and review the meaning of each symbol by referring to the Safety Symbols on page xiii.

Procedure

1. With the room darkened, turn on the incandescent lamp. Observe the light from the bulb. In the data table, draw the spectrum that you expect to see when you view the bulb through the spectroscope. If necessary, use colored pencils to draw the spectrum.
2. Now, use the spectroscope to observe the spectrum of the light from the incandescent bulb. In the data table, draw and describe the spectrum that you observed.
3. Examine the test tube of the chlorophyll solution. Observe the light from the incandescent bulb through this test tube. Record in the data table the color that you see.
4. In the data table, draw the spectrum that you expect to see when you view the chlorophyll solution through the spectroscope.

Name ______________________ Class ________________ Date ____________

5. Hold the test tube of chlorophyll solution against the far end of the spectroscope so that the light from the bulb passes through the solution before entering the spectroscope. In the data table, draw the spectrum of the chlorophyll solution. Record any differences between this spectrum and the one you observed in Step 2. You may note gaps or differences in the brightness of some colors.
6. Repeat Steps 3 through 5 with the test tube of phenolphthalein-sodium hydroxide solution.
7. Repeat Steps 3 through 5 with the test tube of potassium permanganate solution.
8. Return the test tubes to your teacher. Wash your hands thoroughly after carrying out this investigation.

Observations

DATA TABLE

Solution	Color	Drawing of Predicted Spectrum	Drawing of Observed Spectrum	Description of Observed Spectrum
None				
Chlorophyll				
Phenolphthalein-sodium hydroxide				
Potassium permanganate				

Analysis and Conclusions

1. **Analyzing Data** Did passing white light through the colored solutions add colors to the light or remove colors from the light?

____

____

____

2. Formulating Hypotheses What happened to the colors of light that did not pass through the solutions? Explain your answer.

3. Inferring Which colors of light were absorbed in the spectrum of each of the following solutions?

a. Chlorophyll solution

b. Phenolphthalein-sodium hydroxide solution

c. Potassium permanganate solution

4. Drawing Conclusions What is the relationship between the color of a solution and the colors of light that the solution absorbs?

5. Drawing Conclusions What is the relationship between the color of a solution and the colors of light that the solution transmits?

6. Applying Concepts If you shine a red light through a block of red gelatin, the red beam of light is clearly visible in the gelatin. However, if you shine a red light through a block of blue gelatin, the light is not visible in the gelatin. Explain these observations.

Name ______________________ Class __________________ Date ____________

Go Further

The spectroscope that you used in this investigation enabled you to see whether there were any gaps in the spectrum of the light you observed and to judge whether some parts of the spectrum were brighter than others. A more precise instrument called a spectrophotometer enables you to measure the percentage of the light falling on a sample of a solution that the solution absorbs or transmits. The spectrophotometer can make this measurement at any visible wavelength.

Ask your teacher to show you how to use the spectrophotometer. Then, design an experiment to determine whether it is possible to use the spectrophotometer to measure the concentration of a light-absorbing substance in a solution. Write a detailed plan of your experiment. Your plan should state the hypothesis to be tested, identify the manipulated, responding, and controlled variables, and describe the procedures and safety precautions that you will use. Show your plan to your teacher. When your teacher approves your plan, carry out your experiment and report your results and conclusions.

Using Polarized Light

Background Information

Some substances change the direction in which polarized light waves vibrate. These substances are said to be optically active. Sucrose, or table sugar, is optically active. When polarized light passes through a solution of sucrose dissolved in water, the polarization of the light changes—the light waves begin to vibrate in a different direction.

To measure this change, a device called a polarimeter is used. A polarimeter contains two polarizing filters. A container between the two filters holds a sample to be tested for optical activity. If the filters are at right angles to each other, no light can pass through the polarimeter. However, if you place an optically active sample between the filters, it will change the polarization of the light. As a result, some light will pass through the second filter. To measure the optical activity of a sample, you would look through the polarimeter and rotate the second filter until no light is able to pass though the filter. The angle that you rotate the second filter depends on the sample's optical activity.

In this investigation, you will use a polarimeter to determine how the optical activity of a sugar solution is related to the concentration of the solution.

Problem

How is the concentration of a sugar solution related to its optical activity?

Pre-Lab Discussion

Read the entire investigation. Then, work with a partner to answer the following questions.

1. **Inferring** Explain how two polarizing filters can completely block a beam of light.

   ____

   ____

   ____

2. **Designing Experiments** Why will you need to be able to change the angle between the polarizing filters in the polarimeter?

   ____

   ____

   ____

   ____

Name ______________________ Class ______________________ Date ______________

3. **Applying Concepts** Could you determine the optical activity of a solution if the light passed through the sample before it passed through the two polarizing filters? Explain your answer.

____

____

____

____

4. **Controlling Variables** Identify the manipulated, responding, and controlled variables in this investigation.
   a. Manipulated variable

   ____

   b. Responding variable

   ____

   c. Controlled variables

   ____

   ____

5. **Controlling Variables** Why will you need to measure the optical activity of water in Step 9?

____

____

____

Materials *(per group)*

2 cardboard tubes
scissors
transparent tape
metric ruler
glass vial with cap
2 square polarizing filters, approximately 2 cm × 2 cm
duct tape
graph paper with millimeter rulings
bright light source
red pencil
paper towels
10 mL 20% sugar solution
10 mL 30% sugar solution
10 mL 40% sugar solution
unknown sugar solution

Safety

Put on a lab apron. Be careful to avoid breakage when working with glassware. Be careful when handling sharp instruments. Never look directly at the sun. Note all safety alert symbols next to the steps in the Procedure and review the meaning of each symbol by referring to the Safety Symbols on page xiii.

Name ______________________ Class ____________________ Date ______________

Procedure

Part A: Building a Polarimeter

1. Use scissors to cut a cardboard tube open lengthwise. Then, overlap the cut edges to make a slightly smaller tube that just fits inside the second cardboard tube, as shown in Figure 1. Use transparent tape to hold the cut edges of the smaller tube together. **CAUTION:** *Be careful not to puncture or cut skin when using scissors.*

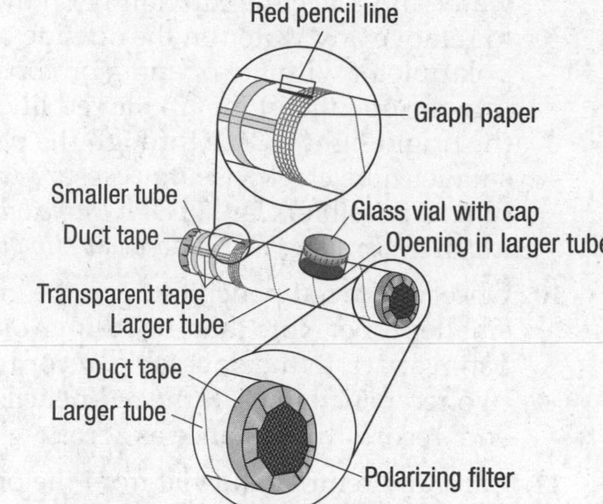

Figure 1

2. Using a metric ruler to measure, make a pencil mark on the side of the larger tube 4 cm from one end of the tube. Hold the glass vial with the center of its base on this mark. Use a pencil to trace the outline of the base of the vial on the tube.
3. Cut out the circle that you traced on the tube in Step 2. The resulting opening in the tube should be just large enough to allow the vial to fit snugly inside the tube, as shown in Figure 1.
4. Use small pieces of duct tape to carefully mount a polarizing filter over one end of the larger tube. Place tape only on the edges of the filter. To avoid getting any dirt or fingerprints on the polarizing filter, handle the filter only by its edges. If necessary, use small pieces of duct tape to cover any gaps between the edges of the filter and the tube. To hold the pieces of duct tape in place, wrap a piece of duct tape around the end of the tube, as shown in Figure 1.
5. Repeat Step 4 with the second polarizing filter and the smaller tube.
6. Cut a strip of graph paper that is 12 cm long and 1 cm wide. Wrap this strip around the open end of the larger tube, as shown in Figure 1. Use transparent tape to attach the strip of graph paper to the tube.
7. Insert the vial into the hole that you made in Step 3. Then, gently insert the smaller tube into the larger tube as far as the smaller tube will go.
8. Hold the polarimeter in one hand. Use your other hand to cover the vial to prevent it from falling out of the larger tube. Then, look at the bright light source through the polarimeter. As you look at the light through the polarimeter, rotate the smaller tube to make the light as dim as possible. Have a member of your group mark a short red pencil line on the strip of graph paper. Extend this line onto the smaller tube, as shown in Figure 1. **CAUTION:** *Do not aim the polarimeter at the sun.*

Name ______________________ Class ________________ Date ____________

Part B: Measuring Optical Activity

9. Remove the vial from the polarimeter. Fill the vial with water and place the cap tightly on the vial. Use a paper towel to remove any water on the outside of the vial. Hold the polarimeter with the opening on top. Carefully put the vial back into the opening. Line up the red lines on both tubes. Look at the bright light source through the polarimeter. Rotate the smaller tube clockwise if necessary until the light is as dim as possible. **CAUTION:** *Immediately wipe up any spilled water. Make sure the vial does not slip out of the polarimeter.*
10. Observe the red pencil lines on the graph paper strip and on the smaller tube. Note that the rulings on the graph paper strip are 1 mm apart. In the data table, record the distance between the two red pencil lines. If the red pencil lines are precisely end to end, record this distance as zero.
11. Carefully remove the vial from the polarimeter. Discard the water in the sink. Rinse out the vial with water and use a paper towel to dry the vial.
12. Repeat Steps 9 through 11 with the 20%, 30%, and 40% sugar solutions. Then, repeat Steps 9 through 11 with the unknown sugar solutions.
13. Make a graph of the data from your observations of the water and the 20%, 30%, and 40% sugar solutions. Plot sugar concentration on the horizontal axis and optical activity on the vertical axis. Draw a straight line as close as possible to all four data points.
14. Find the point on the vertical axis of your graph that corresponds to the optical activity of the unknown sugar solution. Draw a horizontal dotted line from this point to the solid line. Then, draw a vertical dotted line from the point where the two lines meet down to the horizontal axis. The point where the vertical dotted line meets the horizontal axis marks the concentration of the unknown solution. Record this concentration in the data table.

Observations

DATA TABLE

Sugar Concentration (percent)	Optical Activity (mm)
0 (water)	
20	
30	
40	
Unknown ____________	

Name ____________________ Class ______________ Date ____________

Analysis and Conclusions

1. **Analyzing Data** What was the relationship between the concentration of the sugar solutions and their optical activities?

2. **Using Graphs** Was it reasonable to use your graph to determine the concentration of sugar in the unknown solution? Explain your answer.

3. **Evaluating and Revising** When would it be unreasonable to use your graph to determine the concentration of an unknown sugar solution? Explain your answer.

4. **Predicting** How do you think the distance that light passes through the sample affects the observed optical activity?

Go Further

Design an experiment to use your polarimeter to determine the concentration of sugar in liquids such as fruit juices or syrups. Write a detailed plan of your experiment. Your plan should state the hypothesis to be tested, identify the manipulated, responding, and controlled variables, and describe the procedures and safety precautions that you will use. If the liquids you choose to test contain sugar other than sucrose, you will need to make solutions of known concentrations. After your teacher approves your plan, carry out your experiment and report your results and conclusions.

Name ______________________ Class ______________ Date __________

Refraction and Reflection

Background Information

In a vacuum, light travels in a straight line at 3.0×10^8 m/s. The situation is different, however, when light is not in a vacuum. Light can change direction when it passes through, bounces off, or is absorbed by substances. When light rays enter a substance, they change speed and may change direction. This behavior is called **refraction.** When light rays bounce off a surface, or undergo **reflection,** they also change direction. The angle between an incoming ray of light and a line perpendicular to the surface—called the normal line—is the **angle of incidence.** The angle between the reflected ray of light and the normal to the reflecting surface is the **angle of reflection.** If the light enters the substance and is refracted, the angle between the refracted light and the normal is the **angle of refraction.**

In this investigation, you will examine how the direction of light changes during refraction and reflection.

Problem

How do reflection and refraction change the direction of light?

Pre-Lab Discussion

Read the entire investigation. Then, work with a partner to answer the following questions.

1. **Inferring** In what direction will the tennis ball bounce if it is thrown directly at a wall? In what direction will the tennis ball bounce when it hits the wall at an angle? How is the direction influenced by the size of the angle?

____

____

____

____

____

2. **Using Analogies** Think of a photon of light as if it were a tennis ball and a mirror as if it were a wall. Use this analogy to describe what happens when light is reflected from a mirror's surface.

____

____

____

____

____

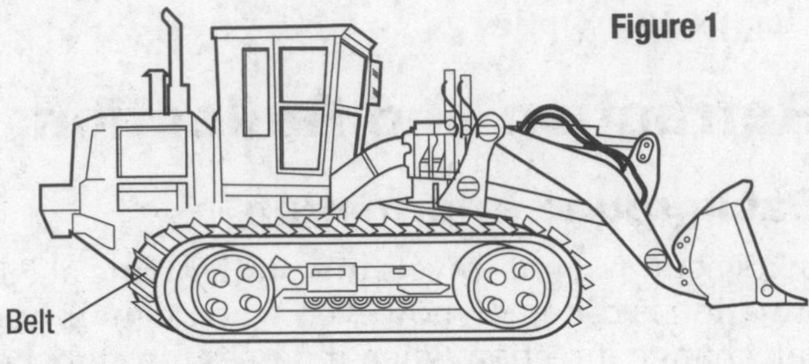

3. **Inferring** Consider the tractor shown in Figure 1. The tractor goes straight as long as both belts are going the same speed.

   a. Suppose the tractor exits a road and enters a field such that both belts enter the field at the same time. If the field slows the speed of the belts, how are the speed and direction of motion of the tractor affected as it enters the field?

   ____

   ____

   ____

4. **Inferring** Suppose the tractor exits the road and enters the field at an angle such that one belt enters the field before the other.

   a. Describe how the speeds of the belts and the direction of motion are affected as the tractor enters the field at an angle.

   ____

   ____

   ____

   b. Suppose that the tractor continues through the field in its new direction until it reaches a road parallel to the first. How will the tractor's final direction on the new road compare to its original direction on the first road? Explain your answer.

   ____

   ____

   ____

5. **Using Analogies** Think of a photon of light as if it were a tractor with belts on each side. Think of the medium that light is traveling through as if it were the surface on which the tractor is traveling. Light moving through air into glass is therefore similar to the tractor moving from the road to the field. Use this analogy to describe what happens when light moves from one medium to another.

   ____

   ____

   ____

   ____

   ____

   ____

Name ______________________ Class ________________ Date ____________

Materials *(per group)*

cardboard (approximately 30 cm × 30 cm)
30-cm ruler
4 straight pins
protractor
unlined paper
small mirror
support for mirror (wood block and glue, tape, or rubber band)
transparent container with a square base (7 cm × 7 cm)

Safety

Be careful when handling sharp instruments. Note all safety alert symbols next to the steps in the Procedure and review the meaning of each symbol by referring to the Safety Symbols on page xiii.

Procedure

Part A: Observing Reflection

1. Place the paper on the cardboard. Stand the mirror in the center of the paper. Support the mirror by gluing, taping, or tying it with a rubber band to a small wooden block. Draw a line along the edge of the mirror. Stick a pin in the paper and cardboard about 4 cm in front of the center of the mirror. Draw a small circle around the pin position and label it *Object*, as shown in Figure 2. **CAUTION:** *Pinpoints can cut or puncture skin, so handle pins carefully.*

Figure 2
(Not to scale)

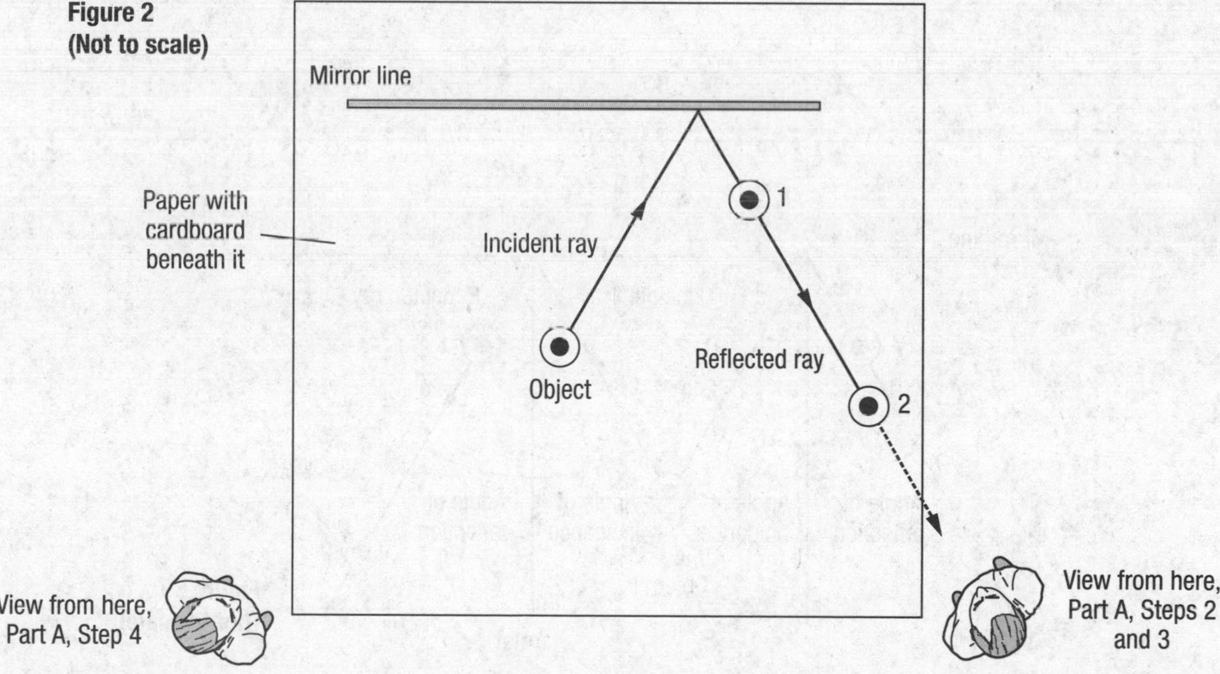

2. Refer to Figure 2. Position your head near the lower-right corner of the paper. Look at the mirror with one eye closed and observe the reflection of the pin. Do not look at the real pin. Insert a pin in the paper near the mirror so that it hides the reflection of the Object pin. Draw a small circle around the pin position and label it *1*.

Name ______________________ Class ______________________ Date ______________

3. Refer to Figure 2. From the same viewing position, place a second pin in the paper near the mirror so that it hides the pin you placed in position 1 and the reflection of the Object pin. Draw a small circle around the pin position and label it 2.
4. Remove the pins from positions 1 and 2. Use them to repeat Steps 2 and 3 from the lower-left corner of the paper. Draw circles around these pin positions and label them 3 and 4.
5. Remove the mirror and all the pins. Using the ruler, draw a solid line through pin positions 1 and 2 and extend it as far as the mirror line. This line is a reflected ray. Draw a line from the Object pin position to the point where the reflected ray leaves the mirror. This line is the incident ray. Label each ray and draw an arrow on the ray to show its direction.
6. Repeat Step 5 for pin positions 3 and 4.
7. Draw two lines perpendicular to the mirror line at the two points where the incident rays and the reflected rays touch. These lines are the normal lines. Label and measure the angles of incidence and reflection for the rays coming from the left and right corners of the paper, as shown in Figure 3. Record your measurements in Data Table 1.

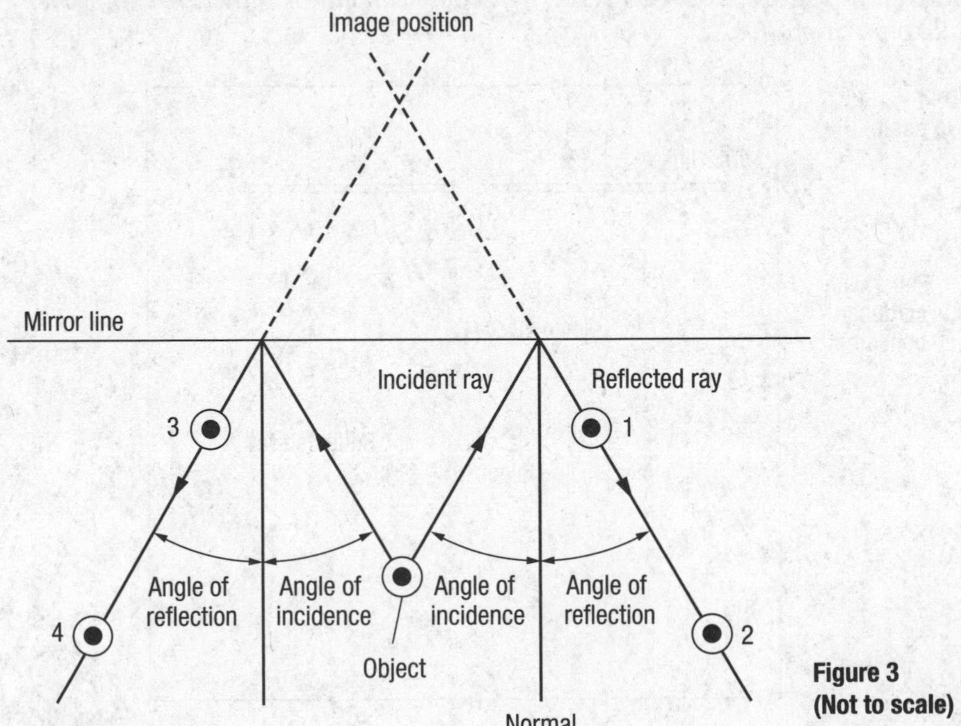

Figure 3
(Not to scale)

8. Using the ruler, draw two dashed lines extending from the two reflected rays beyond the mirror line. Continue these dashed lines just beyond the point where they cross. This point is the position of the Object pin's image in the mirror. Label this point *Image*.

Part B: Observing Refraction

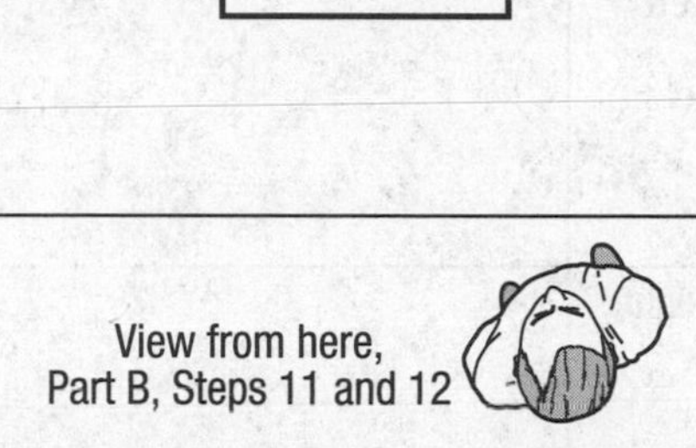

Figure 4
(Not to scale)

9. Fill a transparent square-based container with tap water. Place a piece of unlined paper on a piece of cardboard. Place the container in the center of the paper and trace a line around the edges.
10. Using the ruler, draw a line on your paper at an angle to one edge of the container. Do not draw this line perpendicular to the edge of the container.
11. Place two pins on the line about 3 cm apart from each other. Draw circles around the base of the pins and label the circles *Pin 1* and *Pin 2*, as shown in Figure 4. Look through the bottom edge of the container until you see Pins 1 and 2 positioned exactly behind each other. (They will look like only one pin.)
12. Place two more pins on the lower part of your paper so that they also seem to line up with Pins 1 and 2. (All four pins should appear to be one pin.) Draw circles around the base of these pins and label them *Pin 3* and *Pin 4*.
13. Remove the pins and the container. Using a ruler, draw a line through the positions of Pins 3 and 4 just to where they meet the line made by the container.
14. The line through Pins 1 and 2 represents a ray of light entering the container and is called the incident ray. Label this ray and draw arrows on it to show its direction.
15. The line through Pins 3 and 4 represents a ray of light leaving the container and going to your eye. It is called the emergent ray. Label this ray and draw arrows on it to show its direction.
16. Using the ruler, connect the incident ray and the emergent ray through the container. This line is called the refracted ray. Label this ray and draw arrows on it to show its direction.
17. Using the protractor, construct normal lines (lines perpendicular to the edge of the container) at the points where the incident and emergent rays touch the container. Extend the normal lines into the container area. You should have formed two angles on each side of the container.
18. Two angles are formed with the normal lines as the incident ray touches the side of the container and as the refracted ray touches the opposite side of the container. These two angles are called angles of incidence. Label these two angles *I*.
19. Two angles are formed with the normal lines as the refracted ray enters the container and again as the emergent ray leaves the opposite side of the container. These two angles are called angles of refraction. Label these two angles *R*.

Name ______________ Class ______________ Date ______________

20. Measure the angles of incidence and the angles of refraction and record your measurements in Data Table 2.
21. Using the ruler and a dashed line, extend the emergent ray backward through the container and beyond it.

Observations

DATA TABLE 1

Side	Angle	
	Incidence	Reflection
Left		
Right		

DATA TABLE 2

Pins	Angle	
	Incidence (I)	Reflection (R)
1 and 2		
3 and 4		

Analysis and Conclusions

1. **Analyzing Data** In Part A, how do the distances of the object and image from the mirror compare?

___

___

2. **Analyzing Data** How do the angles of incidence and the angles of reflection in Part A compare in size?

___

___

___

3. **Interpreting Diagrams** Follow the path of one of the incident rays to the mirror and the path of its reflected ray. Repeat for the other incident ray and reflected ray. How does the direction of the incident ray compare to the direction of the reflected ray? As a result, how is the image oriented with respect to the object?

4. **Inferring** The image you see in a mirror is formed from many incident and reflected rays. How would the image be affected if there were no relationship between the angles of the incident and reflected rays?

5. **Relating Cause and Effect** When you look in a plane mirror, the image seems to be "inside" or "behind" the mirror, even though no light rays can pass through the mirror. What kind of image (real or virtual) exists where there are no actual light rays? Explain how the image appears in a place from which no actual light rays are coming.

6. **Analyzing Data** In Part B, as the incident ray enters the container of water, how does it bend with respect to the normal line? As the emergent ray leaves the glass, how does it bend with respect to the normal line?

7. **Analyzing Data** In Part B, How does the angle of incidence of the incident ray compare with the angle of refraction for the emerging ray? How does the angle of refraction for the incident ray compare with the angle of incidence for the emerging ray?

Name ______________________ Class ________________ Date ____________

8. **Analyzing Data** How do the directions of the emergent ray and the incident ray compare?

____

____

9. **Applying Concepts** Why does a light ray bend as it passes from air to a container of water or from the container of water to air at an angle?

____

____

____

____

Go Further

Some substances refract light more than others do. Diamond bends light so much that light approaching at even a small angle reflects inside the diamond instead of passing through. This process is called total internal reflection. It is responsible for diamond's characteristic sparkle.

When the pathway of light is disrupted in this way, it can produce some interesting illusions. Try the following experiments:

1. Put a penny on a flat surface and place an empty, transparent cup directly over the penny. Observe the penny through the side of the cup.
2. Completely fill the cup with water and observe the penny through the side of the cup.
3. Carefully remove the cup and use an eyedropper to put several drops of water on the penny.
4. Put the cup containing the water back on the penny. Observe the penny through the side of the cup.
5. What did you observe in each case? How can your observations be explained.

Harnessing Solar Energy

Background Information

The sun radiates a tremendous amount of energy. Even from a great distance away, sunlight warms Earth. As the cost of fossil fuels rises, solar energy becomes a more attractive alternative energy source. Some people install solar panels on the roofs of their houses. These devices are often used to heat water that is then used as a hot-water source or to heat the house.

In order to make the greatest use of energy from the sun, it is necessary to focus the sun's rays. This can be accomplished by using a curved, or concave, mirrored surface or a magnifying lens.

In this investigation, you will use a mirror to focus the sun's rays and measure the effect it has on the temperature of a sample of water.

Problem

What happens to the thermal energy of a substance when light rays from the sun are focused on it?

Pre-Lab Discussion

Read the entire investigation. Then, work with a partner to answer the following questions.

1. **Applying Concepts** Suppose parallel rays of light strike a plane mirror at an angle. How will the directions of the reflected rays compare with the directions of the incident rays?

____

____

____

2. **Interpreting Diagrams** Two plane mirrors are joined at an angle of 120° and oriented toward two parallel incident rays of light, as shown in Figure 1. Construct the normal lines for each plane mirror, measure the angles of incidence, and draw the reflected rays as dashed lines with arrowheads to show their directions. Are the reflected rays parallel to each other? Explain.

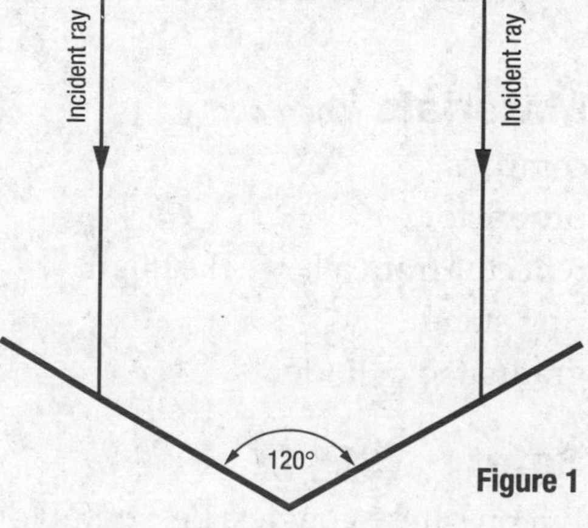

Figure 1

____

____

____

____

____

Name ______________________ Class ____________________ Date ______________

3. **Interpreting Diagrams** A spherical concave mirror is shown in Figure 2. Draw dashed lines to represent the reflected rays and use arrowheads to indicate direction. Label the point at which the rays cross as the Focus. How is this concave mirror similar to the V-shaped mirror in Question 2? How does the concave mirror affect the direction of the incident rays?

____

____

____

____

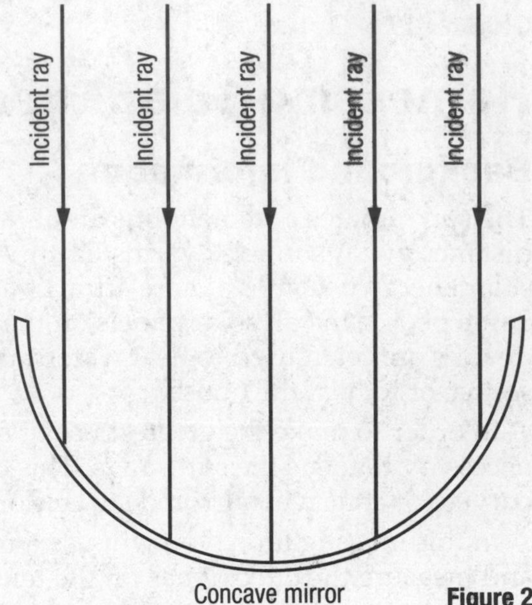

Figure 2

4. **Inferring** How does the amount of light energy at the focus compare to the amount of energy at any other location near the mirror? Explain.

____

____

____

5. **Predicting** Two water-filled test tubes are set up so the sun is shining on them. One of the test tubes is positioned to be at the focus of a concave mirror. How would you expect the temperature of the water in the two test tubes to compare after they have each had sun shining on them for an hour? Explain.

____

____

____

____

Materials *(per group)*

compass
protractor
reflector from a large flashlight
ring stand
graduated cylinder
2 thermometers
2 test tubes
2 test-tube clamps
triangular file
tape

Safety

Put on safety goggles. Be careful to avoid breakage when working with glassware. Be careful when handling sharp instruments. Note all safety alert symbols next to the steps in the Procedure and review the meaning of each symbol by referring to the Safety Symbols on page xiii.

Name ______________________ Class ________________ Date ____________

Procedure

1. Insert one of the test tubes through the hole in the center of a flashlight reflector so that it extends about 1 cm below the bottom of the reflector. The test tube should fit snugly. If the hole is too small, enlarge it with a triangular file. If the test tube is loose, secure it with some tape.
2. Set up a ring stand with two test-tube clamps. Secure the test tube in the reflector and the second test tube in the test-tube clamps, as shown in Figure 3. Place a thermometer into each test tube.

Thermometers
Test tubes
Reflector
Test tube clamps
Ring stand

Figure 3

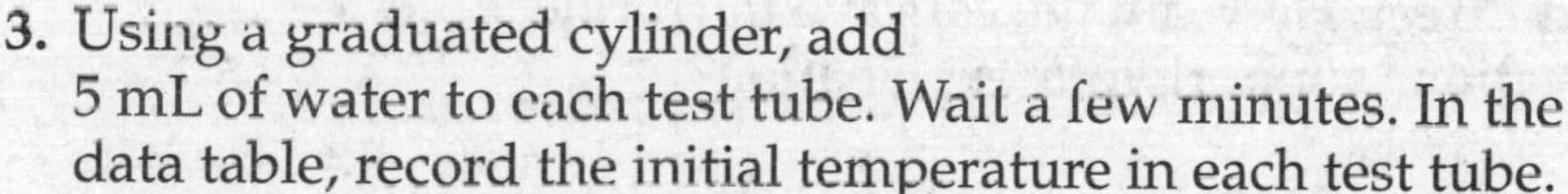

3. Using a graduated cylinder, add 5 mL of water to each test tube. Wait a few minutes. In the data table, record the initial temperature in each test tube.

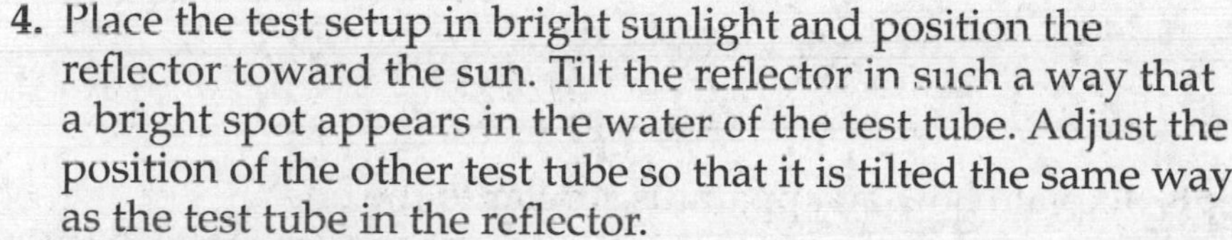

4. Place the test setup in bright sunlight and position the reflector toward the sun. Tilt the reflector in such a way that a bright spot appears in the water of the test tube. Adjust the position of the other test tube so that it is tilted the same way as the test tube in the reflector.
5. Expose the test tubes to the sun for 5 minutes. Observe the temperatures of the water in each test tube and record the values in the data table.

Observations

DATA TABLE

Test Tube	Initial Temperature (°C)	Final Temperature (°C)
With Reflector		
Without Reflector		

Name ______________________ Class ______________________ Date ______________

Analysis and Conclusions

1. **Comparing and Contrasting** How did the temperature in the two test tubes compare? What caused the difference in temperature? How did this result compare to your earlier prediction?

____

____

____

____

2. **Controlling Variables** Why did you need to set up two test tubes with the same amount of water in each?

____

____

____

____

____

____

3. **Relating Cause and Effect** How did the concave mirror heat the water? What observations support your explanation?

____

____

____

4. **Applying Concepts** Explain how an apparatus similar to the one you constructed could be used to change the sun's radiant energy into mechanical energy.

____

____

____

Go Further

With adult supervision, construct a device to heat water by using a magnifying lens. Use a similar apparatus to the one you used in the investigation. Use two test tubes so that you can evaluate the effect of the lens. Attempt to position the lens in such a way that a large amount of sunlight is focused in a small volume of water. Compare the results of your experiment with the results from this investigation. **CAUTION:** *Focused light from the lens can produce very high temperatures.*

Constructing a Telephone

Background Information

The operation of the telephone involves energy conversions. In the transmitter of the telephone, sound waves exert a pressure on a flexible film, or diaphragm, that conducts electricity, and which vibrates with the same frequency as the sound waves. The louder the sound waves are, the larger the vibrations of the diaphragm are. In some older telephone transmitters, finely granulated carbon was placed between the diaphragm and a conducting plate. Changes in the diaphragm's vibrations change the distance between the diaphragm and the plate, causing the electric current through the carbon grains to vary. In this way, the variations in intensity and frequency of sound are converted into changes in current. These current changes form electronic signals that travel over wires. In the receiver of the telephone, the electronic signals are converted back into sound waves by a somewhat similar process.

The first telephone conversation took place on March 10, 1876, between the inventor of the telephone, Alexander Graham Bell, and his assistant, Thomas Watson.

In this investigation, you will build a simple device that changes pressure into an electrical signal, which illustrates the operation of a transmitter in older models of telephones.

Problem

How do energy conversions take place within the transmitter of a telephone?

Pre-Lab Discussion

Read the entire investigation. Then, work with a partner to answer the following questions.

1. **Observing** What process is this investigation meant to test?

____

____

____

____

____

____

____

Name ______________________ Class ______________ Date __________

2. **Controlling Variables** What is the manipulated variable in this investigation?

3. **Controlling Variables** What is the responding variable in this investigation?

4. **Predicting** What do you predict will occur at the transmitting end of the energy conversion?

5. **Predicting** What do you predict will occur at the receiving end of the energy conversion?

Materials *(per group)*

plastic cup
1.5-V lamp with socket
carbon grains
2 copper strips
2 alligator clips
1.5-V dry cell
3 connecting wires, each 30 cm long

Name ______________________ Class ________________ Date ____________

Safety 

Put on safety goggles and a lab apron. Be careful to avoid breakage when working with glassware. Observe proper laboratory procedures when using electrical equipment. Note all safety alert symbols next to the steps in the Procedure and review the meaning of each symbol by referring to the Safety Symbols on page xiii.

Procedure

1. Place the two copper strips on opposite sides of the plastic cup. **CAUTION:** *Metal strips can be sharp and can cut skin.*
2. Half-fill the cup with carbon grains.
3. Using an alligator clip, connect one end of a wire to one of the copper strips. Connect the other end of the wire to one side of the lamp socket. **CAUTION:** *Observe proper laboratory procedures when using electrical equipment.* **CAUTION:** *Wire ends can puncture skin.*
4. Using the other alligator clip, connect another wire to the second copper strip. Connect the other end of this wire to one terminal of the dry cell, as shown in Figure 1.

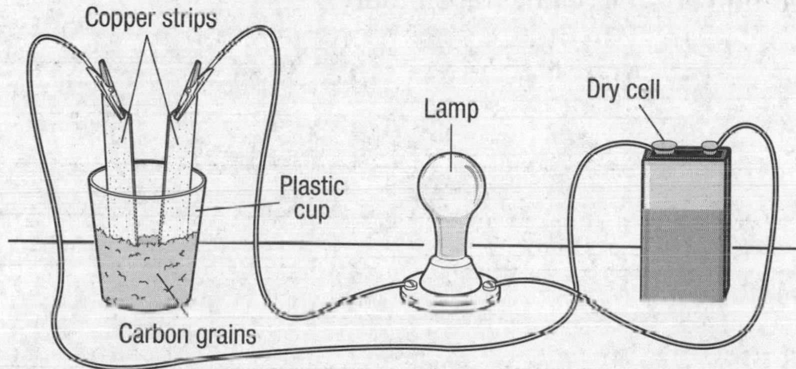

Figure 1

5. Connect a third wire to the other side of the lamp socket. Connect the other end of this wire to the other terminal of the dry cell.
6. Squeeze the lower sides of the plastic cup so that the distance between the copper strips changes. Do not bring the strips into direct contact with each other. Observe how the brightness of the light bulb varies with the pressure applied to the cup.

Observations

____

____

____

____

____

Name ________________ Class ________________ Date ________________

Analysis and Conclusions

1. **Observing** What happened when you squeezed the copper strips together?

2. **Observing** What happened when you stopped squeezing the copper strips together?

3. **Drawing Conclusions** How did pressure on the carbon grains affect the flow of electricity?

4. **Inferring** How is the process observed in this investigation comparable to the operation of a telephone transmitter?

Go Further

Using the Internet or the library, perform additional research about telephone transmitters. How similar were old transmitters to the apparatus in the investigation? How are they different now? What materials are currently used in transmitters? What is piezoelectricity, and how are certain crystal used to produce it? Has the basic process of energy conversion changed significantly? Use the results of your research to write a short report.

Charging Objects

Background Information

An object can become charged in several different ways. When electrons are transferred between objects that are rubbed together, the objects become charged due to friction. An object can sometimes become charged simply by touching it with another charged object. In this case, the object is charged by direct contact, or conduction. An object can also be charged by an object that is already charged, without contact between them. This newly charged object is said to be charged by **induction.** The charge on an object can be detected by using a device called an electroscope.

In this investigation, you will construct an electroscope and use it to explore charging by friction, conduction, and induction.

Problem

How do electrons move when objects become charged?

Pre-Lab Discussion

Read the entire investigation. Then, work with a partner to answer the following questions.

1. **Forming Hypotheses** What hypotheses are to be tested in this investigation?

2. **Predicting** When the balloon is rubbed with flannel, in what manner will the balloon become charged?

3. **Predicting** What type of electron transfer will take place when the electroscope is touched by the balloon?

Name ______________________ Class ______________________ Date ______________

4. Predicting When the charged glass rod is held near the electroscope and then moved away, what type of electron transfer will occur?

____

____

____

____

____

5. Drawing Conclusions What is the purpose of this investigation?

____

____

____

____

____

Materials *(per group)*

scissors
cardboard
glass jar
thick wire
aluminum foil
very thin aluminum foil from a gum wrapper
masking tape
2 balloons
wool flannel
string
glass rod
silk

Safety

Put on safety goggles. Be careful to avoid breakage when working with glassware. Be careful when handling sharp instruments. Observe proper laboratory procedures when using electrical equipment. Note all safety alert symbols next to the steps in the Procedure and review the meaning of each symbol by referring to the Safety Symbols on page xiii.

Procedure

1. To build an electroscope, cut out a circle of cardboard slightly larger than the opening of the glass jar. Use the point of the scissors to make a small hole in the center of the cardboard. **CAUTION:** *Be careful not to cut yourself when handling sharp instruments.*
2. Push the wire through the hole in the cardboard. Bend one end of the wire to form an L-shaped hook, as shown in Figure 1. Crumple the aluminum foil into a ball and push it onto the other end of the wire. **CAUTION:** *Use care when handling wire; it can cut or puncture skin.*

Name ______________________ Class ________________ Date __________

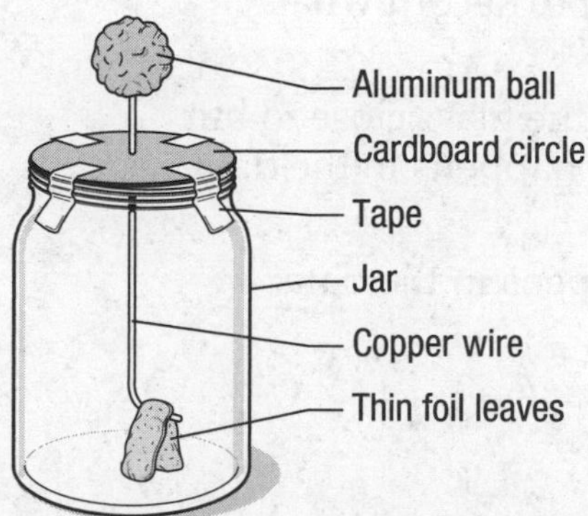

Figure 1

3. Cut a small strip of thin foil from a gum wrapper. Fold the foil strip in half and hang it over the hook so that the two leaves of foil hang down side by side. Lower the cardboard lid assembly onto the jar and tape it in place. **CAUTION:** *Be careful when handling sharp instruments.*
4. Inflate the two balloons and tie the ends so that the air does not escape.
5. To test your electroscope, rub one of the inflated balloons with the wool flannel. This will give the balloon a negative charge and the wool a positive charge. Gently touch the rubbed part of the balloon to the aluminum ball of your electroscope. The foil leaves should move apart. (*Hint: If they do not move, remove the lid from the jar and check that the leaves are not stuck together.*) Touch the top of the electroscope with your hand.
6. Tie a piece of string to the end of each balloon. Rub both balloons with the wool flannel. Hang both balloons by their string and bring the rubbed parts of the balloons together. Observe what happens.
7. Hold the wool flannel near one of the hanging balloons. Observe what happens.
8. Touch one of the charged balloons to the top of the electroscope. Record what happens in the data table.
9. Move the balloon away. Record what happens in the data table.
10. Touch the top of the electroscope with your hand and again record what happens in the data table.
11. Rub the glass rod with the silk. Doing this gives a positive charge to the glass and a negative charge to the silk. Touch the glass rod to the electroscope. Record what happens in the data table.
12. Move the glass rod away from the electroscope. Again, record what happens in the data table. Touch the electroscope with your hand.
13. Rub one of the balloons again with the wool. Move the balloon close to but not touching the top of the electroscope. Record what happens in the data table.

14. Move the balloon away from the electroscope. Record what happens in the data table.
15. Rub the glass rod again with the silk. Hold the glass close to but not touching the electroscope. Record what happens in the data table.
16. Move the glass rod away. Record what happens in the data table.

Observations

DATA TABLE

Procedure Step Number	Action	Observation of Electroscope Leaves
8	Rubbed balloon touches electroscope	
9	After touching, balloon is moved away	
10	Hand touches electroscope	
11	Rubbed glass rod touches electroscope	
12	Rubbed glass rod is moved away	
13	Rubbed balloon held near	
14	Rubbed balloon moved away	
15	Rubbed glass held near rod	
16	Rubbed glass rod is moved away	

Name ________________ Class ________________ Date ________________

Analysis and Conclusions

1. **Observing** After being rubbed with wool flannel, what happened to the balloons in Step 6 when they were brought near each other?

2. **Observing** What happens to an electroscope that indicates that a charged object is near?

3. **Inferring** Recall that rubbing a balloon with flannel gives the balloon a negative charge. Does the balloon gain or lose electrons in this situation? Is this an example of charging by friction, contact, or induction?

4. **Inferring** By what method was the electroscope charged in Step 8? Did the leaves become positively or negatively charged? What happened when the charged glass rod touched the electroscope in Step 11?

5. **Inferring** What happened to the charged electroscope when you touched it with your hand in Step 10? Did the electroscope gain or lose electrons?

6. Inferring Why did the electroscope leaves behave as they did when the charged balloon was brought near in Step 13? Did any electrons from the balloon move into the electroscope?

7. Inferring Why did the electroscope leaves behave as they did when the charged balloon was moved away in Step 14?

8. Classifying Explain what happened when the charged glass rod was held near and then moved away from the electroscope in Steps 15 and 16. Was the electroscope charged by friction, conduction, or induction?

9. Comparing and Contrasting Compare the three methods of charging in terms of electron movement.

Go Further

Design an experiment to compare how much different substances are charged by friction. Show your plan to your teacher. When your teacher approves your plan, carry out your experiment and report your results and conclusions.

Studying Electromagnetic Induction

Background Information

In 1831, Michael Faraday discovered that when a coil of wire is moved in a magnetic field, an electric current is generated, or induced, in the wire. This process is called electromagnetic induction. A current is generated only if the wire is part of a circuit. The current is induced because in the frame of reference of the wire, the magnetic field is changing.

In this investigation, you will move a bar magnet through a coil of wire to induce a current. You will use a simple galvanometer (a second coil of wire wrapped around a compass) to detect the induced current. In this galvanometer, the compass needle responds to the magnetic field produced by the induced current.

Problem

How can you measure an electric current in a a wire using a magnetic compass?

Pre-Lab Discussion

Read the entire investigation. Then, work with a partner to answer the following questions.

1. **Inferring** Why does a compass needle move?

____

____

2. **Inferring** Why does a moving magnet produce a changing magnetic field?

____

____

____

____

3. **Predicting** What will happen when the number of turns in the coil in the 3-m wire is increased? Explain your answer.

____

____

____

____

Name ______________________ Class ______________________ Date ______________

4. **Predicting** What will happen when the magnet is moved back and forth inside the coil? Explain your answer.

____

____

Materials *(per group)*

connecting wire with bare ends, 1 m in length
connecting wire with bare ends, 3 m in length
magnetic compass
bar magnet

Safety

Use caution when connecting wires. Note all safety alert symbols next to the steps in the Procedure and review the meaning of each symbol by referring to the Safety Symbols on page xiii.

Procedure

1. Using a piece of wire 1 m long, wrap a coil with 20 turns of wire around the compass, as shown in Figure 1.

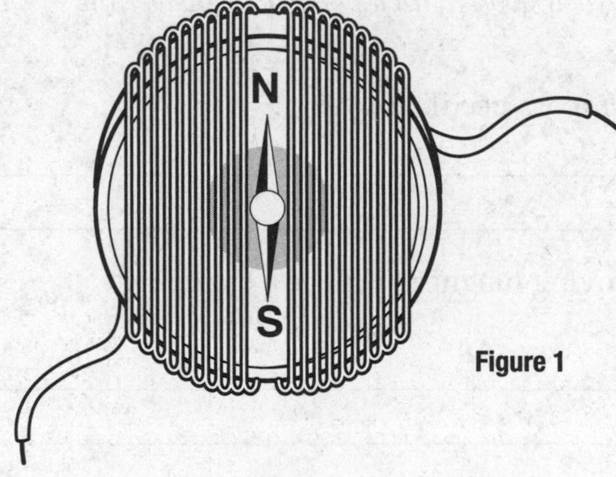

Figure 1

2. Place the compass on a table or other flat surface. Rotate the compass to align the compass needle with the wire.
3. In the middle of the 3-m length of wire, wind a coil with ten turns of wire around your finger. The coil should be large enough for the bar magnet to fit through.
4. Connect the two coils of wire by twisting the bare ends of the wires together, as shown in Figure 2. **CAUTION:** *Be careful when handling the sharp ends of wires; they can puncture skin.* The second coil should be at least 1 m away from the compass so that the magnet does not directly affect the compass needle. Hold the compass in a horizontal position so the needle moves freely.

Name _______________ Class _______________ Date _______________

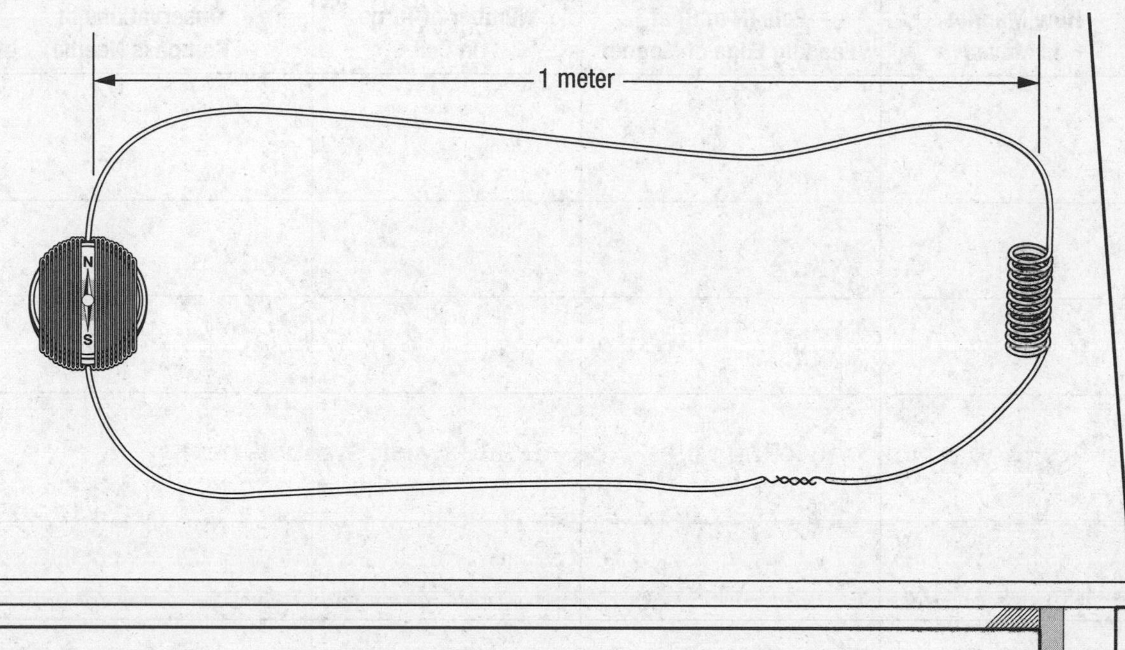

Figure 2

5. Slowly push the north pole of the bar magnet into the coil of wire. Have a partner observe what happens to the compass needle. Record your observations in the data table.
6. Have your partner observe what happens to the compass needle as you slowly pull the magnet out of the coil of wire. Record your observations in the data table.
7. Add ten more loops of wire to the coil in the 3-m wire. Then, repeat Steps 5 and 6.
8. Repeat Steps 5 and 6, but this time make the south pole of the magnet the leading edge.
9. Repeat Steps 5 and 6, but this time move the magnet quickly instead of slowly.
10. Try pushing and pulling the magnet continuously into and out of the coil. Record your observations in the data table.

Name ______________ Class ______________ Date ______________

Observations

DATA TABLE

How Magnet Is Moved	Pole (N or S) at Leading Edge of Magnet	Number of Turns in Coil	Observations of Compass Needle

Analysis and Conclusions

1. **Observing** Explain what you observed happening when you moved a magnet in a coil of wire.

Name ______________________ Class ______________ Date ___________

2. **Drawing Conclusions** How does the number of turns in the coil affect the current in the wire?

3. **Drawing Conclusions** How did changing the pole of the magnet affect the direction of the current in the wire? How can you tell?

4. **Predicting** Would a current be induced in the wire if you did not move the magnet? Why or why not?

5. **Predicting** Would a current be induced if you moved the coil of wire instead of the magnet? Why or why not?

6. **Inferring** What kind of current was induced in Step 10? Explain your answer.

Go Further

What do you think would happen if you made a coil of wire by first winding ten turns of wire in one direction and then winding ten turns in the opposite direction? Try it and find out.

Making a Compass

Background Information

A compass is basically a floating magnet used to find directions. It responds to the magnetic poles of Earth. The north-seeking pole of the floating magnet points in the northern direction and is therefore called the north pole of the compass. The south-seeking pole of the floating magnet points in the southern direction and is therefore called the south pole of the compass.

The Earth's magnetic pole in the northern hemisphere is located in the Hudson Bay region of northern Canada, nearly 1800 km from the geographical North Pole. The magnetic pole in the southern hemisphere is south of Australia.

In this investigation, you will use a permanent magnet and a needle to make a floating compass. You will then test your compass by comparing it to a standard compass.

Problem

How accurate is a classroom compass that you make?

Pre-Lab Discussion

Read the entire investigation. Then, work with a partner to answer the following questions.

1. **Predicting** What do you expect to happen when you hold the north pole of a bar magnet near a compass needle?

____

____

____

2. **Predicting** In what direction do you expect the magnetized needle to point when you magnetize it with the south pole of the bar magnet? Explain your answer.

____

____

____

____

3. **Designing Experiments** Why is it important to stroke the needle with the magnet in only one direction?

____

____

____

4. **Applying Concepts** How do the properties of magnets make it possible to use compasses?

5. **Applying Concepts** Why might the use of a compass mislead you if you were seeking geographic north?

Materials *(per group)*

magnetic compass
permanent bar magnet
file
cork strip or disk, 3 cm in length or diameter
grease pencil
petri dish or other shallow dish
2 needles

Safety

Be careful to avoid breakage when working with glassware. Be careful when handling sharp instruments. Note all safety alert symbols next to the steps in the Procedure and review the meaning of each symbol by referring to the Safety Symbols on page xiii.

Procedure

1. Use the grease pencil to label one point on the side of a petri dish with the letter *N*. Label the point on the opposite side *S*. Label with an *E* the point that is to the right when the *S* is closest to you. Label with a *W* the point that is on the left of *S*. Make an intermediate marking at each of the four positions midway between the pairs of letters.

2. Obtain a bar magnet. If its north and south poles are not marked (with an *N* and an *S*), place one end near the north-pointing end of a magnetic compass. If the compass needle is deflected, the end of the bar magnet is its north pole. If the compass needle is attracted, the end of the bar magnet is its south pole.
3. Use the file to make a straight, shallow groove lengthwise on the cork strip or disk. **CAUTION:** *Be careful when handling sharp instruments.*
4. Hold the needle at its eye end (the end with the opening in it). Stroke the needle at least ten times along the south pole of the bar magnet. The strokes should all be in the same direction and should all start near the eye end of the needle. Do not use a back-and-forth motion. Instead, lift the needle each time you bring it back to its starting position for the next stroke.
5. Move the bar magnet at least a meter from where you are working so that it will not interfere with your observations.
6. Fill the labeled petri dish halfway with water. Float the cork groove side up in the water so that it floats freely.
7. Lay the stroked needle inside the groove in the cork. Observe what happens. Rotate the cork by 90° in either direction. Again, observe what happens.
8. Repeat Steps 4 through 7, using a different needle and stroking the needle along the bar magnet's north pole. You must stroke the new needle in exactly the same direction as in Step 4.
9. To check the accuracy of your floating compass, compare its orientation with that of the standard magnetic compass. Turn the dish so that the *N* and *S* markings you made are oriented like those on the standard compass.

Observations

1. What happened when you floated the cork with the needle that was stroked along the magnet's south pole? What happened when you tried to turn the cork in other directions?

____

____

____

____

2. What happened when you floated the cork with the needle that was stroked along the magnet's north pole? What happened when you tried to turn the cork in other directions?

____

____

____

Name ______________________ Class ________________ Date ____________

Analysis and Conclusions

1. **Observing** Which needle for the floating compass lined up in the same way as the needle of a standard magnetic compass?

2. **Inferring** How could you use your floating compass to find east? To find southwest?

3. **Inferring** What does the magnetic polarity of your compass tell about the polarity of Earth's magnetic poles?

Go Further

Try to improve on the design of your compass. For example, you can find ways to reduce friction in the compass so that the needle aligns with Earth's magnetic field more easily. Think of other designs that do not require the use of liquid in a petri dish. Write a description of your improved design. When your teacher has approved your design, carry it out and test it, using all necessary safety procedures. Report your observations and conclusions.

Identifying Rocks

Background Information

A rock is a solid combination of one or more minerals or other materials. Geologists classify rocks into three major groups (igneous, sedimentary, and metamorphic) based on how the rocks form. To identify rocks, geologists observe a rock's texture—the size, shape, and arrangement of the crystals and other particles that make up the rock.

Igneous rock forms from magma that cools either underground (intrusive rock) or on Earth's surface (extrusive rock). Intrusive rocks cool slowly, allowing crystals to grow larger and giving the rock a coarse-grained texture. Extrusive rocks cool quickly and have a fine-grained, or even glassy, texture.

Sedimentary rock forms from sediment that is squeezed and cemented together. Sedimentary rocks that form from the broken fragments of other rocks are called clastic rocks. The fragments might be fairly large, such as pebbles, somewhat smaller, such as grains of sand, or very small, such as grains of clay. Other kinds of sedimentary rock include chemical rocks, which form when minerals precipitate out of solution, and organic rocks, which form when the shells and skeletons of marine animals become compacted and cemented together over time.

Metamorphic rock forms from rock that has been changed by temperature, pressure, or chemical reactions. Metamorphic rocks may be foliated, in which the particles are arranged in parallel bands, or nonfoliated, in which the particles are not arranged in bands.

In this investigation, you will learn how to identify the three major types of rocks as well as some rock types within each major category.

Problem

What are the identifying properties of rocks?

Pre-Lab Discussion

Read the entire investigation. Then, work with a partner to answer the following questions.

1. **Inferring** What is the purpose of this investigation?

___

___

___

___

___

___

Name ______________________ Class ________________ Date __________

2. **Observing** What property distinguishes the two main types of igneous rock? Explain your answer.

3. **Drawing Conclusions** Chalk is made of tiny fragments of marine animals. What kind of rock is chalk?

4. **Drawing Conclusions** If you have a rock that has parallel bands in it, what kind of rock might you have? Might it be another type of rock? Explain your answer.

Materials *(per group)*

igneous rocks
sedimentary rocks
metamorphic rocks
Hand lens
Dropper bottle of dilute hydrochloric acid (HCl)
Paper towels

Safety

Put on safety goggles and wear plastic disposable gloves when handling chemicals, as they may irritate the skin or stain skin or clothing. Never touch or taste a chemical unless instructed to do so. Note all safety alert symbols next to the steps in the Procedure and review the meaning of each symbol by referring to the Safety Symbols on page xiii.

Procedure

1. Choose one of the rock samples provided by your teacher. Observe its texture, color, and other properties.
2. Use the key in Figure 1 to identify the sample. Begin by reading the first question. Answer yes or no based on your observations.
3. After Yes or No, you will find a phrase telling you to proceed to another question. Continue working through the key in this way until you come to a phrase that identifies your rock sample. In the data table, record the route that you take through the key, using the numbers of the questions. Then, record the type of rock you have identified.
4. Work through the key for each of your samples to identify them.
5. Check your identifications with the true identifications from your teacher.

Figure 1 Key to Identification of Some Rocks

1. Does the rock contain visible interlocking crystals?	Yes: Go to Step 2. No: Go to Step 4.
2. Are all of the crystals the same color and shape?	Yes: nonfoliated metamorphic (possibly marble or quartzite) No: Go to Step 3.
3. Are all of the crystals in a mixed "salt-and-pepper" pattern?	Yes: intrusive igneous (possibly granite or diorite) No: foliated metamorphic (possibly schist or gneiss)
4. Does the rock contain many small holes or have a uniform dark appearance?	Yes: extrusive igneous (possibly pumice or basalt) No: Go to Step 5.
5. Is the rock glassy, like broken black or brown glass?	Yes: extrusive igneous (obsidian) No: Go to Step 6.
6. Is the rock made of strong, flat sheets that can be split in layers?	Yes: foliated metamorphic (slate) No: Go to Step 7.
7. Does the rock contain pebbles, sand, or smaller particles cemented together?	Yes: clastic sedimentary (possibly conglomerate or sandstone) No: Go to Step 8.
8. Does the rock fizz when dilute HCl is added to it?	Yes: chemical or organic sedimentary (limestone or chalk) No: Ask your teacher for help.

Note: Answer Question 8 by placing the rock on a paper towel, then placing a single drop of HCl on the rock. **CAUTION:** *Wear safety goggles and disposable gloves when using the HCl.*

Name ______________ Class ______________ Date ______________

Observations

Letter of Sample	Route Taken	Identity of Rock Sample

Name ______________________ Class ______________ Date ____________

Analysis and Conclusions

1. **Evaluating and Revising** How difficult was it to use the key to identify your rock samples? What problems did you encounter?

2. **Evaluating and Revising** For each sample that you incorrectly identified, retrace the route you took through the key. Do you need to correct your route? If so, write it below. If not, why might you have incorrectly identified the sample?

3. **Generalizing** How helpful is a rock's color in identifying the rock? Explain your answer.

Name ______________________ Class ______________ Date ____________

4. Comparing and Contrasting Which two of the rock samples were the easiest to identify? What properties made them easy to identify?

Go Further

Collect several rock samples from the area around your home or school and attempt to identify them by using the key in this investigation.

Name ______________________ Class __________________ Date ____________

Recovering Oil

Background Information

Crude oil, or petroleum, is usually found beneath nonporous rock in underground deposits. The petroleum can be recovered by a well pipe lowered to the deposit through a drilled hole. In some cases, the petroleum is automatically pushed up by the pressure of underground water. In other cases, however, pressure must be applied by methods involving pumping water into the petroleum deposit. This method works because petroleum is less dense than water and so will float on top of it.

In this investigation, you will use various methods to recover the maximum amount of oil from a pump bottle.

Problem

How does water affect the recovery of oil from a petroleum deposit?

Pre-Lab Discussion

Read the entire investigation. Then, work with a partner to answer the following questions.

1. **Predicting** What do you expect to happen when you add water to the bottle after the first attempt to remove the oil has been made? Do you expect more oil to be brought up after adding cold water or hot water? Explain your answer.

____

____

____

2. **Applying Concepts** Would you expect more oil to be removed by using hot water or cold water? Explain your answer.

____

____

____

____

____

3. **Applying Concepts** How does adding water increase pressure within a petroleum deposit?

____

____

____

____

Name ______________________ Class ________________ Date ____________

4. **Inferring** What properties of oil makes water the preferred substance for pushing oil up to Earth's surface?

____

____

____

____

5. **Controlling Variables** Why must the investigation be repeated with hot water after it has been performed with cold water?

____

____

____

____

____

Materials *(per group)*

plastic bottle with spray pump
plastic tubing to fit the pump nozzle
pebbles (enough to half-fill the plastic bottle)
2 graduated cylinders
200 mL of vegetable or mineral oil
4 250-mL beakers
cold tap water
hot tap water
paper towels
clock or watch

Safety

Be careful to avoid breakage when working with glassware. Use extreme care when working with hot water to avoid burns. Wash your hands thoroughly after carrying out this investigation. Note all safety alert symbols next to the steps in the Procedure and review the meaning of each symbol by referring to the Safety Symbols on page xiii.

Procedure

1. Build a model of an oil pump, as shown in Figure 1. Remove the spray pump top of the spray bottle and half-fill the spray bottle with clean pebbles.

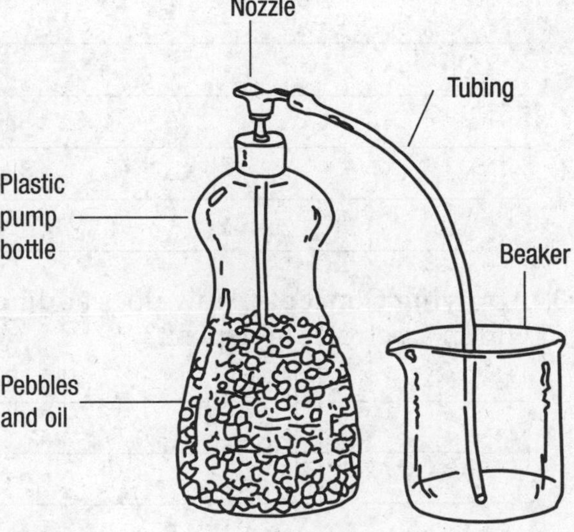

Figure 1

2. Use a graduated cylinder to measure 100 mL of vegetable or mineral oil and pour the oil into the bottle. **CAUTION:** *Be careful to avoid breakage when working with glassware. Be careful not to spill any oil onto your clothing. Immediately wipe up any spilled water or oil.*
3. Place the spray-pump top back onto the bottle while working its tube down through the pebbles. Attach the plastic tubing to the nozzle and place the other end of the tubing into a 250-mL beaker.
4. Use the spray pump to remove as much oil as you can from the bottle within 5 minutes. Use the graduated cylinder to measure the amount of oil removed. Record this information in the data table.
5. Measure 80 mL of cold tap water in the second graduated cylinder and add this water to the spray bottle. Attempt to pump as much liquid as possible into the second beaker within 5 minutes. Let the mixture stand for 1 or 2 minutes so that the oil and water separate. Carefully pour into the first graduated cylinder the oil layer that is on top of the water in the beaker. Record in the data table how much oil you collected.
6. Rinse the bottle and pebbles with hot water to remove any excess oil and wipe them dry with paper towels. Place the used oil in a container designated by your teacher. Clean the first graduated cylinder and add 100 mL of fresh oil.
7. Repeat Steps 1 through 5, but in Step 5, use 80 mL of hot tap water instead of cold water. Record in the data table the amount of oil collected. Place the used oil in a container designated by your teacher. The water with traces of oil can be poured down the sink. **CAUTION:** *Use extreme care when working with hot water to avoid burns. Wash your hands thoroughly after carrying out this investigation.*

Observations

DATA TABLE

	Oil Added to Bottle (mL)	Oil Removed Before Adding Water (mL)	Oil Removed After Adding Water (mL)
Cold water			
Hot water			

Analysis and Conclusions

1. **Analyzing Data** How did your results compare with your prediction?

2. **Observing** Why were you unable to remove all the oil from the bottle when you pumped it in Step 4?

3. **Applying Concepts** Explain the effect of adding cold water.

4. **Applying Concepts** Explain the effect of adding hot water.

Go Further

Repeat the investigation, using different kinds of oil to determine how the density and thickness, or viscosity, of the oil affects recovery. Show your plan to your teacher. When your teacher approves your plan, carry out your experiment and report your results.

Using a Contour Map to Create a Landform

Background Information

Water is responsible for shaping much of Earth. For example, the southeastern part of the United States is part of a coastal plain that was deposited by water. The coastal plain is a flat, fertile plain that gently slopes down to the coast from the mountains farther inland. Much of the coastal plain is underlain with limestone and other water-deposited rocks. The surface soil tends to be chiefly sand or clay. These conditions produce a somewhat flat landscape except where interrupted by unusual rock formations, tectonic uplift, or depressions such as **sinkholes.**

One of the tools that scientists use to study the landscape and its history is a contour map. Contour maps are also called topographic maps. The high and low elevations created by mountains, hills, and valleys cannot be observed on a typical map. Contour maps show differences in elevation, or height above sea level, and outline the shapes, or contours, of the landscape by using contour lines. A contour line connects the points on a map that have the same elevation. The contour interval is the difference in elevation between one contour line and the next contour line.

In this investigation, you will interpret the contour lines of a topographic map and use them to create a three-dimensional model, or landform, of the region shown on the map.

Problem

How can you use a contour map to create a landform?

Pre-Lab Discussion

Read the entire investigation. Then, work with a partner to answer the following questions.

1. **Using Models** What is the advantage of creating a landform from a topographic map?

____

____

____

____

____

____

____

____

Name ______________________ Class ____________________ Date ____________

2. **Applying Concepts** Why does the land vary so much throughout the United States?

3. **Applying Concepts** How does a topographic map illustrate the elevation of the land?

4. **Applying Concepts** What do all contour intervals on a single topographic map have in common? Why is this done?

5. **Using Models** What do narrow contour intervals indicate? What do wide contour intervals indicate? Explain your answers.

Name ______________________ Class __________________ Date ____________

Materials *(per group)*

transparent plastic box with lid
nonpermanent marking pen
enlarged photocopy of a regional contour map
modeling clay
meter ruler

Procedure

1. Place the contour map provided by your teacher inside the lid of the plastic box so that the map can be seen through the top side of the lid. Secure the map to the lid by using small pieces of masking tape near the corners. Using a nonpermanent marking pen, trace the contour map onto the box lid. Then, remove the contour map from the lid.
2. Using the marking pen and a ruler, make a centimeter scale on one of the vertical sides of the transparent box. Start by making a mark at the bottom edge of the box. Then, continue to make marks at centimeter intervals upward along the side of the box until you reach the top of the box, as in Figure 1.
3. Find the lowest elevation on the regional contour map. Write this elevation next to the bottom edge of the box.
4. Find the contour interval for your regional map. Each centimeter mark on the side of the box will represent the same vertical distance as the contour interval. Next to each cm mark, write the elevation in meters.
5. Using modeling clay, construct the first layer of the landform shown in your regional contour map. Start at the lowest elevation and work your way up to the next contour interval.
6. When you have finished the first layer of the landform, check it for accuracy. Do this by placing the lid with the contour map on top of the box. Looking down through the lid, compare the landform with the corresponding contour lines shown on the map, as in Figure 2.
7. Repeat Steps 5 and 6 for each layer of the landform until all of the contour lines of the map have a corresponding level on the landform.

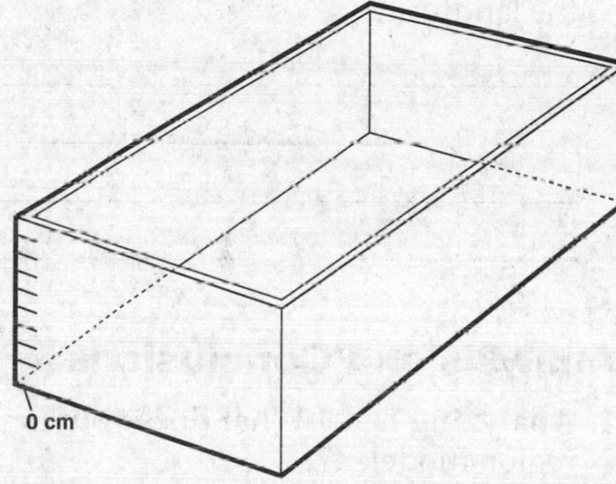

Figure 1

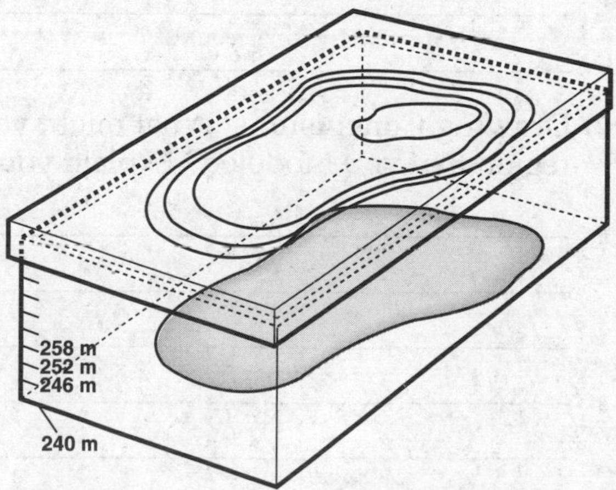

Figure 2

Name ______________________ Class ______________ Date ____________

Observations

1. Describe the shape of the landform you made.

2. How many meters above sea level is the base of the landform?

3. What is the contour interval of the contour map you used to make the landform?

Analysis and Conclusions

1. **Analyzing Data** What does your landform indicate about the region modeled?

2. **Drawing Conclusions** What might you conclude about the type of region that you modeled? Explain your answer.

Name ______________________ Class ______________ Date __________

3. **Using Models** Look at the contour maps in Figure 3. How does the feature in the map for the Southwest differ from the features depicted in the other maps?

4. **Inferring** Compare the contour map for the Southeast with the contour map for the Southwest. Do you think the feature in the map for the Southwest was also formed by water? Explain your answer.

Go Further

Repeat the investigation, using one of the two other maps shown in Figure 3 or find a contour map of a different region and model it with a landform. Be sure to choose a region that does not cover too large an area or does not have too great an elevation change so that your landform will still be reasonably accurate. First, show your selected map to your teacher. When your teacher approves your plan, carry out the investigation.

Southwest—Grand Canyon, Arizona
Contour interval: 50 meters

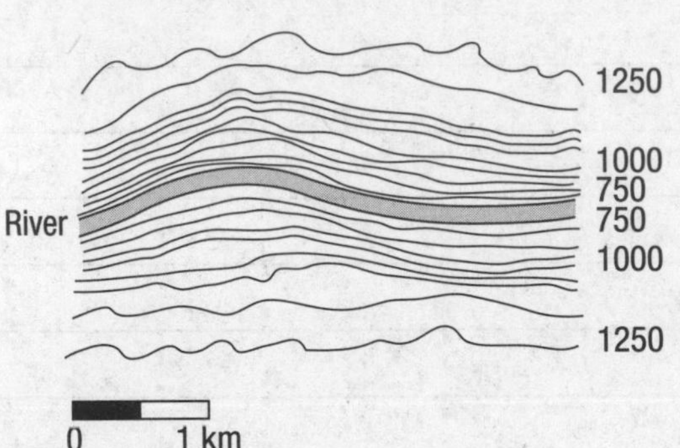

Northeast—Vermont
Contour interval: 30 meters

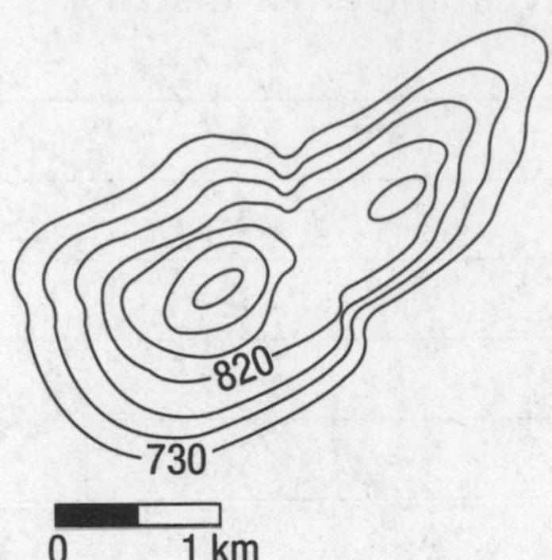

N
W E
S

Southeast—Florida
Contour interval: 3 meters

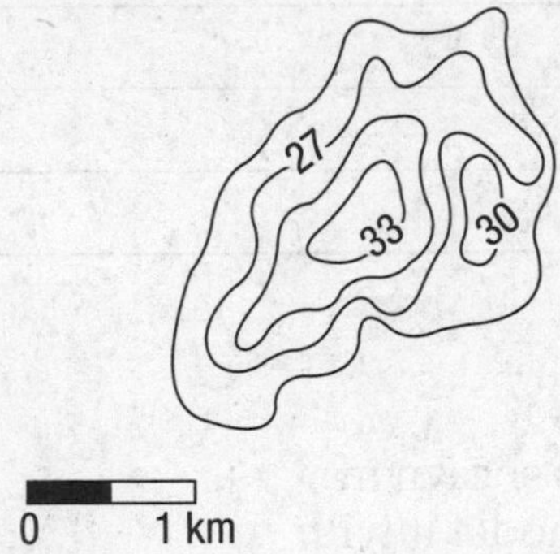

Midwest—Wisconsin
Contour interval: 6 meters

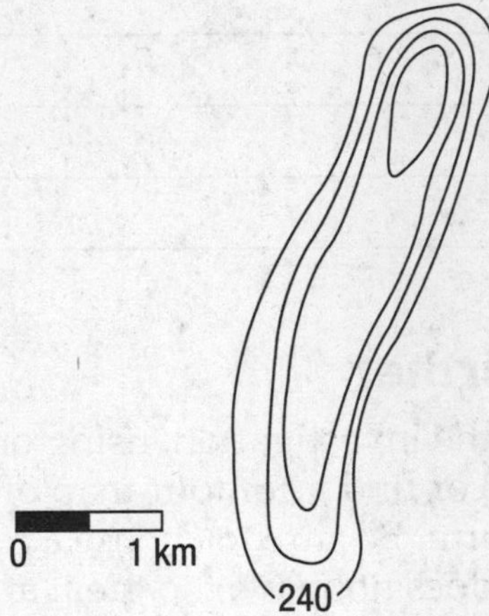

Figure 3

Name ______________________ Class ________________ Date __________

Beach Erosion

Background Information

Ocean waves are examples of kinetic energy transferred through the medium of water. If ocean waves hit a beach at an angle, some of their kinetic energy is transferred to sand and pebbles, causing them to move. Some of the energy is reflected back through the water at right angles to the incoming waves, and some energy is dissipated by heat because of friction.

The kinetic energy transferred to the rocks and sand on the shore causes them to move not in the direction of either the incoming or reflected waves, but in a direction perpendicular to the shore. This is part of the process called **longshore drift.** Sand and small rocks move away from the shore at right angles to the shore as they obtain kinetic energy from the waves. Eventually, the sand and rocks are far from the shore, and so the incoming waves they encounter simply push them along in the direction of the wave. This direction is back toward the shore, but further along than where the rocks and sand originally were. Once they reach a new location on the shore, the rocks and sand once again move away from the shore at right angles. This cycle is repeated so that over time, the sand and small rocks on a beach can move long distances along the shore.

In this investigation, you will create a shoreline model with a beach and rocks. By simulating ocean waves, you will observe how the sand and rocks are moved by the energy from the waves.

Problem

How does the energy in ocean waves affect the material on the shore?

Pre-Lab Discussion

Read the entire investigation. Then, work with a partner to answer the following questions.

1. **Applying Concepts** What happens to the kinetic energy of a wave as the wave comes ashore?

____

____

____

____

2. **Inferring** From your answer to Question 1, what can you infer about the amount of kinetic energy of the waves reflected from the shore compared to the amount of kinetic energy of the incoming waves?

____

____

Name ______________________ Class ______________ Date __________

3. **Controlling Variables** What are the manipulated and responding variables in this investigation?

____

____

____

4. **Controlling Variables** What variables must be kept constant in this investigation so that the results will be meaningful?

____

____

____

____

5. **Predicting** If you perform this investigation long enough, what do you expect will happen?

____

____

____

Materials *(per group)*

large rectangular aluminum baking dish
fine sand
5 very small pebbles, each about 1 cm in diameter
clock or watch
water
ruler or flat stick 10–12 cm long
newspaper

Safety

Put on safety goggles and a lab apron. Note all safety alert symbols next to the steps in the Procedure and review the meaning of each symbol by referring to the Safety Symbols on page xiii.

Procedure

1. Mix the sand with a little water so that it will hold its shape. Use the sand to create a shoreline along one side of the baking dish. Make the sand deeper along the edge of the pan and taper it, as shown in the side view in Figure 1.

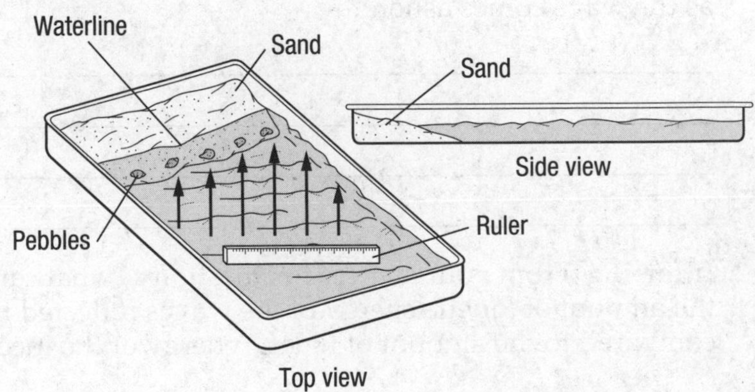

Figure 1

2. Place the dish on a sheet of newspaper so that any water that is spilled over the sides will be absorbed. Add water to the dish very slowly so that you do not disturb the sand. Leave 4 or 5 cm of beach above the water line. **CAUTION:** *Wipe up any spilled liquids immediately to avoid slips and falls.*
3. Place a small pebble every few centimeters along the simulated beach.
4. Set the ruler on edge in the water, as shown in Figure 1. Gently rock the top edge of the ruler back and forth to create waves. Try to keep the intensity with which you rock the ruler steady and uniform so that the waves are nearly the same throughout the investigation. Observe the movement of the sand and pebbles. Record your observations.
5. Restore the pebbles and sand to their original positions. Repeat Step 4 for three minutes.

Observations

Analysis and Conclusions

1. **Observing** In what direction did the reflected waves move with respect to the incoming waves? How did the intensity of the reflected waves compare to the intensity of the incoming waves?

Name ______________________ Class ______________ Date ___________

2. **Interpreting Diagrams** The diagram in Figure 2 shows how a pebble on the shore moves as an incoming wave strikes the beach at an angle. Draw the path that the pebble will take as the next three waves hit the beach.

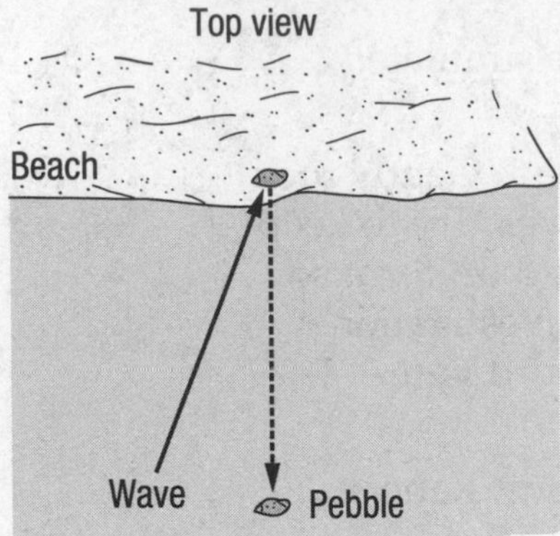

Figure 2

3. **Drawing Conclusions** Based on your investigation, in what direction will beach erosion occur?

____

____

____

____

Go Further

Plan an experiment to show how the angle and intensity of the incoming waves affect longshore drift. Vary the procedure of this investigation accordingly, making sure to account for all controlled, manipulated, and responding variables. Show your plan to your teacher. When your teacher approves your plan, carry out your experiment and report your results.

Recipe for a Cloud

Background Information

The scientific study of clouds was begun in 1803 by Luke Howard, a British meteorologist. However, it was not until the late 1800s that clouds were classified according to their different forms.

Clouds consist of tiny water droplets or ice crystals. These droplets or crystals form when water vapor in the atmosphere condenses. Condensation occurs when air pressure decreases so that the water vapor in the air expands and cools. Therefore, factors such as atmospheric pressure and the relative humidity of the air determine when clouds form and what form they take.

For a cloud to form, there must be a surface of some kind for water vapor to condense on, and so form the small water droplets or (if it is cold enough) ice crystals that make up the cloud. In most cases, small particles of dust provide the surfaces for such condensation. By artificially adding small particles, such as salt or dry ice crystals, to clouds at certain temperatures, condensation can be stimulated, causing rain. Such a process is called cloud seeding.

In this investigation, you will examine how the temperature and humidity of air, as well as the presence or absence of tiny particles in the air, affects the formation of cloud droplets.

Problem

Under what basic conditions do clouds form?

Pre-Lab Discussion

Read the entire investigation. Then, work with a partner to answer the following questions.

1. **Formulating Hypotheses** Write a hypothesis about how you expect pressure, humidity, and the presence of tiny particles in the air to affect cloud formation.

____

____

____

2. **Designing Experiments** Why is it important to this investigation to use a container in which the pressure can be easily and significantly changed?

____

____

____

3. **Controlled Variables** For the first half of the investigation, in which cold water is used, what are the manipulated and controlled variables?

4. **Controlled Variables** What controlled variable is changed in the second half of the investigation, in which hot water is used?

5. **Predicting** Do you expect to observe cloud formation before smoke is added to the container or after it is added? Explain your answer.

Materials *(per group)*

graduated cylinder
gallon glass pickle jar
plastic freezer storage bag (26 cm × 26 cm)
rubber band (15 cm circumference; 0.5 cm width)
cold tap water
hot tap water
safety matches

Safety

Put on safety goggles. Be careful to avoid breakage when working with glassware. Be careful when using matches. Do not reach over an open flame. Tie back loose hair and clothing when working with flames. Note all safety alert symbols next to the steps in the Procedure and review the meaning of each symbol by referring to the Safety Symbols on page xiii.

Procedure

1. Use the graduated cylinder to measure 40 mL of cold water. Pour the water into the jar. Place the plastic bag into the jar so that the top edges of the bag lie just outside the rim of the jar, as shown in Figure 1. **CAUTION:** *Wipe up any spilled liquids immediately to avoid slips and falls.*

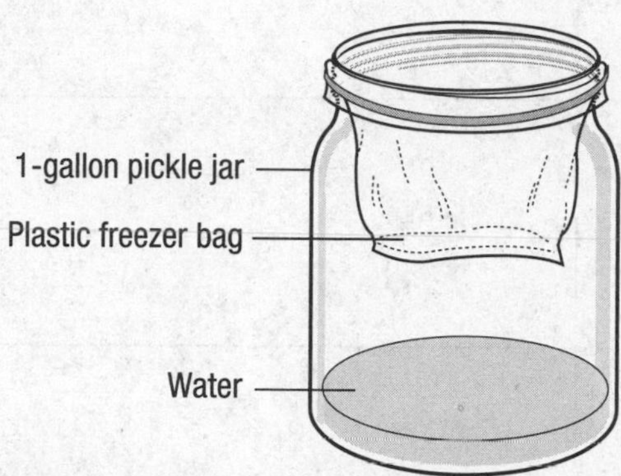

Figure 1

2. Secure the top of the bag to the outer rim of the jar using the rubber band, as shown in Figure 2.

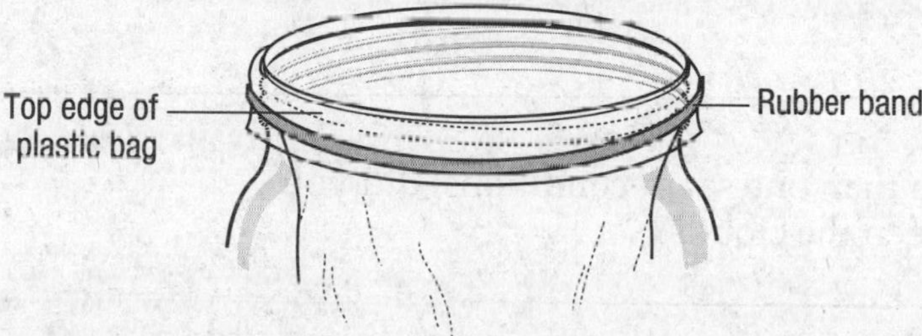

Figure 2

3. Place your hand inside the bag, grab the bag's bottom edge, and rapidly pull the bag out of the jar. Observe the inside of the jar while pulling the bag out. Record your observations in the data table provided on the following page.
4. Remove the rubber band and plastic bag. Light a match, allow it to burn for about 3 seconds, then drop the match into the jar. Quickly place the plastic bag inside the jar, again securing its top edge around the rim of the jar with the rubber band.
5. Repeat Step 3. Again, observe the inside of the jar as you pull the bag rapidly out of the jar. Record your observations in the data table.
6. Remove the plastic bag and rinse out the bottle. Throw away the burnt match as directed by your teacher.
7. Repeat Steps 1 through 6, this time using 40 mL of hot tap water. **CAUTION:** *Be careful not to burn yourself when using hot water.*

Name ______________________ Class ______________ Date __________

Observations

DATA TABLE

Water Type	Smoke	Cloud Formation
Cold	Absent	
Cold	Present	
Hot	Absent	
Hot	Present	

If clouds formed under more than one set of conditions, did you observe any difference between the clouds?

____

____

____

____

____

____

Analysis and Conclusions

1. **Inferring** What effect did pulling the plastic bag out of the jar have on the water vapor inside the jar?

____

____

____

____

____

2. **Drawing Conclusions** What conditions proved most important for forming clouds?

3. **Drawing Conclusions** Did your results support or contradict your hypothesis? Explain your answer.

4. **Designing Experiments** What improvements could you make to the apparatus to provide quantitative information?

5. **Using Models** Relate each ingredient in your cloud-making procedure to the process of making clouds in nature.

6. **Making Generalizations** A topic of discussion in astronomy is terraforming, the process by which other planets can be modified so that their climates are like those on Earth. One important feature of terraforming is starting and maintaining a water cycle in the planet's atmosphere. What conditions would be necessary for rain to be stimulated and maintained on a terraformed planet?

Go Further

Plan an investigation to determine the way that different changes in pressure and different particles sources may affect cloud formation. You can plan your design, using the same equipment used in the investigation or using some or all of the improvements listed in your answer to Question 4 of Analysis and Conclusions. Identify which variables are to be manipulated and which are to be controlled throughout the investigation. Show your plan to your teacher. When your teacher approves your plan, carry out your experiment and report your results and conclusions.

Modeling Global Warming

Background Information

Some atmospheric gases keep Earth much warmer than it would be otherwise. Energy from the sun is transferred to Earth through radiation and is absorbed by the surface of Earth. Then, some of this energy is transferred back toward space through the process of radiation. Carbon dioxide, water vapor, and other gases in the atmosphere absorb some of this radiated energy, making the atmosphere warmer. The warm atmosphere re-radiates this energy, some of which is directed back toward Earth's surface. This entire process is called the greenhouse effect.

In this investigation, you will describe how carbon dioxide affects the temperature of the atmosphere. You will also understand more about the process that results in the greenhouse effect.

Problem

Does carbon dioxide really affect the atmosphere's temperature?

Pre-Lab Discussion

Read the entire investigation. Then, work with a partner to answer the following questions.

1. **Posing Questions** Write a question that summarizes the purpose of this investigation.

____

____

____

2. **Controlling Variables** What is the manipulated variable in this investigation?

____

____

____

____

3. **Controlling Variables** What are the controlled variables in this investigation?

____

____

____

____

4. Controlling Variables What is the responding variable in this investigation?

____

____

____

____

____

____

5. Predicting Predict the outcome of this investigation.

____

____

____

____

____

____

Materials *(per group)*

2 clear 2-L plastic bottles

2 one-hole rubber stoppers with a Celsius non-mercury thermometer inserted into each

funnel

plastic spoon

baking soda

vinegar

25-mL graduated cylinder

bright incandescent lamp or flood lamp

Safety

Put on safety goggles and a lab apron. Be careful to avoid breakage when working with glassware. Use extreme care when working with heated equipment or materials to avoid burns. Observe proper laboratory procedures when using electrical equipment. Note all safety alert symbols next to the steps in the Procedure and review the meaning of each symbol by referring to the Safety Symbols on page xiii.

Procedure

1. Fill a bottle with carbon dioxide by adding baking soda and vinegar to the bottle. **CAUTION:** *Leave the bottle open until the bubbling stops.*

Name ______________ Class ______________ Date ______________

2. Put a one-hole stopper containing a thermometer in the bottle of carbon dioxide. Put the other stopper with its thermometer in the bottle of air. In the data table, record the initial temperature for each bottle.

3. Shine a lamp on both bottles at the same angle from a distance of 30 cm. In the data table, record the temperature of each bottle every two minutes for 20 minutes. **CAUTION:** *Lamps can get very hot. Be sure not to come too close to the lamps when they are in use.*

Observations

DATA TABLE

Elapsed Time (minutes)	Temperature in Bottle With Air (°C)	Temperature in Bottle With Carbon Dioxide (°C)
0		
2		
4		
6		
8		
10		
12		
14		
16		
18		
20		

Name ______________________ Class ________________ Date ____________

Analysis and Conclusions

1. **Comparing and Contrasting** What was the difference in the temperatures of the two bottles at the end of the experiment?

2. **Inferring** What can you infer about how carbon dioxide affects air temperature?

3. **Drawing Conclusions** What do your observations suggest about the effect of carbon dioxide on global warming?

4. **Applying Concepts** How do you think your conclusions for this investigation could be applied to situations that you observe in your everyday life?

Go Further

Conduct this investigation on a larger scale. Set up terrariums next to sunlit windows in two large, clear, wide-mouth bottles. Place plants in only one of the terrariums. Record the temperature of each terrarium at the same time of day over several days. Write a report of your observations and your conclusions based on your analysis of the data.

Deflecting an Asteroid

Background Information

Although asteroids and comets often have well-defined orbits, these orbits can be disturbed by the gravitational forces of massive bodies that the asteroids or comets encounter. Such gravitational disturbances, or perturbations, cause the asteroid or comet to change direction and follow a new orbital path.

The perturbation of an asteroid or comet depends on its speed and how close it approaches the more massive body. Sometimes the perturbations are strong enough that the asteroid or comet is captured by the more massive body. In these cases, the asteroid or comet orbits or collides with the larger object.

In this investigation, you will simulate the perturbation of an asteroid's motion by observing how a magnet deflects a steel ball bearing from its path.

Problem

How does the amount an object is deflected from its path depend on its speed and its distance from a perturbing force?

Pre-Lab Discussion

Read the entire investigation. Then, work with a partner to answer the following questions.

1. **Formulating Hypotheses** Write a hypothesis about how you expect the speed of the ball bearing and the distance of the magnet from the ball bearing's path to affect the deflection of the ball bearing.

____

____

____

____

____

____

____

2. **Using Models** What force is being modeled in this investigation by the magnet?

____

____

____

____

3. **Controlling Variables** What are the manipulated and controlled variables in this investigation?

4. **Controlling Variables** What is the responding variable in this investigation?

5. **Predicting** Assuming that all other conditions are the same, how would placing the magnet near the target produce different results from placing it near the end of the tube? Explain your answer.

Materials *(per group)*

cardboard tube, 30 cm long
steel ball bearing, 1.5 cm in diameter
magnet (preferably a strong alnico or rare-earth type)
3 books, each about 3 cm thick
wooden block, at least 6 cm long on each side
meter stick
paper strip, 60 cm × 4 cm
masking tape
pencil

Name ______________________ Class ________________ Date ____________

Procedure

1. Set up the materials, as shown in Figure 1. Center the block (target) in the middle of the paper strip and tape the edges of the strip to the table surface.

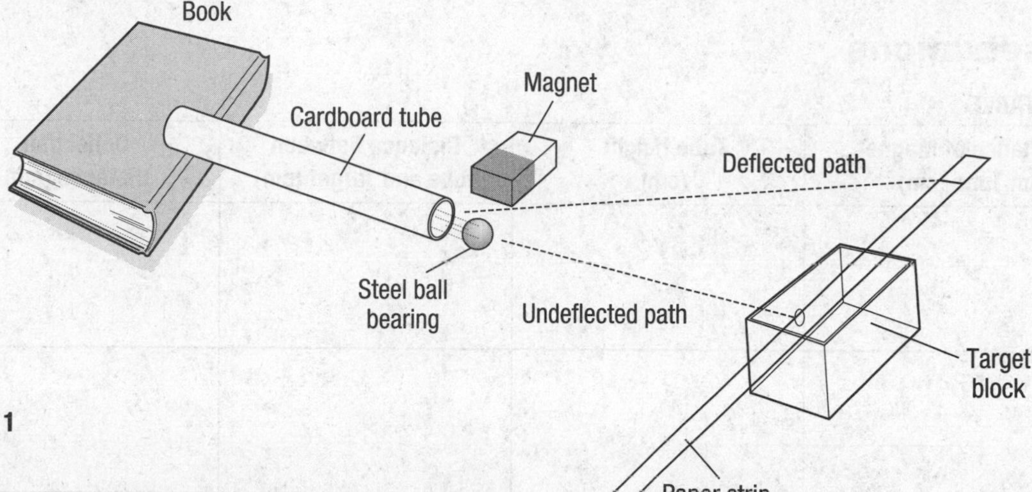

Figure 1

2. Place the cardboard tube so that one end is supported on the top edge of one of the books and the other end is on the table. The target block should be in a direct line with the tube so that a ball bearing rolled down the tube will strike the center of the block, as shown by the undeflected path in Figure 1.
3. The distance from the end of the cardboard tube to the target block should be between 50 and 75 cm. Measure the actual distance and record the value in the data table.
4. Measure the height of the tube above the table (that is, the thickness of the book). Record the value in the data table.
5. Place the magnet 6 cm to the side of the lower end of the cardboard tube. Roll the ball bearing down the tube and observe how it deviates from the straight path it followed before the magnet was introduced. Adjust the position of the magnet so that the ball bearing is deflected enough to miss the target. (*Hint:* Depending on how strong the magnet is, you may have to try positioning the magnet farther or closer to the side of the tube so as to keep the ball bearing from attaching itself to the magnet or from not causing any deflection at all).
6. Repeat the trial, marking on the paper strip the point where the ball bearing crosses the strip. Measure the distance from the center of the block to the mark and record the value in the data table.
7. Place a second book on top of the first book, measure the tube height, and record the value in the data table. Repeat Step 6 and record your observations in the data table.
8. Place a third book on top of the first two books, measure the tube height, and record the value in the data table. Repeat Step 6 and record your observations in the data table.

Name ______________________ Class ______________ Date ____________

9. Repeat Steps 6 through 8, after halving the distance between the magnet and the end of the tube. Record your observations in the data table.
10. Repeat Steps 6 through 8, placing the magnet against the end of the tube. Record your observations in the data table.

Observations

DATA TABLE

Distance of Magnet From Tube (cm)	Tube Height (cm)	Distance Between Tube and Target (cm)	Deflection Distance (cm)

Name ____________ Class ____________ Date ____________

Analysis and Conclusions

1. **Observing** What effect did raising the height of the tube have on the deflection of the ball bearing?

2. **Applying Concepts** How does the speed of the ball bearing relate to the amount of deflection? Explain your answer.

3. **Observing** What effect did moving the magnet closer to the opening of the tube have on the deflection of the ball bearing?

4. **Drawing Conclusions** Did your results support or contradict your hypothesis? Explain your answer.

5. **Designing Experiments** How might you redesign the experiment so that the deflecting force was provided by gravity instead of by magnetism?

6. **Designing Experiments** How would the design improvement you have suggested in Question 5 allow you to test spherical objects with different masses?

7. **Inferring** From you observations, infer why a small gravitational force could cause an asteroid to travel far off course as it moves through the solar system.

8. **Inferring** A concern about asteroids is that they might collide with Earth, causing tremendous destruction. Why is this concern greater for asteroids moving at high speeds than for those moving at lower speeds?

Go Further

Design an experiment to determine how the mass of an asteroid affects the deflection by a given force. Your plan can use the same materials used in this investigation or some or all of the improvements you suggested in Question 5. Specify which variables are to be manipulated and which need to be controlled throughout the experiment. Submit your procedure and design to your teacher for approval before conducting your experiment. Record your observations and report your results.

Exploring Orbits

Background Information

All bodies that move in closed orbits around the sun follow a path described by an **ellipse.** An ellipse is an oval-shaped figure that is characterized by two quantities. The first of these quantities is the width of the ellipse, which is called the major axis.

Along the major axis and on either side of the center of the ellipse are two points called the foci. For elliptical orbits, the sun is at one focus. The distance between the foci is called the focal length of the ellipse, as shown below. This distance determines the eccentricity of the ellipse. Eccentricity is an indicator of how elongated an ellipse is. Ellipses can be very elongated, or they can be nearly circular. The planets of the solar system have orbits with different major axes and eccentricities.

In this investigation, you will draw some elliptical shapes, calculate the eccentricity of these ellipses, and compare them to the orbital eccentricities of Earth and other planets in the solar system.

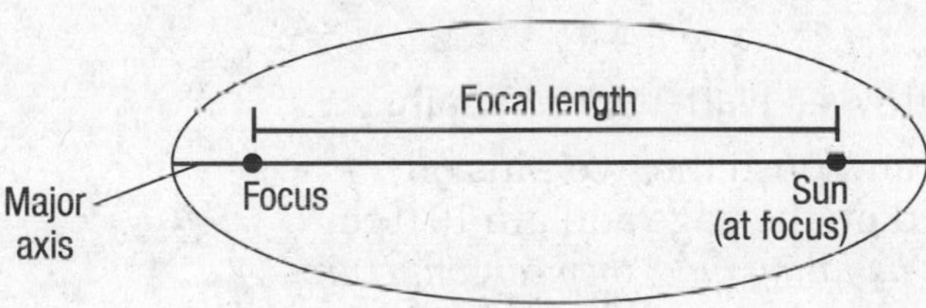

Problem

What do the elliptical orbits of the planets look like?

Pre-Lab Discussion

Read the entire investigation. Then, work with a partner to answer the following questions.

1. **Predicting** Predict the shapes of the planets' orbits (more circular or more flattened).

____

2. **Applying Concepts** What is the one thing that the elliptical orbits of all planets, asteroids, and most comets have in common?

____

3. **Controlling Variables** What is the manipulated variable for the various ellipses drawn?

____

4. **Controlling Variables** What are the responding variables for the various ellipses drawn?

____

5. **Designing Experiments** What purpose do the two pushpins serve in this investigation?

____

Materials *(per group)*

3 sheets of paper
heavy corrugated cardboard
2 pushpins
metric ruler
string, 30 cm in length
colored pencils
tape
calculator

Safety

Be careful when handling sharp instruments. Note all safety alert symbols next to the steps in the Procedure and review the meaning of each symbol by referring to the Safety Symbols on page xiii.

Procedure

1. Fold a sheet of paper in half lengthwise. Flatten it out again.
2. Place the paper on the cardboard and push the two pins on the crease so that they are centered on the page and are 10.0 cm apart. **CAUTION:** *Be careful when handling pins; they can puncture skin.* (*Hint:* As the focal length for ellipses in this investigation becomes smaller, you may have to tape additional sheets of paper above and below to show the entire ellipse).
3. Label one of the pushpins as the sun.
4. Take the string, tie it in a loop, and place it around the pins. Using one of the colored pencils, gently pull the string taut. Keep the string taut without pulling the pins out of the cardboard and carefully drag the pencil around the pins to draw an ellipse, as shown in Figure 1.
5. Remove the pin that is not labeled as the sun. In its place, draw a noticeable dot the same color as the ellipse.
6. Use the metric ruler to measure the length of the major axis and focal length. Record these values in the data table.
7. Reposition the second pin so that it is now 8.0 cm from the other pin. Repeat Steps 4 through 6, using a different colored pencil.

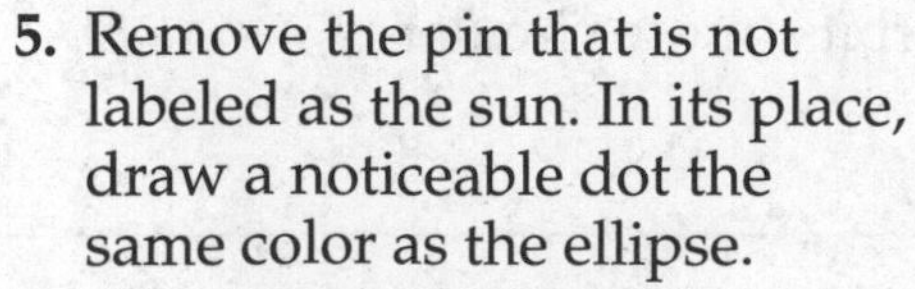

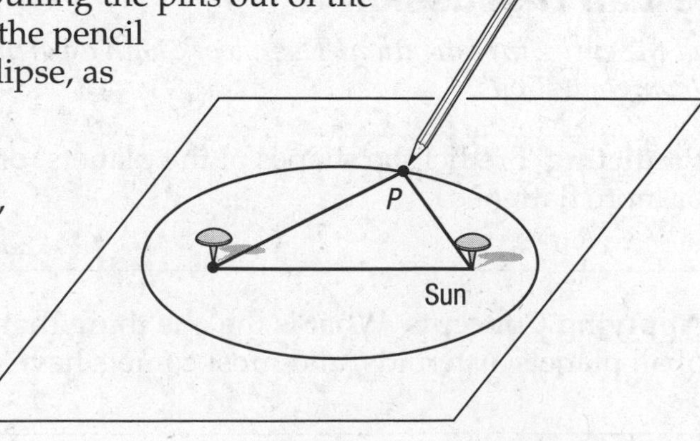

Figure 1

8. Repeat Step 7, using distances of 6.0 cm, 4.0 cm, and 2.0 cm between the pins.
9. The eccentricity for each ellipse is calculated by dividing the focal length by the length of the major axis:

$$\text{Eccentricity} = \frac{\text{Focal length}}{\text{Major axis}}$$

Calculate the eccentricity for each ellipse and record the values in the data table.
10. Label each ellipse on your diagram with its matching eccentricity.

Observations

DATA TABLE

Ellipse (color)	Major Axis (cm)	Focal Length (cm)	Eccentricity

Name ____________________ Class ______________ Date __________

Analysis and Conclusions

1. **Drawing Conclusions** Did the investigation results confirm your prediction? Explain why or why not.

2. **Compare and Contrast** Compare the following values for planetary eccentricities to those you calculated for your ellipses. What can you state about the orbits of the various planets?

Planet	Eccentricity
Mercury	0.206
Venus	0.007
Earth	0.017
Mars	0.093
Jupiter	0.048
Saturn	0.056
Uranus	0.047
Neptune	0.009
Pluto	0.250

Go Further

Research the orbits of various smaller bodies in the solar system, such as asteroids or comets. Use the materials from this investigation and researched values for the major axis and eccentricity to produce drawings of these objects' orbits. Include in your report all values used and your drawings.

Measuring the Diameter of the Sun

Background Information

The sun is approximately 150,000,000 km from Earth. To understand how far away this is, consider the fact that light travels approximately 300,000 km/s. At this incredible speed, it takes the light from the sun a little over 8 minutes to reach Earth.

Even though the sun is very far away, it is still possible to make an accurate measurement of its size. This can be done by making two simple measurements and then setting up and solving a proportion problem. You can estimate the diameter of the sun by solving the following proportion problem.

$$\frac{\text{Diameter of sun}}{\text{Distance to sun}} = \frac{\text{Diameter of sun's image}}{\text{Distance between two cards}}$$

If you can determine three of the terms in a proportion problem, the fourth term, such as the diameter of the sun, can be solved mathematically.

In this investigation, you will construct a simple device and use it to collect data that will enable you to calculate the diameter of the sun.

Problem

What is the diameter of the sun, and how can it be determined?

Pre-Lab Discussion

Read the entire investigation. Then, work with a partner to answer the following questions.

1. **Inferring** What is the purpose of this investigation?

____

____

____

2. **Calculating** To prepare for this calculation, solve for x in the following proportion problems.

   a. $\frac{x}{5} = \frac{100,000}{20}$

   ____

   ____

   b. $\frac{5}{x} = \frac{200,000}{50}$

   ____

   ____

Name ______________________ Class __________________ Date ____________

3. **Inferring** Why is it important to never look directly at the sun?

____

____

____

4. **Applying Concepts** In what way is the process of proportional relationships practical for determining the diameter of the sun?

____

____

____

5. **Predicting** Would you expect error in the value you calculate for the sun's diameter? Explain your answer.

____

____

Materials *(per group)*

2 index cards (10 cm × 15 cm)
drawing compass
meter stick
metric ruler
tape

Safety

Be careful when handling sharp instruments. Never look directly at the sun. Note all safety symbols next to the steps in the Procedure and review the meaning of each symbol by referring to the Safety Symbols on page xiii.

Procedure

Part A: Measuring Distances and Calculating Ratios

1. In Figure 1, measure the base of each of the two triangles. Record your measurements in Data Table 1.
2. Measure the altitude (distance from tip to base) of each of the two triangles. Record your measurements in Data Table 1.
3. Determine the ratio between the base of the large triangle and the base of the small triangle. Record this ratio in Data Table 1.
4. Determine the ratio between the altitude of the large triangle and the altitude of the small triangle. Record this ratio in Data Table 1.
5. Think about how these two ratios compare. In Part B of this lab, you will use a similar procedure to determine the diameter of the sun. The base of the small triangle will represent the diameter of the image of the sun on a card. The altitude of the small triangle will represent the distance between the two cards

Name ______________________ Class ______________ Date __________

in the device you will construct. The altitude of the large triangle will represent the distance from Earth to the sun. The base of the large triangle will represent the diameter of the sun, which you will determine. **CAUTION:** *Never look directly at the sun.*

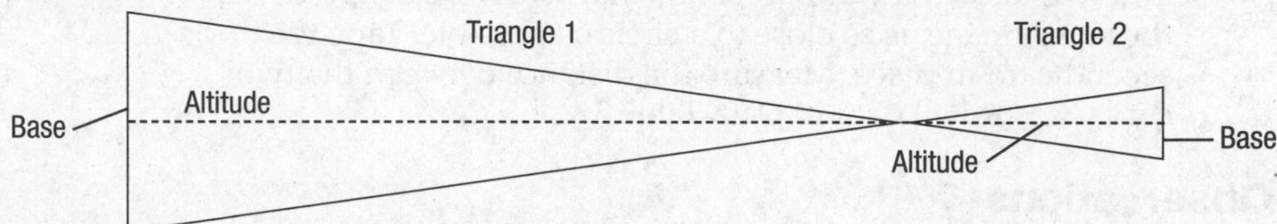

Figure 1

Part B: Determining the Diameter of the Sun

6. Using scissors, cut I-shaped slits in each card in the positions shown in Figure 2. The meter stick should be able to slide through the slits, but the slits should be small enough so that the meter stick fits snugly. **CAUTION:** *Be careful when handling sharp instruments.*

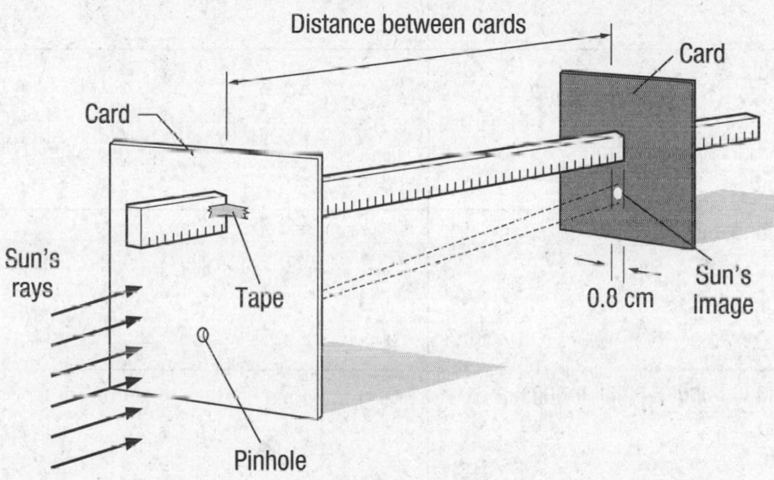

Figure 2

7. With the tip of the compass, punch a pinhole in one of the cards, in the position shown in Figure 2. Tape this card to the meter stick at the 5-cm mark so that it is perpendicular to the meter stick. **CAUTION:** *Be careful when handling sharp instruments.*

8. On the other card, draw two parallel lines exactly 0.8 cm (8 mm) apart, directly above the slit, as shown in Figure 2. Slide this card onto the meter stick. Do not tape this card to the meter stick.

9. While outdoors on a sunny day, position the meter stick so that the taped card is directly facing the sun and casts a shadow over the movable card. **CAUTION:** *Never look directly at the sun.* You should be able to see a bright circle on the movable card caused by the sun's rays passing through the pinhole on the first card.

10. The bright circle on the second card is an image of the sun. Slide the movable card until the image of the sun fits exactly between the two parallel lines you drew earlier.
11. Make sure that both cards are perpendicular to the meter stick. You will know they are perpendicular when the bright circle, the sun's image, is as close to a circle as possible. Tape the second card in place. Measure the distance between the two cards. Record all data in Data Table 2.

Observations

DATA TABLE 1

Base of small triangle (Triangle 1)	
Altitude of small triangle (Triangle 1)	
Base of large triangle (Triangle 2)	
Altitude of large triangle (Triangle 2)	
Ratio of base of large triangle to base of small triangle	
Ratio of altitude of large triangle to altitude of small triangle	

DATA TABLE 2

Distance between two cards (cm)	
Diameter of sun's image (cm)	

Name ______________________ Class ______________________ Date ______________

Analysis and Conclusions

1. **Calculate** Using the formula below, calculate the diameter of the sun. Show your work.

$$\frac{\text{Diameter of sun (km)}}{\text{Distance to sun (km)}} = \frac{\text{Diameter of sun's image (cm)}}{\text{Distance between two cards (cm)}}$$

2. **Calculate** The actual diameter of the sun is 1,391,000 km. Using the formula below, determine the amount of error in your calculated value for the sun's diameter. Show your work.

$$\text{Percentage of error} = \frac{\text{Difference between your value and the correct value}}{\text{Correct value}} \times 100$$

3. **Analyze Data** What could account for your error in calculating the sun's diameter?

____

____

____

____

____

4. **Apply Concepts** How might the technique used in this investigation be useful in making other astronomical measurements?

____

____

____

____

5. **Relate Cause and Effect** How might clouds in the sky affect the accuracy of your measurement in this investigation?

____

____

____

____

____

Name ____________________ Class ________________ Date ____________

Go Further

A sunspot moves along the sun's equator. If the sunspot takes 14 days to move from one side of the sun to the other, calculate how fast the sunspot is moving. Explain why this value is also the speed at which the sun's surface is moving at the equator.

1. Using the actual value for the diameter of the sun and the formula below, calculate the circumference of the sun. The value of p (pi) is approximately 3.14.

$$\text{Circumference} = \pi \times \text{Diameter}$$

2. The sunspot moved only halfway around the sun, so to calculate the distance it traveled in 14 days, divide the value for the circumference by 2.

3. To calculate the distance traveled by the sunspot in one day, divide the distance you calculated in Step 2 by 14.

4. ____

____

____

Modeling Rotation of Neutron Stars

Background Information

Angular momentum measures an object's tendency to continue to spin. If the mass of the spinning object is being pulled closer to the axis of the spin (shrinking in size), then the speed of the spin must increase in order to conserve momentum. For example, when a spinning skater pulls in his arms, he spins faster because his mass is less spread out.

Stars also spin on an axis. When a supergiant with 15 times the sun's mass collapses into a neutron star, much of the star's mass is lost in a supernova explosion. Although the mass decreases somewhat, the diameter of the star drastically decreases. A star that is a supergiant may have a diameter of several million kilometers and may rotate on its axis about once a month. The neutron star into which a supergiant develops may be only a few kilometers across but may rotate thousands of times per second.

In this investigation, you will use a rotating square of cardboard and weights to model the effect of mass distribution on rotation rate.

Problem

Why do neutron stars rotate so rapidly?

Pre-Lab Discussion

Read the entire investigation. Then, work with a partner to answer the following questions.

1. **Inferring** What is the purpose of this investigation?

 ____

 ____

 ____

2. **Observing** After a supergiant becomes a neutron star, what is its size and mass, and what happens to its rotation speed?

 ____

 ____

 ____

3. **Inferring** How will this investigation answer the question of why neutron stars rotate with such great speed?

 ____

 ____

 ____

Name ______________________ Class ________________ Date ____________

4. **Predicting** What would you predict would be the outcome of this investigation?

____

____

Materials *(per group)*

pencil with eraser
square of stiff cardboard, at least 35 cm wide
pushpin
masking tape
2 identical small weights
centimeter ruler
clock or watch with second hand

Safety 

Put on safety goggles. Be careful when handling sharp objects. Make sure that weights stay attached and do not fly off and hit anyone. Note all safety alert symbols next to the steps in the Procedure and review the meaning of each symbol by referring to the Safety Symbols on page xiii.

Procedure

1. Draw lines along the two diagonals of the cardboard square, as shown in Figure 1. Punch a hole through the center of the cardboard with the pushpin. Then, push the pushpin into the eraser end of the pencil. Check that the cardboard is able to spin freely. If it sticks, use the pushpin to widen the hole. **CAUTION:** *Be careful when handling sharp objects.*

2. **Measure** Attach a piece of masking tape to one corner of the square. Then, attach the two weights to the cardboard so that each weight is 30 cm from the center, as shown in Figure 1. The weights should both lie along one of the two diagonals that pass through the center. The card is still balanced because the weights are equidistant from the center.

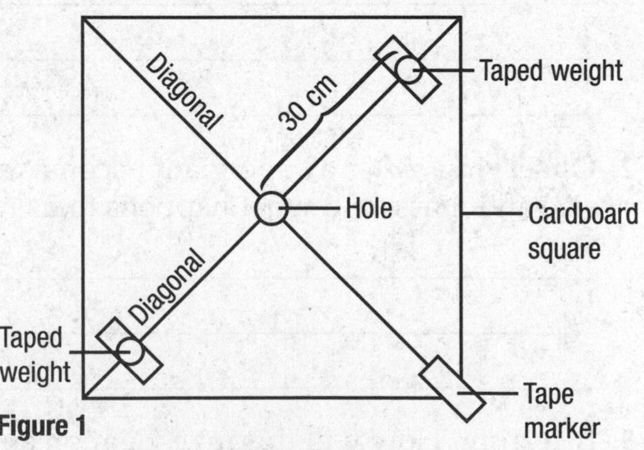

Figure 1

3. Hold the pencil in front of you and perpendicular to your body so that the square of cardboard rotates below eye level and parallel to your body. Try to give each spin of the square the same force. **CAUTION:** *Make sure that weights stay attached and do not fly off and hit anyone.*

4. Spin the square. Watch the taped corner as it goes by and count the number of times it passes in 5 seconds. (If the square slows down during this time, adjust the pushpin so that it turns with less friction. Then, try again.) In Data Table 1, record the number of rotations.
5. Move the weights inward toward the center so that each is 20 cm from the center and tape them down. Spin and count the rotations. Make sure that you apply the same force you did before. In Data Table 1, record the number of rotations.
6. Repeat Step 5, but this time, tape the weights so that each is only 10 cm from the center. In Data Table 1, record the number of rotations.

Observations

DATA TABLE 1

Distance of Weights from Center of Square	Number of Rotations (spins)
30 cm	
20 cm	
10 cm	

Analysis and Conclusions

1. **Calculate** Calculate the rotation rate for each case by dividing the number of spins by 5 seconds.

Name ______________________ Class ________________ Date ____________

2. **Infer** Explain why the rate of rotation of a neutron star is so great compared to that of the star from which it was formed.

____

____

____

____

____

____

3. **Infer** Suggest reasons why this model might not give accurate results.

____

____

Go Further

What happens to the rotation rate when mass decreases? Repeat Step 5 two more times, but for the first repetition, use weights that are about one-half the mass of the initial weights used. For the second repetition, use weights that are one-fourth the mass of the initial weights used. Create a data table in which to record your results.

Name ______________________ Class ________________ Date ____________

Determining the Thickness of Aluminum Foil

Many products such as aluminum foil are too thin to measure easily. However, it is important for manufacturers to know how thick these products are. They wouldn't be useful if they were made too thick or too thin. In this lab, you will use the same method that manufacturers use to determine the thickness of aluminum foil.

Problem How can you determine the thickness of aluminum foil?

Materials

- metric ruler
- aluminum foil
- scissors
- balance
- graph paper

Skills Measuring, Calculating, Using Graphs

Procedure

1. Cut out three squares of aluminum foil with sides of the following lengths: 50 mm, 100 mm, and 200 mm.
2. To determine the area of the 50-mm foil square, measure the length of one of its sides and then square it. Record the length and area in the data table.

DATA TABLE

Length (mm)	Area (mm^2)	Mass (g)	Volume (mm^3)	Thickness (mm)
Density of aluminum = ______________ g/mm^3				

3. Place the foil square on the balance to determine the mass of the foil. Record the mass of the foil square in the data table.
4. You will need the density of aluminum foil to calculate the volume of the foil square from its mass. The density of aluminum foil is 2.71 g/cm^3. Convert cm^3 to mm^3 and record the density of aluminum foil (in g/mm^3) on the line provided at the bottom of the data table.
5. To determine the volume of the foil square, divide its mass by its density in g/mm^3. Record the volume in the data table.
6. To determine the thickness of the foil square, divide its volume by its area. Record this thickness in the data table.
7. Repeat Steps 2 through 6, using the 100-mm foil square.
8. Repeat Steps 2 through 6, using the 200-mm foil square.
9. Construct a graph of your data on a separate sheet of graph paper. Plot length on the horizontal axis and thickness on the vertical axis. Draw a straight line connecting all three points.

Analyze and Conclude

1. **Measuring** How many significant figures were there in your measurement of the length of each square of aluminum foil?

____

____

2. **Using Graphs** What effect, if any, did the length of the square have on your estimate of the thickness of the foil?

____

____

3. **Comparing** Which estimate of thickness was most precise? Explain your answer.

____

____

____

____

____

____

____

4. **Controlling Variables** What factors limited the precision of your measurements?

____

____

Name ______________________ Class ________________ Date __________

Using Properties to Identify Materials

Forensic chemists test the physical and chemical properties of materials found at a crime scene. They also do similar tests on the materials found on a suspect's skin or clothing. These materials are often complex mixtures, such as soil, which contain many substances. In this lab, you will compare the properties of three known materials with two samples of "evidence." These samples represent evidence from a crime scene and evidence from a suspect's shoe. Although your materials and equipment are less complex than those used by forensic chemists, your overall method will be similar to the methods they use.

Problem Can the properties of materials that appear similar be used to tell them apart?

Materials

- 2 spot plates
- glass-marking pencil
- 5 laboratory spatulas
- cornstarch
- baking soda
- baking powder
- wash bottle of water
- vinegar
- iodine solution
- sample from crime scene
- sample from suspect's shoe

Skills Observing, Inferring, Predicting

Procedure

Part A: Properties of Known Substances

1. Use a glass-marking pencil to label 15 wells A through O on the spot plates. Make a mark next to each well, not in the well.
2. Use a spatula to place a small amount of cornstarch in wells A, B, and C. In the data table, record any physical properties of the cornstarch that you observe.

DATA TABLE

Sample	Description	Result of Adding Water	Result of Adding Vinegar	Result of Adding Iodine
Cornstarch				
Baking soda				
Baking powder				
Crime scene sample				
Sample from suspect's shoe				

3. Use a clean spatula to place a small amount of baking soda in wells D, E, and F. Record any physical properties of baking soda that you observe.
4. Using a clean spatula, place a small amount of baking powder in wells G, H, and I. Record any physical properties of baking powder that you observe.

5. Fill wells A, D, and G with water. Record any observed changes.
6. Fill wells, B, E, and H with vinegar. Record any observed changes.
7. Add one drop of iodine solution to wells C, F, and I. Record any changes that you observe. **CAUTION:** *Iodine solution is corrosive and poisonous. It can stain skin and clothing. Rinse any iodine spills with water.*

Part B: Properties of Unknown Substances

8. **Predicting** Look at the sample from the crime scene and the sample from the suspect's shoe. Based on your observations, predict whether testing will show that the samples are identical.

____

____

9. Use a clean spatula to place a small amount of the sample from the crime scene in wells J, K, and L. In the data table, record any physical properties of the sample that you observe.
10. Use a clean laboratory spatula to place a small amount of the sample from the suspect's shoe in wells M, N, and O. In the data table, record any physical properties of the sample that you observe.
11. Fill wells J and M with water. In the data table, record your observations.
12. Fill wells K and N with vinegar. In the data table, record your observations.
13. Add 1 drop of iodine solution to wells L and O. In the data table, record your observations.
14. Rinse all materials off the spot plates and flush them down the drain with at least ten times as much water. Dispose of your plastic gloves as directed by your teacher. **CAUTION:** *Wash your hands thoroughly with soap or detergent before leaving the laboratory.*

Analyze and Conclude

1. **Analyzing Data** Were you able to use the ability to dissolve in water to distinguish all three materials? Explain your answer.

____

____

____

2. **Drawing Conclusions** Are the samples from the suspect's shoe and from the crime scene identical?

____

____

3. **Evaluating and Revising** Did the data you collected support your prediction? Explain your answer.

____

____

____

Name ______________________ Class ____________________ Date ____________

Investigating Changes in Temperature During Heating of Solids

Lauric acid is a solid that is found in coconuts and processed foods that are made with coconut oil. Lauric acid is also used to make some soaps and cosmetics. In this lab, you will measure the temperature of ice and of lauric acid as these solids are heated and melt. You will graph the data you collect and compare the heating curves for ice and lauric acid.

Problem What happens to the temperature of a substance during a phase change?

Materials

- 500-mL beaker
- crushed ice
- thermometer
- hot plate
- clock or watch with second hand
- test tube of lauric acid with thermometer
- glass stirring rod
- graph paper

Skills Measuring, Using Graphs

Procedure

Part A: Heating Ice

1. Fill a 500-mL beaker halfway with crushed ice. **CAUTION:** *Use care when handling glassware to avoid breakage. Wipe up any spilled ice immediately to avoid slips and falls.*
2. Place the beaker on a hot plate. Don't turn the hot plate on yet. Insert a thermometer into the ice. It takes several seconds for the thermometer to adjust to the temperature of its surroundings. Wait 20 seconds and then measure the temperature of the ice. Record this temperature next to the 0 minutes entry in the data table.

DATA TABLE

Time (minutes)	Temperature of Water (°C)	Temperature of Lauric Acid (°C)
0		
1		

Name ______________________ Class ________________ Date ____________

3. Turn the hot plate to a low setting. **CAUTION:** *Be careful not to touch the hot plate because contact with the hot plate could cause a burn.*
4. Observe and record the temperature at one-minute intervals until all the ice has changed to liquid water. Circle the temperature at which you first observe liquid water and the temperature at which all the ice has changed to liquid water.
5. After all the ice has melted, make five more measurements of the temperature at one-minute intervals. Turn off the hot plate.
6. On a separate sheet of graph paper, graph your data with time on the horizontal axis and temperature on the vertical axis.

Part B: Heating Lauric Acid

7. Empty the water from the beaker into the sink. Fill the beaker halfway with cool tap water.
8. Place a test tube containing lauric acid and a thermometer into the beaker. If necessary, add or remove water from the beaker so that the surface of the water is above the surface of the lauric acid but below the opening of the test tube.
9. Place the beaker on the hot plate. After 20 seconds, measure the temperature of the lauric acid. Record this temperature next to the 0 minutes entry in the data table.
10. Repeat Steps 3 through 6, using the lauric acid instead of the ice. To keep the temperature the same throughout the water bath, use the glass stirring rod to stir the water after you take each temperature measurement.

Analyze and Conclude

1. **Using Graphs** Describe the shape of your graph for ice.

____

____

____

2. **Analyzing Data** What happened to the temperature of the ice-water mixture during the phase change?

____

3. **Drawing Conclusions** What happened to the energy that was transferred from the hot plate to the ice during the phase change?

____

____

____

____

4. **Comparing and Contrasting** Compare the shapes of the ice and lauric acid graphs. Compare the melting points of ice and lauric acid.

____

____

Using Flame Tests

Forensic scientists use various approaches to distinguish substances. In this lab, you will observe the flame colors of several substances and use the data to determine the identity of an unknown substance.

Problem How can the color of a flame be used to distinguish substances?

Materials

- solutions of calcium chloride, boric acid, potassium chloride, copper(II) sulfate, sodium chloride, and an unknown
- Bunsen burner
- nichrome wire loop
- dilute solution of hydrochloric acid
- wash bottle with distilled water

Skills Observing, Predicting, Using Data Tables

Procedure

Part A: Observing Flame Colors

1. Light the Bunsen burner. **CAUTION:** *Put on safety goggles and a lab apron. Tie back loose hair and clothing before working with a flame.*
2. Dip the wire loop into the calcium chloride solution and then place the loop in the flame. Observe and record the color of the flame in the data table.

DATA TABLE

Solution	Flame Color
Calcium chloride	
Potassium chloride	
Boric acid	
Copper(II) sulfate	
Sodium chloride	
Unknown	
Identity of unknown	

Name ______________________ Class __________________ Date ____________

3. Clean the loop by dipping it into hydrochloric acid. Then, while holding the loop over a sink, rinse away the acid with distilled water. **CAUTION:** *Keep hydrochloric acid away from your skin and clothing. Do not breathe in its vapor.*
4. Repeat Steps 2 and 3 with each of the other solutions. Be careful not to transfer any solution from one container to another. **CAUTION:** *These chemicals are poisonous. Do not let them get on your skin.*

Part B: Examining an Unknown Solution

5. Obtain the unknown solution from your teacher.
6. Repeat Steps 2 and 3, using the unknown solution. Compare your observations with the other data that you recorded to identify the unknown. **CAUTION:** *Wash your hands thoroughly before leaving the laboratory.*

Analyze and Conclude

1. **Comparing and Contrasting** Is there a relationship between the color of the flame and the color of the solution?

____
____
____
____

2. **Formulating Hypotheses** How do these substances produce light of different colors?

____
____
____
____
____
____
____

3. **Drawing Conclusions** A forensic scientist does a flame test on a substance that was found at a crime scene. What might the scientist conclude if the flame turns green?

____
____
____
____

Name ______________________ Class __________________ Date __________

Predicting the Density of an Element

Density is a useful property for identifying and classifying elements. In this exploration, you will determine the densities of three elements in Group 4A—silicon, tin, and lead. Then, you will use your data to predict the density of another element in Group 4A—germanium.

Problem Can the densities of elements within a group be used to help predict the density of another element in the group?

Materials

- unlined white paper
- scissors
- metric ruler
- balance
- forceps
- silicon
- tin
- lead shot
- 50-mL graduated cylinder
- graph paper
- periodic table

Skills Measuring, Observing, Using Graphs, Calculating

Procedure

Part A: Measuring Mass

DATA TABLE

Element	Mass of Paper (g)	Mass of Paper and Element (g)	Mass of Element (g)	Volume of Water (cm^3)	Volume of Water and Element (cm^3)	Volume of Element (cm^3)	Density of Element (g/cm^3)
Silicon							
Tin							
Lead							

1. Cut out three 10-cm × 10-cm pieces of paper from a sheet of unlined white paper. Label one piece of paper Silicon, the second Tin, and the third Lead. Find the mass of each piece of paper and record it in the data table.
2. Using forceps, place the silicon onto the paper labeled Silicon. Find the mass of the silicon and the paper. Record this mass in the data table. Then, subtract the mass of the paper from the mass of the silicon and paper. Record the mass of silicon in the data table. Set the paper containing the silicon aside for now.
3. Repeat Step 2 to find the masses of tin and lead.

Part B: Measuring Volume

4. Place 25 mL of water in the graduated cylinder. Measure the volume of the water to the nearest 0.1 mL. Record the volume (in cm^3) in the data table. (*Hint:* 1 mL = 1 cm^3)
5. Tilt the graduated cylinder and carefully pour the silicon from the paper into the graduated cylinder. Make sure that the silicon is completely covered by the water. Measure and record the volume of the water and silicon in the data table. Then, subtract the volume of water from the volume of the water and silicon. Record the result in the data table.
6. Repeat Steps 4 and 5 to find the volumes of tin and lead.

Part C: Calculating Density

7. To calculate the density of silicon, divide its mass by its volume.

$$\text{Density} = \frac{\text{Mass}}{\text{Volume}}$$

Record the density of silicon in the data table.

8. Repeat Step 7 to find the densities of tin and lead.
9. Make a line graph that shows the relationship between the densities of silicon, tin, and lead and the periods in which they are located in the periodic table. Place the number of the period (from 1 to 7) on the horizontal axis and the density (in g/cm^3) on the vertical axis. Draw a straight line that comes as close as possible to all three points.
10. Germanium is in Period 4. To estimate the density of germanium, draw a dotted vertical line from the 4 on the horizontal axis to the solid line. Then, draw a dotted horizontal line from the solid line to the vertical axis. Read and record the density of germanium.

____

____

11. Wash your hands with warm water and soap before you leave the laboratory.

Name ______________ Class ______________ Date ______________

Analyze and Conclude

1. **Classifying** List lead, silicon, and tin in order of increasing density.

2. **Comparing and Contrasting** How does your estimate of the density of germanium compare with the actual density of germanium, which is 5.5 g/cm^3?

3. **Calculating** Use the formula for percent error (PE) to calculate a percent error for your estimate of the density of germanium.

$$PE = \frac{\text{Estimated value} - \text{Accepted value}}{\text{Accepted value}} \times 100$$

4. **Drawing Conclusions** How does the density of the elements change from silicon to lead in Group 4A?

Name ______________________ Class ________________ Date ____________

Improving the Dyeing of Nonpolar Fabrics

Most natural fibers, such as cotton and wool, consist of large molecules that have regions with a partial positive or partial negative charge. These polar molecules have a strong attraction for dyes that contain either polar molecules or ions.

The molecules in some manufactured fibers, such as nylon, are nonpolar molecules. These synthetic fibers are difficult to dye. Molecules of other synthetic fibers, such as polyester and rayon, have only a few polar regions. As you might suspect, polyester and rayon have intermediate attractions for dyes. In this lab, you will investigate a process for improving a fiber's ability to absorb and retain dye.

Problem How can you increase the dye-holding capacity of nonpolar fibers?

Materials

- tongs
- 2 fabric test strips
- hot dye bath containing methyl orange
- clock or watch
- paper towels
- scissors
- soap
- hot iron(II) sulfate solution

Skills Observing, Drawing Conclusions

Procedure

Part A: Dyeing Without Treatment

1. Use the tongs to immerse a fabric test strip in the methyl orange dye bath. **CAUTION:** *The dye bath is hot. Do not touch the glass. The dye will stain skin and clothing.*
2. After 7 minutes, remove the strip from the dye bath. Allow as much of the dye solution as possible to drip back into the bath. Rinse off the excess dye with water in the sink.
3. Place the strip on a paper towel to dry. Be careful to avoid splashes when transferring the strip between the dye bath and paper towel. Record your observations in the data table.

DATA TABLE

Dye Treatment	Dyeing of Fibers	Colorfastness of Fibers
Methyl orange		
Iron sulfate and methyl orange		

4. After the fabric strip is dry, test it for colorfastness, or the ability to hold dye. Cut the strip in half lengthwise and wash one half of the strip in the sink with soap and water.
5. Allow the washed half-strip to dry and then compare the washed half to the unwashed half. Record your observations in the data table. Staple the half-strips to a sheet of paper and label each half-strip to indicate how you treated it.

Part B: Dyeing With Treatment

6. Use the tongs to place the second fabric strip in the iron(II) sulfate solution for 25 minutes. Then, use the tongs to lift the strip and allow it to drain into the iron(II) sulfate solution. Wring the strip as dry as possible over the solution. **CAUTION:** *The strip will be hot. Allow it to cool before touching it. Wear plastic gloves.*
7. Repeat Steps 1 through 3, using the strip that you treated with iron(II) sulfate.
8. To test the strip for colorfastness, repeat Steps 4 and 5.
9. Clean up your work area and wash your hands thoroughly with warm water and soap before leaving the laboratory.

Analyze and Conclude

1. **Comparing and Contrasting** How did the color of the untreated strip compare with the color of the treated strip?

____

2. **Comparing and Contrasting** How did the colorfastness of the untreated strip compare to the colorfastness of the treated strip?

____

3. **Applying Concepts** Silk blouses and shirts can be purchased in many intense colors. Why do you think silk is able to hold a variety of intense dyes?

____

____

4. **Drawing Conclusions** How does iron(II) sulfate affect the ability of a fabric to absorb dyes? (*Hint:* What kind of compound is iron(II) sulfate?)

____

____

5. **Predicting** A care label might read *Wash in cold water only.* What might happen to the color of a piece of clothing with this label if you washed the clothing in hot water?

____

____

Manipulating Chemical Equilibrium

Chemical reactions tend to go to equilibrium. It is possible to shift the equilibrium by changing the conditions under which the reaction occurs. Factors that can affect chemical equilibrium include the concentration of reactants and products, temperature, and pressure. In this lab, you will observe a chemical reaction and use your observations to predict how one factor will shift the equilibrium of the reaction. Then, you will perform an experiment to test your prediction.

Problem How can you change the equilibrium of a chemical reaction?

Materials

- iodine-starch solution
- 150-mL beaker
- 4 dropper pipets
- spot plate
- ascorbic acid (vitamin C) solution
- chlorine bleach (sodium hypochlorite, NaOCl) solution

Skills Formulating Hypotheses, Designing Experiments, Observing

Procedure

Part A: Observing a Reversible Reaction

1. Pour 50 mL of iodine-starch solution into the 150-mL beaker. The dark color of this solution is caused by the presence of iodine molecules (I_2) within the grains of starch. **CAUTION:** *Handle iodine solutions with care. Iodine is toxic.*
2. Use a dropper pipet to transfer 3 drops of iodine-starch solution from the beaker to one well on the spot plate.
3. Use another clean dropper pipet to add 1 drop of ascorbic acid solution to the iodine-starch solution on the spot plate. Continue to add ascorbic acid solution to the mixture on the spot plate, 1 drop at a time, until the mixture becomes clear. When an iodine molecule reacts with ascorbic acid, the iodine molecule is reduced and breaks down into two colorless iodide ions ($2I^-$).
4. Use the third clean dropper pipet to transfer one drop of colorless iodide solution to a second well on the spot plate.
5. Use the last clean dropper pipet to add bleach solution to the drop of colorless iodide solution, one drop at a time. Continue until the dark color of the iodine-starch solution reappears. **CAUTION:** *Bleach can damage skin and clothing*. The chlorine bleach (NaOCl) oxidizes iodide ions (I^-), converting them to iodine molecules (I_2).

Name ______________________ Class ________________ Date ____________

6. Write a chemical equation showing the equilibrium between iodine molecules and iodide ions. This equation does not need to be balanced. Label the two sides of your equation to indicate which substance appears dark and which appears colorless.

____

____

Part B: Design Your Experiment

7. **Predicting** Select one of the solutions used earlier that affects the equilibrium between iodine molecules and iodide ions. Record your prediction of the change you will observe in an iodine-starch solution as you add the solution that you selected.

____

____

____

8. **Designing Experiments** Design an experiment to test your prediction. Your experimental plan should describe in detail how you will perform your experiment.

____

____

____

9. Construct a data table like the sample data table shown in which to record your observations. (*Hint:* Your data table may not be exactly like the sample data table.)

SAMPLE DATA TABLE

Initial Solution	Solution Added	Quantity Added	Color of Resulting Mixture

10. Perform your experiment only after your teacher has approved your plan. Record your observations in your data table. **CAUTION:** *Wash your hands with soap or detergent before leaving the laboratory.*

Analyze and Conclude

1. **Analyzing Data** What factor did you investigate? How did it affect the equilibrium between iodine molecules and iodide ions?

2. **Predicting** How would you expect the equilibrium to change if you added more iodide ions to the mixture? Explain your answer.

3. **Calculating** When chlorine bleach (sodium hypochlorite, NAOCl) oxidizes iodide ions to iodine molecules, sodium hypochlorite is reduced to sodium chloride (NaCl) and water (H_2O). Write a balanced chemical equation for this reaction, beginning with the reactants sodium hypochlorite, iodide ions, and hydrogen ions (H^+).

4. **Drawing Conclusions** How does the addition of more product affect the chemical equilibrium of a reaction?

Preparing a Salt by Neutralization

In this lab, you will prepare table salt by reacting hydrochloric acid (HCl) with sodium hydroxide (NaOH). To be sure that all of the acid and base have reacted, you will use phenolphthalein. You will first have to test the colors of this indicator with a known acid and base. After the acid and base have reacted, you will measure the pH of the solution with pH paper. Finally, you will evaporate the water and collect the sodium chloride.

Problem How can you produce a salt by neutralization?

Materials

- 3 dropper pipets
- labels
- 10-mL graduated cylinder
- test tube rack
- 2 10-mL test tubes
- distilled water
- hydrochloric acid
- sodium hydroxide solution
- 3 stirring rods
- phenolphthalein solution
- 2 25-mL beaker
- pH paper
- large watch glass
- 100-mL beaker
- hot plate

Skills Observing, Measuring, Analyzing Data

Procedure

Part A: Preparing for the Experiment

1. Place about 10 mL of distilled water in a 25-mL beaker. Set the graduated cylinder on the table and add distilled water to the 5-mL mark. Be sure that the *bottom* of the meniscus is on the 5-mL line.
2. To determine the number of drops in 1 mL, use a clean dropper pipet to add 1 mL of water to the graduated cylinder. Hold the dropper pipet straight up and down with the tip of the dropper pipet just inside the mouth of the cylinder. As your partner watches the liquid level in the cylinder, add drops of water one at a time while counting the drops. Continue adding drops until the liquid level reaches 6 mL. In the data table, record the number of drops in 1 mL.
3. Label one clean dropper pipet *Hydrochloric acid (HCl)* and the other *Sodium hydroxide (NaOH)*.
4. Using the HCl dropper pipet, add 3 mL of hydrochloric acid to a clean test tube. **CAUTION:** *Hydrochloric acid is corrosive. In case of spills, clean thoroughly with water.* Add 2 to 3 drops of phenolphthalein to the test tube. Use a clean stirring rod to mix the hydrochloric acid and indicator. Record your observations.

DATA TABLE

Material(s)	Observation
1 mL	______ drops
HCl + phenolphthalein	______ (color)
NaOH + phenolphthalein	______ (color)
Drops of HCl used	______ drops
mL of HCl used	______ mL
Drops of NaOH used	______ drops
mL of NaOH used	______ mL
pH of final solution	______

5. Using the dropper pipet labeled NaOH, add 3 mL of sodium hydroxide solution to a clean test tube. **CAUTION:** *Sodium hydroxide is corrosive. In case of spills, clean thoroughly with water.* Add 2 to 3 drops of phenolphthalein to the test tube. Use a clean stirring rod to mix the sodium hydroxide solution and indicator. Record your observations.

Part B: Making the Salt

6. Using the HCl dropper pipet, add 4 mL of hydrochloric acid to a clean 25-mL beaker. Record the number of drops you used. Add 2 to 3 drops of phenolphthalein to the beaker.
7. Use the NaOH dropper pipet to add sodium hydroxide drop by drop to the beaker of hydrochloric acid and phenolphthalein, stirring constantly. Count the drops as you add them. As a pink color remains longer, add the drops more slowly.
8. Continue to add and count the drops of sodium hydroxide until a light pink color remains for at least 30 seconds. (*Hint:* If you add too much sodium hydroxide, add a few more drops of hydrochloric acid until the color disappears.) Record any additional drops of hydrochloric acid that you added. Then, carefully add sodium hydroxide until 1 drop produces a lasting pink color. Record the total number of drops of sodium hydroxide used.
9. Use a piece of pH paper to determine the pH of the final solution. Record the pH. If the pH is higher than 7.0, add hydrochloric acid drop by drop, testing the pH with pH paper after each drop, until the pH is equal to 7.0. Record the pH and the total number of drops of HCl you added.
10. Use the solution in the beaker to fill the watch glass halfway.
11. Fill the 100-mL beaker about half full of water. Place the beaker on top of the hot plate.
12. Set the watch glass on top of the beaker.
13. Turn on the hot plate to a low setting. Adjust the heat as the water in the beaker warms. The water should simmer, but not boil. **CAUTION:** *Do not touch the hot plate or the beaker.* Heat until a solid is visible at the edges of the water in the watch glass and the water is nearly evaporated. Turn off the heat.
14. Allow the remaining water to evaporate. Observe the contents of the watch glass. Record your observations.

____

15. When the watch glass has cooled, dispose of the contents as directed by your teacher. Clean up your equipment. Wash your hands with soap and water.

Name ______________________ Class ________________ Date ____________

Analyze and Conclude

1. **Comparing and Contrasting** What was the total amount of hydrochloric acid used to make the neutral solution? What was the total amount of sodium hydroxide? How do the amounts compare?

____

____

____

____

2. **Drawing Conclusions** What do you conclude about the concentrations of hydrochloric acid and sodium hydroxide in the solutions?

____

____

3. **Predicting** If the acid had been twice as concentrated as the base, how would your data have changed?

____

____

Name ______________________ Class ________________ Date ____________

Comparing Vitamin C in Fruit Juices

Various brands of juices often claim to be good sources of vitamin C, but which juices are the best sources? Vitamin C is an organic acid called ascorbic acid. Like other organic acids, vitamin C reacts with indicators to produce a color change. This reaction can be used to determine the amount of vitamin C present in foods, such as fruit juices. In this lab, you will add an indicator to a sample of apple juice. The indicator will change color when all the vitamin C has reacted. Then, you will test and compare the vitamin C content in other juices with the results for apple juice.

Problem Which juice provides the most vitamin C?

Materials

- apple juice
- a variety of other fruit juices
- test tubes and rack
- 10-mL graduated cylinder
- methylene blue indicator
- dropper pipet
- stirring rods
- graph paper

Skills Observing, Measuring, Analyzing Data

Procedure

Part A: Measuring Vitamin C in Apple Juice

1. Use a graduated cylinder to measure 10 mL of apple juice. Pour the juice into a test tube.
2. Add a drop of methylene blue indicator to the test tube. Stir until the color of the indicator disappears.
3. Add more indicator, one drop at a time, stirring after each addition. Count the drops that you add. Stop adding the indicator when the last drop of indicator does not change color. Record the number of drops that you used in the data table.

DATA TABLE

Type of Juice	Number of Drops
Apple	

Name ______________________ Class ______________ Date __________

Part B: Measuring Vitamin C in Other Juices

4. Formulate and record a hypothesis about which juice will have the greatest amount of vitamin C. You will need to decide which variables must be kept the same, as well as how to account for bits of solid in some juices.

____

____

5. List the steps in your procedure and write the names of each of the juices to be tested in the left column of the data table.

____

____

____

____

____

____

____

6. Have your teacher check your procedure before you begin your experiment.

Analyze and Conclude

1. Using Graphs Make a bar graph of your data. Which juice required the most drops of indicator? Which required the least?

____

____

____

2. Drawing Conclusions Based on your data, which juice contained the most vitamin C? How did you reach this conclusion?

____

____

3. Evaluating and Revising What unexpected problems did you encounter? Explain how you could revise your procedure to avoid these problems.

____

____

____

____

____

Modeling a Chain Reaction

In a nuclear fission chain reaction, a nucleus is struck by a neutron, which causes the nucleus to split into two smaller nuclei and to release other neutrons. If these neutrons strike other nuclei, a chain reaction can occur. In this lab, you will model a nuclear fission chain reaction, using dominoes.

Problem How can you make a model of a nuclear fission chain reaction?

Materials

- 20 dominoes
- watch with a second hand, or stopwatch
- metric ruler

Skills Observing, Using Models

Procedure

1. Stand 15 dominoes in a single straight row in such a way that the distance between them is about one-half of their height. Knock over the first domino. Measure and record the time it takes for all the dominoes to fall.

   ____

2. Repeat Step 1 two more times. Then, average the three time measurements to get a more accurate time.

   ____

3. Arrange 15 dominoes, as shown below, so that each domino will knock over two others. Observe what happens when you knock over the first domino. Measure and record how long it takes for the whole set of dominoes to fall over.

   ____

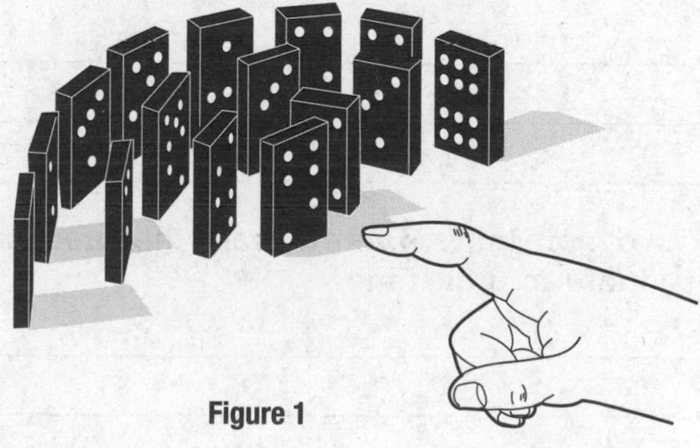

Figure 1

4. Repeat Step 3 two more times. Average the three time measurements to get a more accurate time.

5. Set up 15 dominoes again as you did in Step 3. This time, however, hold a metric ruler on end, in the middle of the arrangement of dominoes. Knock over the first domino. Observe what happens.

6. Set up 15 dominoes as you did in Step 3, but this time, place 5 additional dominoes behind and at right angles to 5 randomly chosen dominoes for support, as shown below. The 5 supported dominoes represent atoms of a different isotope that must be struck with more energy to undergo fission.

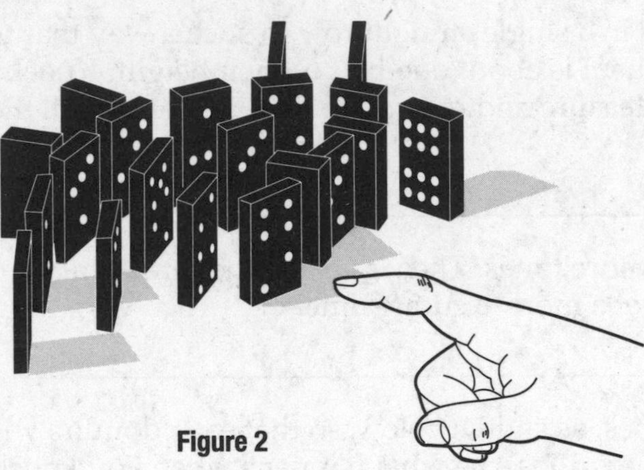

Figure 2

7. Knock over the first domino. Measure and record the time it takes for the dominoes to fall and how many dominoes fall.

8. Repeat Steps 6 and 7 two more times. Then, average the three time measurements to get a more accurate time.

Name ______________________ Class ________________ Date ____________

9. Repeat Steps 6 through 8, but this time, place supporting dominoes behind only 3 dominoes.

10. Repeat Steps 6 through 8, but this time, place a supporting domino behind only 1 domino.

Analyze and Conclude

1. **Calculating** What was the average fall time for the arrangement of dominoes in Steps 1 and 2? In Steps 3 and 4?

2. **Applying Concepts** What type of reaction was modeled in Steps 3 and 4?

3. **Using Models** In your falling-dominoes model of nuclear fission chain reactions, what did a standing domino represent? What did the fall of a domino represent?

4. **Using Models** In your falling-dominoes model of nuclear fission chain reactions, what did the striking of one domino by another represent? What did the metric ruler represent?

5. **Analyzing Data** Before a sample of an easily fissionable isotope is used, it is refined by removing less fissionable isotopes of the same element. On the basis of your observations in Steps 6 through 10, explain why this refinement is necessary.

6. **Inferring** What factors do you think would affect the rate of a nuclear fission chain reaction?

7. **Drawing Conclusions** What do you think would happen to the nuclear fission chain reaction if control rods were not present?

8. **Evaluating and Revising** What are some of the limitations of using falling dominoes to model a nuclear fission chain reaction? Suggest how you might revise this model to make it more representative of a chain reaction.

Name ______________________ Class ______________________ Date ______________

Investigating the Velocity of a Sinking Marble

In this lab, you will graph the motion of a marble falling through shampoo.

Problem What does a distance-time graph look like for a marble falling through shampoo?

Materials

- clear shampoo
- 100-mL graduated cylinder
- 2 small marbles
- stopwatch
- forceps
- masking tape
- metric ruler
- 10-mL graduated cylinder
- long glass stirring rod
- dropper pipet
- graph paper

Skills Measuring, Observing, Using Tables and Graphs

Procedure

1. Wrap a small amount of masking tape around the tips of the forceps. This will allow you to grip the marble with it.
2. Measure the distance between the 10-mL gradations on the 100-mL graduated cylinder. Record the new distance in the first row of the data table.

DATA TABLE

Distance (mm)	First Marble Time (s)	Second Marble Time (s)

3. Multiply this distance by 2 and write the result in the second row of the data table. For the third row, multiply the distance by 3. Continue until you have written distances in 10 rows.
4. Slowly pour 100 mL of clear shampoo into the 100-mL graduated cylinder.
5. Be ready to observe the marble as it falls through the shampoo. Grasp the marble with the forceps and hold the marble just above the shampoo-filled graduated cylinder.

Name ______________________ Class ______________ Date ____________

6. Say "Go!" as you drop the marble into the shampoo. At the same moment, your partner should start the stopwatch.
7. Each time the lower edge of the marble reaches a 10-mL mark on the cylinder, say "Now." Your partner should note and record the time on the stopwatch.
8. Continue calling out "Now" each time the marble reaches a 10-mL mark until it comes to rest on the bottom of the cylinder. Say "Stop!"
9. Use the 10-mL graduated cylinder to add about 8 mL of water to the 100-mL graduated cylinder. Use the glass stirring rod to mix the water and shampoo gently but thoroughly.
10. With the dropper pipet, remove enough liquid from the graduated cylinder to decrease the volume to 100 mL.
11. Repeat Steps 5 through 8, using another marble.
12. Wash all supplies as instructed by your teacher.

Analyze and Conclude

1. **Using Tables and Graphs** Use the data you collected to make a distance-time graph for each of the two marbles.

____

____

____

____

2. **Observing** Explain the motion of the marbles as they fell through the shampoo. How did you show this motion on your graph?

____

____

____

____

____

3. **Inferring** Based on your graph, were the marbles accelerating? Explain your answers.

____

____

____

4. **Calculating** Use the data table to calculate the average speed of each marble.

____

____

____

Name ______________________ Class ________________ Date __________

Investigating a Balloon Jet

In this lab, you will examine the relationships among force, mass, and motion.

Problem How does a jet-powered device move?

Materials

- string, 3 m in length
- drinking straw
- 4 long balloons
- masking tape
- stopwatch
- meter stick
- 2 threaded nuts
- 2 chairs

Skills Applying Concepts

Procedure

1. Insert the string through the straw and tie each end of the string to the back of a separate chair. Pull the chairs apart until the string is tight and horizontal.
2. Blow up the balloon and then hold the balloon's opening closed. In the data table, record the length of the balloon. Have a classmate attach the balloon lengthwise to the straw, using tape.
3. While continuing to hold the balloon's opening closed, slide the balloon jet to the end of the string.
4. Release the balloon. Measure the time during which the balloon jet moves. Measure the distance that the balloon jet travels along the string. Record the distance and time values in the data table for 0 Nuts Used, Trial 1.

DATA TABLE

Number of Nuts Used	Trial Number	Time (seconds)	Distance (centimeters)	Average Velocity (cm/s)
0	1			
0	2			
2	1			
2	2			
Length of inflated balloon (centimeters)				

5. Repeat Steps 2 through 4 with a new balloon. Make sure to inflate the balloon to the same size as in Step 2. Record your results in the data table for 0 Nuts Used, Trial 2.
6. Repeat Steps 2 through 5 twice more with a new balloon. This time, tape two nuts to the balloon before releasing it. Record your results in the data table for 2 Nuts Used, Trials 1 and 2.
7. Calculate and record the average velocity for each trial. The average velocity is equal to the distance divided by the time.

Analyze and Conclude

1. **Applying Concepts** Use Newton's second and third laws to explain the motion of the balloon jet.

____

____

____

____

____

____

____

____

____

____

____

____

____

____

____

2. **Analyzing Data** How did adding mass (nuts) to the balloon jet affect its motion?

____

____

____

____

____

____

____

Determining Buoyant Force

In this lab, you will analyze recorded data to determine the buoyant forces acting on objects.

Problem How does the buoyant force determine whether an object sinks?

Materials

- string
- rock
- spring scale
- can
- plastic tub
- sponge
- paper towels
- 100-g standard mass
- wooden block tied to a fishing weight
- 250-mL graduated cylinder

Skills Measuring, Calculating

Procedure

1. Tie one end of the string around the rock. Tie the other end to the spring scale. Suspend the rock from the spring scale and measure and record its weight in air in the data table.

DATA TABLE

Object	Weight in Air (N)	Apparent Weight in Water (N)	Buoyant Force (weight in air – apparent weight in water, N)	Volume of Displaced Water (mL)	Weight of Displaced Water (N)
Rock					
100-g standard mass					
Wood block with fishing weight					

2. Place the can in an upright position in the plastic tub. Completely fill the can with water. Wipe up any water that has spilled into the tub. **CAUTION:** *Wipe up any water that spills on the floor to avoid slips and falls.*
3. Lower the rock into the water until it is completely submerged. Record in the data table the apparent weight in water of the submerged rock. Remove the rock from the can.
4. Without spilling any water, carefully remove the can from the tub. Pour the water from the tub into the graduated cylinder. Record in the data table the volume of displaced water .
5. Repeat Steps 1 through 4, first with the 100-g standard mass and then with the wooden block that is tied to a fishing weight.
6. To determine the buoyant force on each object, subtract its apparent weight in water from its weight in air. In the data table, record these values.

7. Calculate the weight of the water that each object displaces. (*Hint:* 1.0 mL of water has a weight of 0.0098 N.) In the data table, record these weights.

Analyze and Conclude

1. **Observing** What force is responsible for the difference between the weight of each object in the air and its apparent weight in water?

2. **Analyzing Data** How is the buoyant force related to the weight of water displaced?

3. **Forming Operational Definitions** Define buoyant force and describe two ways you can measure it or calculate it.

4. **Drawing Conclusions** Explain what causes an object to sink or to float, using the terms *buoyancy, weight, force, density,* and *gravity.*

Name ______________________ Class ______________ Date ____________

Determining Mechanical Advantage

Many complex machines have an adjustable mechanical advantage. In this lab, you will learn how adjusting the mechanical advantage of a bicycle affects the bicycle's performance.

Problem How does mechanical advantage affect the performance of a bicycle?

Materials

- board with 2 nails
- 4 thread spools, 3 with different diameters
- rubber band
- masking tape
- multispeed bicycle (one or more per class)
- meter stick
- thick leather glove

Skills Measuring, Calculating

Procedure

Part A: Modeling the Mechanical Advantage of a Bicycle

1. Use a piece of masking tape to label each nail on the board. Label one nail *Pedals* and the other nail *Wheel*. To model the pedals and rear wheel of a bicycle, place a spool on each nail in the board and join the spools with a rubber band, as shown in Figure 1.

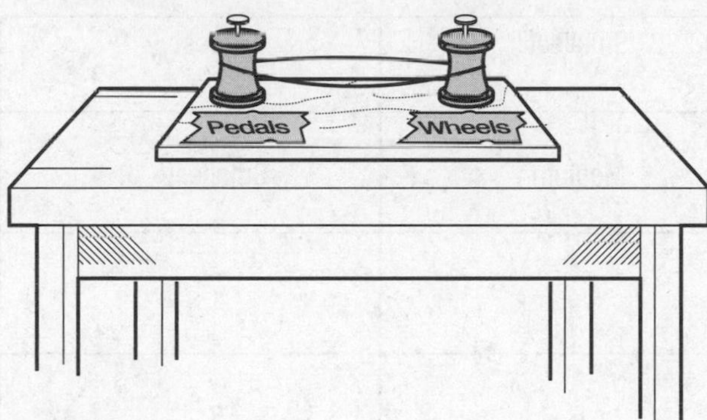

Figure 1

2. Use a pencil to make a reference mark on the edge of each spool. These marks will help you observe the motion of the spools as they turn.
3. **Measuring** Use a ruler to measure the radius of each spool in your model. Record these measurements in the data table for Part A.

Name ______________ Class ______________ Date ______________

DATA TABLE: PART A

Pedal Spool Radius (cm)	Revolutions of Pedal Spool	Wheel Spool Radius (cm)	Revolutions of Wheel Spool	IMA
	5			
	5			
	5			

4. The pedal spool represents the pedals and the gears attached to them. The wheel spool represents the rear wheel and its gears. Using the reference marks, observe the wheel spool as you turn the pedal spool through five complete revolutions. In the data table, record the number of revolutions of the wheel spool.
5. Replace the wheel spool with a spool of a different diameter. Repeat Steps 2 through 4 for each diameter of wheel spool.
6. **Calculating** The ideal mechanical advantage (IMA) of a bicycle is equal to the distance the pedals move divided by the distance the rear wheel moves. For your model,

$$\text{IMA} = \frac{5 \times \text{Pedal radius}}{(\text{Revolutions of wheel}) \times (\text{Wheel radius})}$$

Calculate the mechanical advantage of each spool combination that you used. Record these values in the data table.

Part B: Analyzing Bicycle Gears

7. **Measuring** Work in groups of three. Use a meter stick to measure the radius of the pedals and the rear wheel, as shown in Figure 2. Record these measurements in the data table for Part B.

DATA TABLE: PART B

Size of Pedal Gear	Smallest	Smallest	Largest
Size of Rear Wheel Gear	Largest	Medium	Smallest
Pedal Radius (cm)			
Revolutions of Pedal	5	5	5
Rear Wheel Radius (cm)			
Revolutions of Rear Wheel			
IMA			

8. One person should hold the bicycle with its rear wheel slightly off the floor. While a second person turns the pedals, a third person should use the bicycle's gear shifters to place the chain on the smallest pedal gear and the largest rear wheel gear. **CAUTION:** *Keep your hands out of the spokes, chain, and gears.*
9. One person should put on a heavy leather glove, while a second person holds the bicycle with its rear wheel slightly off the floor.

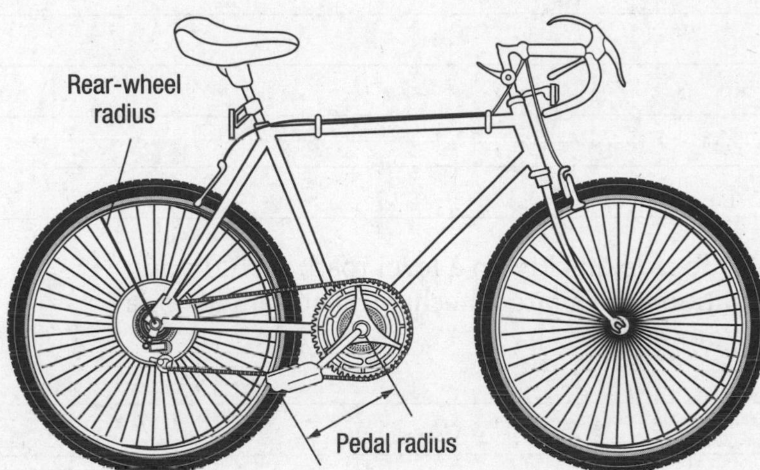

Figure 2

10. The third person should slowly turn the pedals through five complete revolutions. The person who is wearing the glove should gently hold the rear tire tread so that the wheel turns only as fast as the pedals force it to move. This person should also observe the position of the valve stem to count the number of revolutions of the rear wheel. In the data table, record the number of revolutions of the rear wheel.
11. Repeat Steps 8 through 10, once using the smallest pedal gear and a mid-sized rear-wheel gear, and then again using the largest pedal gear and the smallest rear-wheel gear.
12. **Calculating** Use the equation in Step 6 to calculate the mechanical advantage of the bicycle for each gear combination you used. Record these values in the data table.

Name ______________________ Class ________________ Date ____________

Analyze and Conclude

1. **Analyzing Data** Which combination of pedal and rear-wheel gears provided the greatest mechanical advantage? The least mechanical advantage?

2. **Applying Concepts** To ride quickly on a level road, would you select a gear combination with a large mechanical advantage or a small one? Explain your answer.

3. **Drawing Conclusions** To decrease the force needed to ride a bicycle up a steep hill, would you select a gear combination with a large mechanical advantage or a small one? What size rear-wheel gear would you use to race on a flat road? Explain.

Name ______________________ Class ______________ Date ____________

Investigating a Spring Clip

There are many ways to use potential energy. A spring clip is a device used to hold weights on a barbell. The spring clip stores energy when you compress it. In this lab, you will determine how the distance you compress a spring clip is related to the force you apply and to the spring's potential energy.

Problem How does the force you apply to a spring clip affect its elastic potential energy?

Materials

- clamp
- spring clip
- masking tape
- metric ruler
- 50-newton spring scale
- graph paper

Skills Measuring, Using Tables and Graphs

Procedure

1. Using the clamp, firmly attach one handle of the spring clip to a tabletop, with the other handle facing up and away from the table, as shown. **CAUTION:** *Be careful not to pinch your fingers with the clamp or spring clip.*
2. Remove the plastic cover from the upper handle of the spring clip. Hook the spring scale to the spring clip handle, as shown, and use masking tape to secure it. Have your teacher check your setup for safety before proceeding.
3. Have a classmate hold the ruler next to the spring clip, as shown. Record the starting position of the handle. (The reading on the spring scale should be zero.)

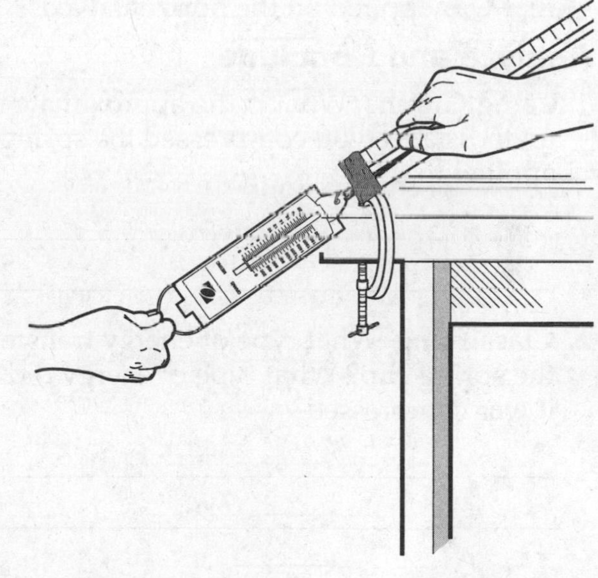

____

4. Slowly pull the spring scale down at a right angle to the upper handle until the handle moves 0.1 cm. In the data table, record the force and the position of the upper handle. Slowly release the scale back to the starting position.

Name ____________ Class ____________ Date ____________

DATA TABLE

Force (N)	Position of Upper Handle (cm)	Total Distance Moved (cm)

5. Repeat Step 4, this time pulling the handle 0.2 cm from the starting position.
6. Repeat Step 4 a few more times, pulling the handle 0.1 cm farther each time. Continue until the spring scale reaches its maximum force.
7. Calculate the distance the handle moved each time you pulled it and record these values in the data table. Graph your data. Place the distance the handle moved on the vertical axis and the force that was applied on the horizontal axis.

Analyze and Conclude

1. **Using Graphs** What is the approximate relationship between the total distance you compressed the spring clip and the force you applied to it?

____

____

2. **Classifying** What type of energy transfer did you use to compress the spring clip? What type of energy did the spring clip gain when it was compressed?

____

____

____

3. **Drawing Conclusions** What relationship exists between the distance the spring clip was compressed and its potential energy? (*Hint:* The elastic potential energy of the spring clip equals the work done on it.)

____

____

Name ______________________ Class ______________________ Date ______________

Using Specific Heat to Analyze Metals

In this lab, you will determine the specific heat of steel and aluminum. Then, you will use specific heat to analyze the composition of a metal can.

Problem How can you use specific heat to determine the composition of a metal can?

Materials

- 10 steel bolts
- balance
- 50-cm length of string
- clamp
- ring stand
- boiling water bath (shared with class)
- thermometer
- 500-mL graduated cylinder
- ice water
- foam cup with lid
- aluminum nails
- crushed can

Skills Calculating, Designing Experiments

Procedure

Part A: Determining Specific Heat

1. Measure and record the mass of 10 steel bolts.

DATA TABLE

	Water	Steel Bolts	Aluminum Nails
Mass (g)			
Initial temperature (°C)			
Final temperature (°C)			
Specific heat (J/g•°C)	4.18		

2. Tie the bolts to the string. Use a clamp and ring stand to suspend the bolts in the boiling water bath. **CAUTION:** *Be careful not to splash boiling water.* After a few minutes, record in the data table the water temperature as the initial temperature of the bolts.
3. Use a graduated cylinder to pour 200 mL of ice water (without ice) into the foam cup. Record the mass and temperature of the ice water. (*Hint:* The density of water is 1 g/mL.)
4. Use the clamp to move the bolts into the cup of ice water. Cover the cup and insert the thermometer through the hole in the cover.
5. Gently swirl the water in the cup. Record the highest temperature as the final temperature for both the water and the steel bolts.
6. Calculate and record the specific heat of steel. (*Hint:* Use the equation $Q = m \times c \times \Delta T$ to calculate the energy the water absorbs.)
7. Repeat Steps 2 through 6 with aluminum nails to determine the specific heat of aluminum. Use a mass of aluminum that is close to the mass you used for the steel bolts.

Name ______________________ Class ______________ Date ____________

Part B: Design Your Own Experiment

8. Designing Experiments Design an experiment that uses specific heat to identify the metals a can might be made of.

9. In the space below, construct a data table in which to record your observations. After your teacher approves your plan, perform your experiment.

Analyze and Conclude

1. Comparing and Contrasting Which metal has a higher specific heat—aluminum or steel?

____

____

2. Drawing Conclusions Was the specific heat of the can closer to the specific heat of steel or of aluminum? What can you conclude about the material in the can?

____

____

3. Evaluating Did your observations prove what the can was made of? If not, what other information would you need to be sure?

____

____

____

____

4. Inferring The can you used is often called a tin can. The specific heat of tin is 0.23 J/g°C. Did your data support the idea that the can was made mostly of tin? Explain your answer.

____

____

Name ______________________ Class ________________ Date ____________

Investigating Sound Waves

Sound is produced when a vibrating source causes a medium to vibrate. In this lab, you will investigate how the vibrating source affects characteristics of the sound produced.

Problem What determines the frequency and amplitude of the sound produced by a vibrating object?

Materials

- meter stick
- 2 cardboard tubes
- scissors or scalpel
- 2 rubber bands
- wax paper
- balloon
- small mirror
- transparent tape
- flashlight

Skills Observing, Inferring, Drawing Conclusions, Controlling Variables

Procedure

Part A: Investigating How Length Affects Pitch

1. Hold one end of a meter stick down firmly on a table so that 20 centimeters of the meter stick extends past the edge of the table. Pluck the end of the meter stick that extends past the table to produce a vibration and a sound. Observe the vibration and sound of the meter stick.
2. Repeat Step 1, but this time allow 40 centimeters of the meter stick to extend past the edge of the table. Observe and record how the length of the vibrating part of the meter stick affects the pitch.

____

____

____

____

3. Repeat Step 1, but this time allow 60 centimeters of the meter stick to extend past the edge of the table. Record your observations.

____

____

____

____

Name ______________________ Class ________________ Date ____________

4. Investigate the relationship between length and frequency for a vibrating column of air, as you did with the vibrating meter stick. Make a kazoo by cutting a hole in the middle of one of the cardboard tubes. Make the hole approximately 1 centimeter in diameter. Use a rubber band to fasten the piece of wax paper over one end of the tube. **CAUTION:** *Be careful when cutting with sharp instruments; always cut away from yourself and away from nearby people.*
5. Make a second kazoo by cutting the second tube 10 centimeters shorter than the first tube. Using the short tube, repeat Step 4.
6. Hold the shorter kazoo in front of your mouth and hum into the open end, keeping your pitch steady. Repeat this action with the longer kazoo, making sure to hum exactly as you did before. Observe and record how the length of the kazoo affects the pitch of the sound.

____
____
____
____
____
____
____

Part B: Investigating How Frequency Affects Pitch and How Amplitude Affects Loudness

7. Cut the neck off of the balloon. Replace the wax paper on the longer kazoo with the cut-open balloon. Wrap the rubber band several times around the end of the cardboard tube. The rubber band should hold the balloon tightly stretched over the end of the tube. Use tape to attach the small mirror onto the balloon on the end of the tube.
8. Have a classmate shine a flashlight on the mirror, as shown, while you hum into the kazoo. Your classmate should position the flashlight so that a spot of light is reflected on the wall. It may be necessary to darken the room. Observe how the spot of light moves when you hum into the kazoo. Make a note of your position and the position and angle of the kazoo and the flashlight.

____
____
____
____
____
____
____

Name ______________________ Class __________________ Date ____________

9. Without changing how loudly you hum, use your voice to raise the pitch of your humming. Observe and record how the movement of the spot of light differs from your observations in Step 8. Make sure you do not change your distance from the wall or the angle at which the light from the flashlight strikes the mirror attached to the kazoo.

____

____

____

____

10. Repeat Step 9, but this time hum at a lower pitch than you did in Step 8.

____

____

____

11. Repeat Steps 9 and 10, but this time vary the loudness of your humming while keeping the pitch constant.

____

____

____

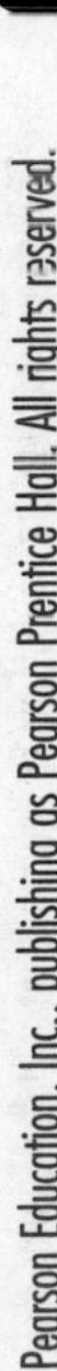

Name ______________________ Class ______________ Date __________

Analyze and Conclude

1. **Observing** What happened to the frequency of the meter stick's vibration when you made the overhanging part longer?

2. **Inferring** How did the frequency of the meter stick's vibration affect the pitch of its sound?

3. **Inferring** How did the kazoo's length affect its pitch?

4. **Analyzing Data** When you changed the pitch of your humming, how did it affect the frequency of vibration of the mirror?

5. **Analyzing Data** How is the amplitude of the kazoo's vibration related to its loudness?

6. **Controlling Variables** Explain why it was important to keep loudness constant when you changed the pitch of your humming in Step 9.

Mixing Colored Lights

What is color? How many different colors can be formed from a combination of only three colors? In this exploration, you will examine what happens when lights of three different colors are mixed.

Problem How can you produce a range of colors from three lights of different colors?

Materials

- sources of red, blue, and green light
- tape
- large sheet of white paper

Skills Observing

Procedure

1. Tape a large sheet of white paper to the wall.
2. Dim the room lights. Turn on the red light source and shine it on the large sheet of white paper. In the data table, record the colors you observe on the paper. **CAUTION:** *Do not touch lamps when they are on. They may be hot.*

DATA TABLE

Light Sources	Colors of Lights	Colors of Shadows
Red only		
Blue only		
Green only		
Red and blue		
Red and green		
Blue and green		
Red, blue, and green		

3. Place your hand between the light source and the paper. Record the color of your hand's shadow.
4. Repeat Steps 2 and 3 with the blue and then with the green light source.

5. Now turn on the red and blue light sources and allow their beams to overlap. Record your observations in the data table.
6. Place your hand in the overlapping beams of light. Note the colors of any shadows that your hand makes. Record your observations in the data table.
7. Repeat Steps 5 and 6 with the red and green light sources. Then repeat Steps 5 and 6 with the blue and green light sources.
8. Turn on all three light sources and allow their beams to overlap. Record your observations in the data table.
9. Place your hand in the overlapping red, green, and blue beams. Note the colors of any shadows that your hand makes on the white paper. Record your observations in the data table.

Analyze and Conclude

1. **Observing** What happened when two colored lights overlapped?

____

2. **Analyzing Data** How did the combination of two colored lights produce the shadows you observed?

____

____

____

____

3. **Applying Concepts** Explain how combining three colored lights produced the colors you observed.

____

____

____

4. **Drawing Conclusions** From the shadows you observed when using three colored lights, what can you conclude about how colors of light combine? Explain your answer.

____

____

____

____

____

____

____

____

Name ______________________ Class ________________ Date ____________

Selecting Mirrors

In this lab, you will compare several mirrors and select the type that is best for a specific use.

Problem What mirror shape is best for magnifying images? For providing a wide view?

Materials

- plane, convex, and concave mirrors
- 2 metric rulers
- roll of string
- protractor

Skills Observing, Measuring

Procedure

Part A: Comparing Magnification

1. Place the plane mirror on a tabletop with its mirror side facing up. Position a metric ruler horizontally across the center of the mirror.
2. Hold the other metric ruler horizontally against your nose, just below your eyes, as shown below. Make sure the ruler's markings face away from you. Look down at the mirror.

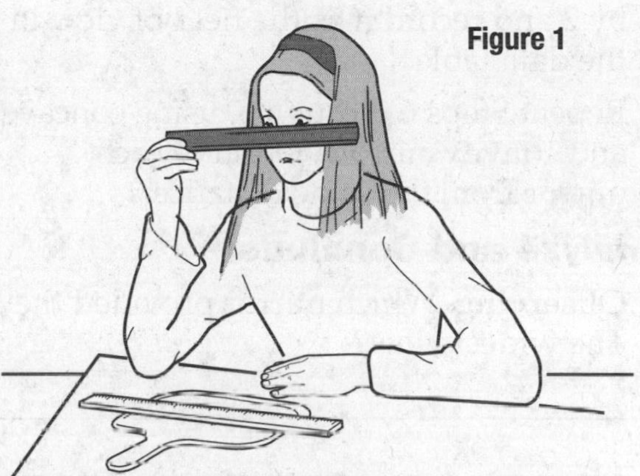

Figure 1

3. Use the ruler resting on the mirror to measure the actual length of the image of a 3-cm-long portion of the ruler you are holding. In the data table, record the size of the image.

DATA TABLE

Mirror	Size of Image	Magnification	Field of View
Plane			
Concave			
Convex			

4. Repeat Steps 1 through 3, using concave and convex mirrors. Observe each image from the same distance.
5. Divide each image size you measured by 3 cm to determine its magnification. Record the magnification in the data table.

Part B: Comparing Fields of View

6. Tie a string to a ruler. Hold the protractor, mirror, and free end of the string. Have a classmate hold the ruler vertically off to one side of the mirror. Position a third classmate (the observer) directly in front of and about 2 meters away from the mirror, as shown in Figure 2.
7. Have the classmate holding the ruler slowly move toward the observer while keeping the string tight. The observer should look directly into the mirror and say "Stop!" as soon as the reflection of the ruler can be seen.
8. Measure the angle the string makes with the protractor. Multiply this angle by 2 and record it as the field of view in the data table.
9. Repeat Steps 6 through 8, using concave and convex mirrors. Observe each mirror from the same distance.

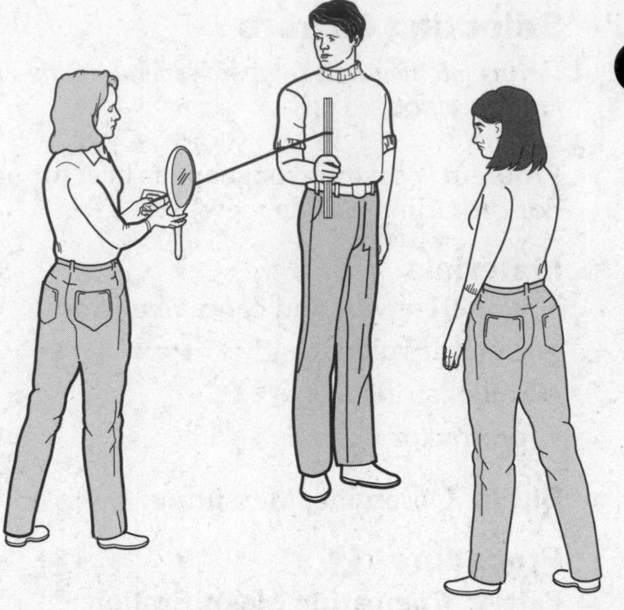

Figure 2

Analyze and Conclude

1. **Observing** Which mirror provided the greatest magnification? The widest view?

____

____

____

2. **Applying Concepts** Which mirror shape would work best for a dentist who needs to see a slightly magnified image of a tooth? Explain your answer.

____

____

3. **Drawing Conclusions** Could one of the mirrors be used both to view a wide area and to magnify? Explain your answer.

____

____

____

____

____

____

Evaluating Electrical Safety

Electric appliances must be safely insulated to protect users from injury. In this lab, you will play the role of a safety engineer determining whether an electric power supply is safely insulated.

Problem How much resistance is needed in series with a known resistance to reduce the voltage by 99 percent?

Materials

- 9-volt battery
- battery clip
- multimeter
- 3 alligator clips
- 4 resistors: 1-ohm, 10-ohm, 100-ohm, 1000-ohm

Skills Calculating, Using Tables

Procedure

1. Attach the battery clip to the battery. **CAUTION:** *The circuit may become hot.*
2. Use an alligator clip to attach one wire of the 1-ohm resistor to one of the battery clip's wires, as shown in Figure 1.
3. Clip one wire of the 1000-ohm resistor to the free end of the 1-ohm resistor. Clip the other wire of the 1000-ohm resistor to the free wire of the battery clip.
4. The 1-ohm resistor represents the current-carrying part of the appliance. The 1000-ohm resistor represents the insulation for the current-carrying part. Place one of the multimeter's electrodes on each wire of the 1-ohm resistor. Record the voltage difference.

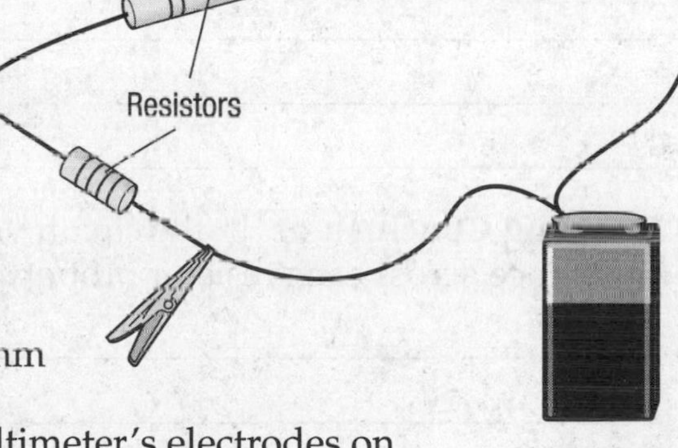

Figure 1

Data Table

Resistance (ohms)		Voltage difference (volts)	
Current-Carrying	Insulating	Current-Carrying	Insulating
1	1000		
1	100		
10	1000		
10	100		

5. Place the multimeter's electrodes on the wires of the 1000-ohm resistor. Record the voltage difference.
6. To model a reduction in the resistance of the insulation, repeat Steps 4 and 5, replacing the 1000-ohm resistor with a 100-ohm resistor. Disconnect the resistors from the battery clip.
7. **Predicting** Record your prediction of how increasing the resistance of the current-carrying part of the appliance will affect the voltage difference across the insulating part.

____

____

____

____

8. To test your prediction, repeat Steps 2 through 6, using a 10-ohm resistor to represent the current-carrying part of the appliance.

Analyze and Conclude

1. **Calculating** When the resistance of the current-carrying part was 1 ohm and the resistance of the insulating part was 100 ohms, what was the ratio of the voltage differences across the current-carrying part and the insulating part?

____

____

____

____

2. **Drawing Conclusions** In the circuit you built, what is the voltage difference across each resistor proportional to?

____

____

____

____

3. **Applying Concepts** You know the resistance of the current-carrying part of an appliance. What should the resistance of the insulation be to reduce the voltage by 99 percent?

____

____

____

____

Investigating an Electric Generator

All generators have two main parts—a magnet and a wire that is wrapped into a coil. The arrangement of these parts varies, depending on the size and power of the generator and whether it produces direct or alternating current. In this lab, you will determine how several variables affect the current produced by a simple generator.

Problem How do the direction in which the magnet moves and the number and direction of the turns in the coil affect the current that a generator produces?

Materials

- cardboard tube
- 5-m length of insulated wire
- metric ruler
- multimeter
- bar magnet
- graph paper

Skills Observing, Using Graphs

Procedure 

Part A: Changing the Number of Turns

1. Slip the wire between your hand and the tube so that 15 cm of wire extends from the tube. Use your other hand to wrap the long end of the wire around the tube 10 times in a clockwise direction, as shown in Figure 1. Make sure all the turns are within 10 cm of the end of the tube. **CAUTION:** *Be careful not to cut yourself on the sharp ends of the wire.*

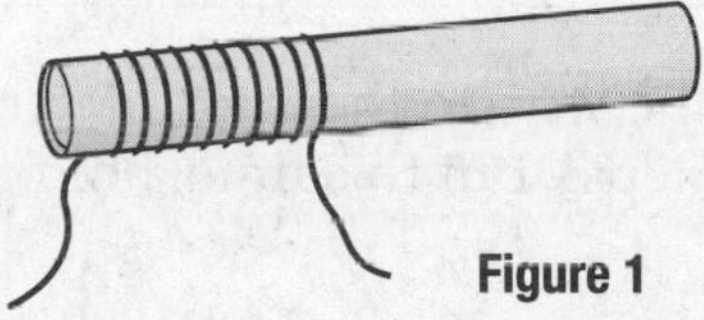

Figure 1

2. Connect both ends of the wire to the multimeter. Set the multimeter to measure current.
3. Hold the bar magnet by its south pole. Observe the multimeter as you quickly insert the bar magnet into the open end of the cardboard tube that is wrapped with the wire coil. Repeat this step if necessary as you adjust the scale of the multimeter. Record the maximum current in the data table.

DATA TABLE

Number of Turns	Direction of Turns	Pole Inserted	Current (mA)
10	Clockwise	North	
20	Clockwise	North	
30	Clockwise	North	
30	Clockwise	South	
30	Counterclockwise	South	

4. Disconnect the multimeter from the end of the wire that is farther from the turns.
5. **Predicting** Record your prediction of how increasing the number of turns in the coil will affect the current.

____

____

____

6. To test your prediction, wrap the wire around the end of the tube 10 more times in the same direction that you wound it previously—clockwise. You should now have a total of 20 turns. Reconnect the wire to the multimeter.
7. Repeat Step 3.
8. Again, disconnect the multimeter from the same end of the wire. Wrap the wire clockwise around the tube 10 more times for a total of 30 turns. Reconnect the wire to the multimeter.
9. Repeat Step 3 and then disconnect the multimeter from the same end of the wire.

Part B: Changing Other Properties of the Generator

10. **Predicting** Record your prediction of how reversing the direction of the magnet will affect the current.

____

____

____

11. To test your prediction, reconnect the wire to the multimeter exactly as you did before. Repeat Step 3, but this time, hold the magnet by its north pole.
12. **Predicting** Record your prediction of how reversing the direction of the turns in the coil will affect the current if you hold the magnet by its south pole.

____

____

____

13. To test your prediction, remove the wire from the tube. Now wrap 30 turns of wire in the opposite direction—counterclockwise.
14. Repeat Step 3, holding the magnet by its south pole.
15. Construct a graph using the data from the first three rows in the data table. Plot the number of turns on the horizontal axis and the current on the vertical axis.

Name ______________________ Class ________________ Date ___________

Analyze and Conclude

1. **Inferring** What caused a current in the wire?

2. **Using Graphs** Based on your graph, what is the relationship between the number of turns and the amount of current?

3. **Analyzing Data** Explain the effect that reversing the direction of the magnet or the direction of the turns had on the direction of the current.

4. **Predicting** Explain whether a generator could be built with a stationary magnet and a coil that moved.

Name ______________________ Class ______________ Date __________

5. Evaluating and Revising Did your observations support your predictions? If not, evaluate any flaws in the reasoning you used to make the predictions.

Name ______________________ Class ____________________ Date __________

Using Earthquakes to Map Plate Boundaries

In this lab, you will analyze data from several earthquakes to determine how the plates in the northwestern United States are moving.

Problem How can you use earthquake data to infer the movement of tectonic plates?

Materials

- graph paper

Skills Inferring, Analyzing Data

Procedure

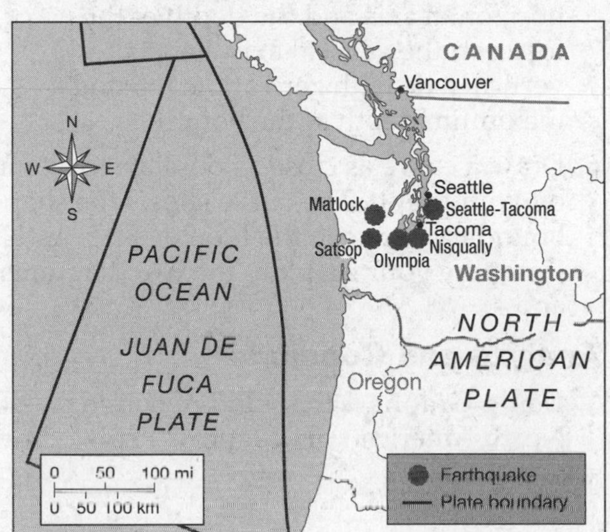

1. Examine the map of Oregon and Washington states. Earthquakes occur in the western parts of these states as a result of the movements of two plates—the Juan de Fuca Plate, which lies under the Pacific Ocean, and the North American plate.
2. Examine the table of earthquake data. Record any patterns that you observe.

____

____

DATA TABLE

Year	Location of Epicenter	Distance From Coast (km)	Depth of Focus (km)
1949	Olympia	116	53
1965	Seattle-Tacoma	141	63
1999	Satsop	58	41
2001	Nisqually	108	52
2001	Matlock	60	41

3. Draw a diagram showing how the edges of the Juan de Fuca and North American plates would move if they formed a convergent boundary. Use Figure 30 on page 682 of your textbook to help you draw this diagram.

4. Draw a diagram showing how the edges of the two plates would move if they formed a transform boundary. Use Figure 30 again to help you draw this diagram.

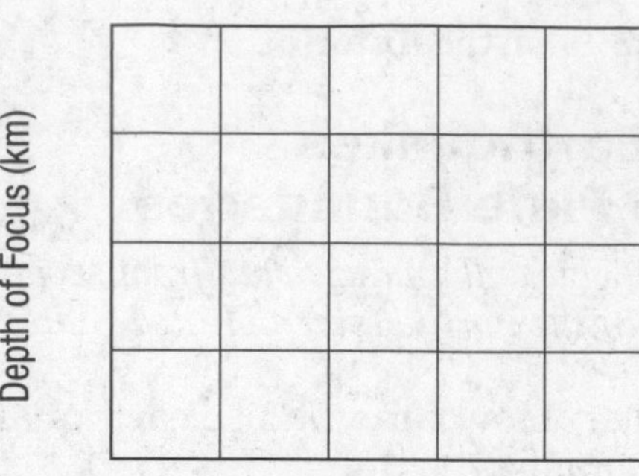

5. Use the information in the data table to construct a graph showing the location and depth of earthquakes. Plot the distance from the coast on the horizontal axis and the depth of the focus on the vertical axis. Label the vertical axis with zero at the top and maximum depth at the bottom.
6. Draw a curve as close as possible to all the points you plotted on your graph. The curve shows the shape and position of the boundary between the Juan de Fuca and North American plates. Compare your graph to the two diagrams you drew in Steps 3 and 4.

Analyze and Conclude

1. **Using Graphs** What kind of boundary do the Juan de Fuca and North American plates form? Explain how your graph supports your answer.

____

____

2. **Inferring** What does your graph suggest about the direction in which the Juan de Fuca and North American plates are moving?

____

____

3. **Predicting** In California, the Pacific plate and the North American plate meet along a transform boundary called the San Andreas fault. Would you expect to observe a similar curve in a graph of the earthquake data from the San Andreas fault? Explain your answer.

____

____

4. **Drawing Conclusions** Based on your data, how is earthquake depth related to distance from a convergent plate boundary? Explain your answer.

____

____

Modeling Erosion

Moving water is the major cause of erosion on Earth. In this lab, you will investigate some factors that affect the rate of erosion by moving water.

Problem What are some of the factors that affect the rate of water erosion?

Materials

- metric ruler
- large sheet of cardboard
- plastic wrap
- newspaper
- soil
- blocks
- pencil
- paper cup
- scissors
- drinking straw
- modeling clay
- paper towels
- small rocks

Skills Using Models, Inferring

Procedure

1. Measure and record the length of the cardboard in centimeters. Wrap the cardboard with plastic wrap to keep it dry.
2. Put several sheets of newspaper on a flat surface. Place cardboard on the newspaper and spread a thin layer of soil over the cardboard.
3. To model a hillside, raise one end of the cardboard about 5 cm from the flat surface by placing blocks under one end.
4. Using a pencil, make a hole in a paper cup 1 cm from the bottom.
5. Cut the straw in half with the scissors and insert the end of one of the halves 2 cm into the hole in the cup.
6. Use modeling clay to seal the hole around the straw. Make sure that the clay forms a tight seal around the straw.
7. Place the cup in the middle of the raised end of the cardboard so that the straw is pointing downhill, as shown.
8. Place your finger over the straw's opening as another student fills the cup with water.
9. Remove your finger. Record your observations in the data table.

Name ______________________ Class ______________ Date ____________

DATA TABLE

Elevation of Cardboard	Slope of Cardboard	Rocks	Observations

10. Clean the cardboard with paper towels and cover it again with soil. Put used soil in the trash.
11. Now use blocks to raise the end of the cardboard 15 cm above the flat surface. Repeat Steps 7 through 10.
12. Lower the end of the cardboard to 5 cm above the flat surface. Repeat Steps 7 through 10 again, but this time place a small rock on the cardboard directly in front of the straw. In the data table, record your observations about how water moves around the rock.
13. Repeat Step 12, but this time place a pile of several small rocks on the cardboard directly in front of the straw. In the data table, record your observations about how water moves around the rocks.

Analyze and Conclude

1. **Observing** Does water erosion create smooth curves or sharp angles?

   ____

2. **Analyzing Data** How did increasing the elevation of the cardboard affect the speed of the water?

   ____

3. **Calculating** The slope of a hillside is equal to its height divided by the horizontal distance it covers. Using the length of the table under the cardboard and the height it was raised, calculate and record the slope of the model hillside in each row of the data table.

   ____

   ____

   ____

4. **Inferring** What is the relationship between the slope of a hillside and the rate of erosion?

   ____

5. **Analyzing Data** Compare the movement of the water with one rock and several rocks in front of the straw. Explain any differences you observed.

   ____

   ____

Determining Relative Humidity

To measure relative humidity, you can use a sling psychrometer. This device contains two thermometers. An absorbent wick keeps the bulb of one thermometer wet. As you spin the psychrometer, air flows over the wet bulb, increasing the rate of evaporation. In this lab, you will discover how a sling psychrometer measures the relative humidity of the surrounding air.

Problem How can you measure the relative humidity of the air?

Materials

- sling psychrometer
- relative humidity chart from Appendix G
- clock or watch with second hand

Skills Using Tables, Formulating Hypotheses

Procedure

1. Wet the cotton wick of the sling psychrometer with water.
2. Observe the temperature of the wet-bulb thermometer. Then, spin the psychrometer for 30 seconds. **CAUTION:** *Take care not to spin the psychrometer near anyone or anything.*
3. Repeat Step 2 until the temperature of the wet-bulb thermometer remains constant. Then, in the data table, record the temperature of both thermometers.

DATA TABLE

Location	Dry Bulb Temp. (°C)	Wet Bulb Temp. (°C)	Relative Humidity (%)
Classroom			

4. Calculate the difference between your dry-bulb and wet-bulb temperatures.
5. In the relative humidity chart, find the row and column that list the dry-bulb temperature and the difference in temperature that you calculated. The number located where this row and column meet is the relative humidity of the classroom. Record the relative humidity in the data table.

6. Place the psychrometer on a flat surface. Observe the temperature of the wet-bulb thermometer every 30 seconds until it remains constant. Then, repeat Steps 2 through 5 at a location your teacher indicates.

Analyze and Conclude

1. **Analyzing Data** Why did the two thermometers have different temperatures?

2. **Formulating Hypotheses** Explain how the relative humidity of the air affected the difference between the temperatures of the two thermometers.

3. **Drawing Conclusions** What do you think caused the difference in relative humidity between the two locations?

4. **Predicting** How would the relative humidity change if you cooled the air in the classroom?

Modeling the Solar System

You may have seen models and illustrations that compare the sizes of the planets, but do not accurately show their relative distances from the sun. In this lab, you will compare the sizes of the planets to their distances from the sun.

Problem How can you model both the relative sizes and distances of the planets in the solar system?

Materials

- calculator
- large sheet of unlined paper
- meter stick
- scale models of the sun and planets

Skills Calculating, Using Models

Procedure

1. To model the relative sizes of the planets' orbits, convert the distances of the planets from the sun in astronomical units to kilometers, using Figure 3 on pages 792 and 793 of your textbook. Record these distances in scientific notation.

____

____

____

____

2. Use the meter stick to draw a straight line down the entire length of the large sheet of unlined paper. Measure and record the length of this line in centimeters.

____

____

3. Label one end of the line *sun* and the other end *Pluto*.
4. To calculate the scale of your model, divide the length of the line in centimeters by Pluto's average distance from the sun in kilometers.

____

____

____

5. To determine Neptune's position, multiply Neptune's average distance from the sun by the scale of your model. Mark Neptune's position on the line in your model.
6. Repeat Step 5 for each of the remaining planets in the solar system.

7. Your teacher will provide a set of scale models of the sun and planets. Use a meter stick to measure and record the diameter of the model of Jupiter.

8. To determine the scale of the planet models, divide the diameter of the model of Jupiter in centimeters by the actual diameter of Jupiter, which can be found in Figure 20 on page 811 of your textbook.

9. To determine the size of the solar system at the scale of the planet models, multiply the actual distance from Pluto to the sun by the scale of the planet models. Convert the result from centimeters to meters and record this distance.

Analyze and Conclude

1. **Using Models** How big would a model of the solar system be at the scale of the planet models you used? Explain your answer.

2. **Analyzing Data** What difficulty would you have including the relative sizes of the planets on the paper model you made in Steps 1 through 6?

3. **Drawing Conclusions** Explain why it is difficult to model the sizes and distances of the planets at the same scale.

Investigating Parallax

Astronomers use parallax to measure the distances to nearby stars. In this lab, you will investigate the effect of distance on parallax. You will observe how an object appears to move against a distant background as you look at it first through one eye, and then through the other.

Problem How is parallax related to the distance to a star?

Materials

- unlined paper
- tape
- marker
- pencil
- meter stick
- index card
- graph paper

Skills Measuring, Using Models

Procedure

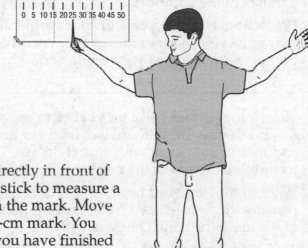

1. Tape three sheets of unlined paper to the wall horizontally, at eye level. Use a marker to draw 11 vertical marks 5 centimeters apart on the paper, as shown in Figure 1. The marks represent a distant background against which you will view a closer star. Label the marks in multiples of five from left to right, starting with 0 and ending with 50.

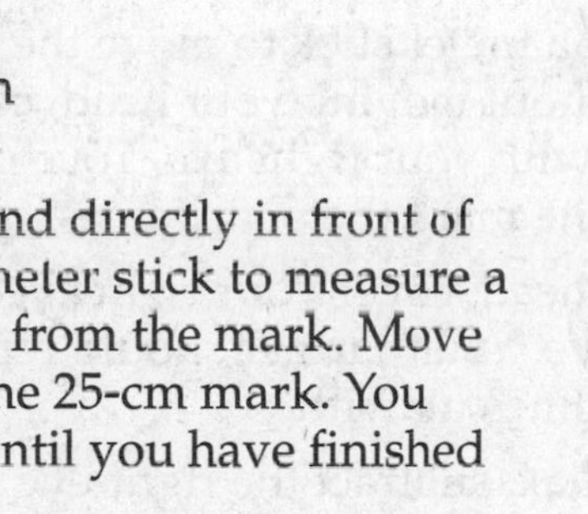

2. Facing the sheets of paper, stand directly in front of the 25-cm mark. Then, use a meter stick to measure a perpendicular distance of 7 m from the mark. Move to that spot and face toward the 25-cm mark. You must remain at this position until you have finished collecting all data.

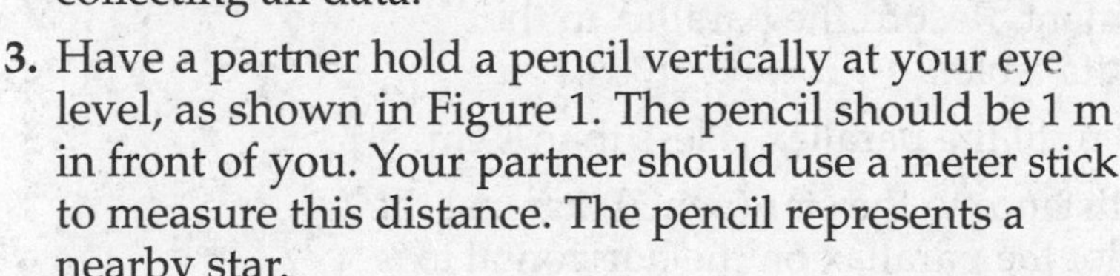

3. Have a partner hold a pencil vertically at your eye level, as shown in Figure 1. The pencil should be 1 m in front of you. Your partner should use a meter stick to measure this distance. The pencil represents a nearby star.

Figure 1

4. Hold an index card over your left eye and look at the pencil with your right eye. Your right eye represents Earth's position at one point in its orbit. Move your head so the pencil lines up with the mark labeled 0.

5. Now, without moving your head, hold the index card over your right eye and look at the pencil with your left eye. Your left eye represents Earth's position at the opposite end of its orbit six months later. Note the number of the mark that lines up with the pencil. If the pencil is between two marks, estimate its position to the nearest whole number. Your partner should record this number in the appropriate place in the data table.

DATA TABLE

Distance to Star (m)	Right Eye (cm)	Left Eye (cm)	Parallax (cm) (Difference)
1.0	0		

6. To determine the parallax, subtract the right-eye measurement (zero, in this case) from the left-eye measurement. Record the parallax in the appropriate place in the data table.
7. **Predicting** How do you and your partner think the parallax will change as your partner moves the pencil away from you? Your partner should record your prediction.

 ____

8. Have your partner use a meter stick to move the pencil 0.5 m toward the marks. Without moving your head, cover your left eye and look at the pencil with your right eye. Your partner should record the number of the mark the pencil lines up with.
9. Without moving your head, cover your right eye and look at the pencil with your left eye. Your partner should record the number of the mark the pencil lines up with.
10. To determine the parallax, subtract the right-eye measurement from the left-eye measurement. Record the parallax in the appropriate place in the data table.
11. Repeat Steps 8 through 10 until the parallax is less than 1 cm.
12. Construct a graph of the distance to the star (pencil) against the parallax you calculated. Plot the parallax on the horizontal axis and the distance on the vertical axis.

Name ______________________ Class ______________ Date ___________

Analyze and Conclude

1. **Using Graphs** What does your graph show is the relationship between the distance to the pencil and the pencil's parallax?

2. **Analyzing Data** Was your prediction in Step 7 correct? Explain your answer.

3. **Drawing Conclusions** Assume that a parallax of less than 1 cm is too small to be measured. What is the maximum distance at which the pencil would still have a parallax you can measure?

4. **Applying Concepts** Parallax can only be used to measure the distances to nearby stars. Why can't this method be used to find the distances to far-away stars?

5. **Inferring** Astronomers usually make two measurements of the position of a star six months apart, when Earth is at opposite sides of its orbit. How is this useful in determining the star's parallax?